BENJAMIN FRANKLIN:
POOR RICHARD's ALMANACKS

POOR RICHARD:
THE
ALMANACKS
for the Years 1733-1758

By RICHARD SAUNDERS, Philom.

Wherein are retain'd in their Entirety the *Author's Prefaces*, *Proverbs*, *Verses*, & entertaining *Remarks*; Together with those Chronological, Historical, and Scientific *Observations* which the *Author* has illumin'd with his characteristic *Wit & Wisdom*.

Now containing *An Introduction*
By *VAN WYCK BROOKS*
and *Embellish'd with Illustrations*
By *NORMAN ROCKWELL*

**PADDINGTON
PRESS LTD**
**THE TWO CONTINENTS
PUBLISHING GROUP**

Library of Congress Cataloging in Publication Data
*Franklin, Benjamin, 1706-1790.
  Poor Richard: the almanacks for the years 1733-1758.*

*"Contains the text of each of the twenty-six issues
of Poor Richard's almanack...For the most part,
meteorlogical and astronomical material has been omitted,
as well as a few factual articles..."*
*Reprint of the ed. published by the Limited Editions
Club, Philadelphia.*
  I. Rockwell, Norman, 1894-   II. Title.
[PS749.A3 1976]   818'.1'07   75-27943
ISBN 0-8467-0120-0

IN THE UNITED STATES
PADDINGTON PRESS LTD
TWO CONTINENTS PUBLISHING GROUP
30 East 42 Street
New York City, N.Y. 10017

IN THE UNITED KINGDOM
PADDINGTON PRESS LTD
231 The Vale
London W3 7QS

IN CANADA
distributed by
RANDOM HOUSE OF CANADA LTD
5390 Ambler Drive
Mississauga, Ontario LGW 1Y7

Publisher's Note

A new illustrated *Poor Richard's Almanacks* was published by the Limited Editions Club in 1964 in an edition limited to 1,500 copies. This new volume contains everything in that limited edition, including all of the illustrations by Norman Rockwell.

Presented here is virtually all of the text of Benjamin Franklin's original *Almanacks* – prefaces, verses, historical and scientific observations. The *Almanacks*, published annually between 1733 and 1758, were one of the most popular and influential publications of their time. In colonial America they were read by one out of every hundred citizens, enjoying a popularity second only to the Bible; in France alone they went through fifty-six editions. The introduction to this edition, written by the American author and critic Van Wyck Brooks, describes the *Almanacks* in detail.

Norman Rockwell's illustrations consist of six full-color oil paintings and some forty line drawings, each illustrating a typical aphorism. Rockwell is undoubtedly America's most famous illustrator, as well as a great exponent of genre painting. Until 1963 he had been creating covers for *The Saturday Evening Post*, for which he is perhaps best known.

Norman Rockwell is a thoroughly conscientious craftsman. When he is preparing to assemble a period piece he researches very carefully so as to obtain the greatest accuracy of detail. We here append a collection of notes he submitted concerning his paintings for this *Poor Richard's Almanacks:*

1. *Double-page Philadelphia scene:* The authority with us in Philadelphia explained to us that no one knows the architecture of Franklin's shop or its exact location, except that it was on Market Street near Christ Church. That is Christ Church in the background. Note the scaffolding. This is supposed to be at the time (1752) that Franklin organized a lottery to raise funds for the completion of the steeple. It is quite plausible that next door was a grog shop, because he often complained of his apprentices rushing the growler. Though at this time he was still a royalist, he was called to the door by the excitement over the appearance of the British general and his lady.

2. *Scene in printing shop:* Franklin as a young man wore a wig (as in the portrait by Robert Feke, *ca.* 1738) but when he was working he wore a

Publisher's Note

sort of scarf over his shaved head (as in the portrait by C. Dixon, 1767). Later on he did not wear a wig (as in all other portraits). In the picture I show Franklin re-writing for his *Almanack*, in his own style and as dictated by the requirements of the printed page, sayings from earlier sources.

3. *Night scene outside tavern:* Franklin also wrote sayings out of his own experience, and I am trying to show humorously an inspiration for one of his many epigrams on the futility of drunkenness. In the upper background you see the tower of Independence (Carpenters') Hall as it was in Franklin's early days.

4. *Scene in blacksmith shop:* Franklin was quite a young man (*ca.* 30), wore a wig, and was something of a dandy at this period. For the Franklin stove, which brought him great popular fame, he followed the experiments of Desagulier and Gauger, but he perfected their studies and applied them by having a practical stove actually made.

5. *Double page of characters reading the Almanack:* I don't know that there is much to be said about this picture except that the *Almanack* was read by all who could read at that time, was tremendously popular, and inspired widespread reactions both friendly and otherwise.

6. *Franklin with French court ladies:* This is completely from my imagination, but I was amused by the idea of the robust old gentleman, much adored by the French court ladies, young and old, amusing them by reading the homespun philosophy of Poor Richard.

TABLE OF CONTENTS

AN INTRODUCTION

POOR RICHARD had no rival in popularity among the publications of the American colonies. Benjamin Franklin began it in 1732, when he was twenty-six, and carried it on for twenty-five years, using the name of Richard Saunders, who said he was poor but his wife was proud and "could not sit spinning in her shift" while he did nothing but gaze at the stars. When ten thousand copies a year were sold, his wife got a pair of shoes, two new shifts, and a new warm petticoat, and she grew so pacific that he could sleep more quietly than in his three foregoing years. Poor Richard liked pudding while he lived better than praise after he was dead. Balzac said that Franklin was the inventor of the hoax, and few hoaxes have been more successful than the "Bonhomme Richard" after whom John Paul Jones named his ship. Paul Jones waited for months at Brest for the ship which the French king promised him; then, remembering Poor Richard's remark, "If you'd have it done, go; if not, send," he went to Versailles and procured the ship at once.

Almanacs at the time were calendars and road-books with lists of places where one could stay and descriptions of the highways, the names of British kings and the rulers of Europe, dates of eclipses, days for courts and fairs. They contained a chronicle of "remarkable things," the founding of Philadelphia and the date when three whole bullocks were roasted on the ice of the Thames, together with the changes of the moon, prognostications about the weather, recipes, jokes, maxims, and cautionary rhymes. Pedlars carried them in their packs with needles and pins and china bowls, worsted stockings, gloves and looking glasses; and they were strung on a stick and hung by the fireplace, often with records of the family written in for forty years. They were sometimes paid for in wheat and potatoes, a handful of nails or a bottle of rum. But for those who could pay anything, almanacs were virtually indispensable, and *Poor Richard* reached one in every hundred of the population. Scattered among the proverbs were Franklin's rules of health and "hints for those that would be rich." There were many remarks that were permanently wise: "Fish and visitors stink after three days." "He that lies down with dogs shall rise up with fleas."

Franklin's own time of prosperity was just beginning in the year when he initiated *Poor Richard's Almanack*. He had paid off his debts and opened a shop near the Philadelphia market place, selling books, paper and parchment, perfumed soap and Rhode Island cheese, pamphlets, bohea tea, coffee and sack. His wife, when she was not at the tub, stitched pamphlets and sold inkhorns, and Franklin himself was sometimes seen trundling home a wheelbarrow that was loaded with paper bought at some near-by shop. Bred a tradesman, he had set up a newspaper and, managing the printing-press, he made lampblack and cast type. Soon to be the chief printer of the province, and the most genial and cheerful of men, he was full of homely wisdom and common sense. Since running away from Boston and walking the fifty miles from Perth Amboy across New Jersey, he had founded the Junto — it met first in a tavern, then in a hired room — the club that was to last for thirty years. The Junto discussed such questions as "What is Wisdom?" and "Can a Man Arrive at Perfection or Is This Impossible?" and out of it sprang the American Philosophical Society.

Franklin had organized the first police force and the first fire company in the colonies, and when six French privateers were planning to sack Philadelphia, he opposed the pacifist Quakers and got up a troop to defend the town. He took the lead in street lighting, paving the city's streets and founding the hospital of which he was president of the board, as he became later the president of the first Abolition society.

It was he mainly, who formed the academy that was to become the University of Pennsylvania. He had written for the Junto two dialogues on the question whether one should seek reasonable virtue or pleasure, and he had conceived a plan for arriving at moral perfection, wishing to live without committing any kind of fault.

The proverbs of *Poor Richard's Almanack* were not all Franklin's own. They were, he said, "the wisdom of many ages and nations," and he borrowed them freely from Dryden and Pope, La Rochefoucauld and Rabelais, changing the words, reworking them, and including popular adages. His rule for writing, he once said, was to be "smooth, clear, and short," and he added notes each year and revised the text several times.

An Introduction

His sayings soon passed into everyday speech and were quoted in sermons, on the title pages of pamphlets, or as mottoes in newspapers. Down to the Revolution they were universally known, and "As Poor Richard says . . . . " was a common popular phrase.

In the twenty-fifth almanac, in 1758, Franklin went through the previous issues and made up a harangue, "Father Abraham's Speech" or "The Way to Wealth," composed of a string of adages from the almanac. Poor Richard was supposed to have been at a country auction when a wise old man, Father Abraham, got up to speak. The people had been summoned by crier and bell and they had been plied with rum so that they were ready to pay prices they would never have offered if they had been sober. The times were bad, trade was dull, the French and Indian War continued, and one of the company called to Father Abraham, "What do you think of the times? Won't these heavy taxes ruin the country? How shall we ever be able to pay them? What would you advise us to do?"

Then Father Abraham, who had risen, replied, "If you'd have my advice, I'll give it you in short, for many words won't fill a bushel, as Poor Richard says." Franklin believed that only thrift could cure the hard times, so Father Abraham, inculcating frugality and industry, was listened to as never before: "A fat kitchen makes a lean will. . . . Keep thy shop and thy shop will keep thee. . . . If you would have a faithful servant, serve yourself. . . . Fools make feasts and wise men eat them. . . . A ploughman on his legs is higher than a gentleman on his knees."

Most of the colonists, Franklin said, were "middling people" who were obliged to work and save to prosper and survive, and the popularity of the proverbs was due to this. But there were constant new editions in England, Scotland, and Ireland, and there were fifty-six editions in French translations. Great numbers were bought by noblemen and priests in order to distribute them among their poor tenants and parishioners. *The Way to Wealth* was soon translated into Russian, Welsh, and Chinese, into Catalan, Bohemian, Polish, and Gaelic.

Franklin may have been thrifty, but he was far from penurious, as the well-known story of Whitefield's sermon shows. He went to hear Whitefield, resolved to give nothing, but he softened as the sermon went on. First he gave his coppers, then his silver, and finally emptied his pocket, including five gold coins — and presently, he published a volume of Whitefield's sermons.

Franklin had been working with leisure in mind, and in 1748 he retired from the printing business in which he had brought out the first novel printed in America. This was Samuel Richardson's *Pamela*. He bought a farm of three hundred acres in New Jersey and planned to indulge himself there in the most agreeable kind of life. The tradesman had arrived at freedom and, becoming interested in electrical experiments, he soon made himself a master of them. He moved into a new house and worked with a saltcellar, a vinegar cruet, and a pump handle. He was surprised by the "wonderful effect of pointed bodies, both in drawing off and throwing off the electrical fire."

This presently suggested the lightning rod, which Franklin invented. He had set out to prove that lightning was electricity, which many others had suspected, and his proof was confirmed in France in 1752. He was virtually the only American scientist at that day and the first among the world's electricians, and his writings on electricity were translated into French, German, and Italian. This man who had caught and tamed the lightning became at once immensely famous, a member of the Royal Society, of all the important learned societies in Europe, and better known than any other American there. He was, said Kant, a "new Prometheus who stole fire from Heaven." Turgot devised, in praise of him, a phrase in Latin which may be rendered: "He snatched the lightning from the sky and the sceptre from tyrants." This was after the Revolution in which Franklin played a major part and long after he had turned from business to science.

In spite of the message of *Poor Richard's Almanack*, he was an open-handed man who refused to patent the lightning rod or the Franklin stove either, one of the most useful of his many inventions, and he gave away his salary as Postmaster General for the relief of soldiers who were wounded in the Revolution. He invented a rolling press for making copies of letters, an artificial hand and arm for placing books on high shelves, bifocal eyeglasses to assist his reading, and the water-glass harmonica, popular especially among German musicians. He played tunes on the harmonica himself, accompanying the Scottish airs that a young acquaintance sang to her harpsichord. Franklin also learned to play the harp, the guitar, and the violin; and, while the only foreign tongue he spoke was French, he was able to read Spanish, Italian, and German.

Postmaster of Philadelphia as early as 1737, Franklin had become Postmaster General in 1753. His rule in regard to public office was: "Never ask, never refuse, nor ever resign," and no other man in America had seen so much of the country or knew so many of its influential men. Save for Charleston in the Carolinas he had visited every post office, and he wished to bring and keep together ingenious men of all the colonies — his real motive in founding the American Philosophical Society. As Postmaster, he read most of the newspapers, and Philadelphia was the centre of mail from Boston and the South as well, so that when Franklin went to France, as envoy before Jefferson, he knew America better than anyone else. He arranged for sending, from England to John Bartram, American botanist to the king, seeds to be planted in the colonies, as he had sent over the first kohlrabi and the first Scotch cabbage seeds. He introduced Chinese rhubarb that is used in medicine; and when he found a discarded osier basket, brought from Europe and thrown away, he planted shoots that grew up into the first yellow willow in the country.

Crossing the ocean, Franklin noted every day the temperature of the air and water. Studying the common cold, he wrote letters on sun spots and swimming and on flies apparently drowned in wine but revived by the sun. Convivial in taverns, he had written several drinking songs, as he had written in boyhood a ballad on Blackbeard the pirate — in the days when the *Spectator* was his model of prose; and among his subjects of speculation were population and smallpox, whirlwinds and waterspouts, geology and salt mines. He wrote on the structure of the earth, on Scottish tunes, on tides in rivers, the origin of northeast storms, botany and insects, silkworms, astronomy, the effect of oil on water, the use of copper on roofs, the causes of earthquakes. He wrote, moreover, on the heating of churches, the vegetable origin of coal, the consumption of smoke in stoves, and the census in China. Poor Richard had become a universal genius whose first book to be printed in Europe was *Reflections on Courtship and Marriage*, and who, long before he retired at the age of eighty-two, had become one of the most famous men in the world.

Franklin was regarded as a friend of humankind in France, where John Adams said he was better known than Frederick the Great or even Voltaire, where he was expected to restore the golden age, and where his phrase *ça ira* — it will all come right in the end — became the song of the French Revolution. "All jollity and pleasantry," as James Boswell found him, he was represented in France in busts and prints, in statue-ettes, on snuff-boxes, on rings and in miniatures, on handkerchiefs and dishes and in medallions of various sizes. All these images showed him as patriarchal, old, and wise, and his face became as familiar, he said, as that of the moon. Poor Richard was beloved and esteemed on two continents, in Philadelphia, in all America and in France as well.

This edition of *Poor Richard's Almanack* is truly unique. As a rule, books bearing that title are merely a collection of adages, occasionally with added prefaces and verses, while here is presented, in chronological sequence, the complete text of the original almanacs; only the astronomical data and other factual pieces are omitted. Moreover, the text preserves the typographical flavor of Franklin's own composition. The result is a real contribution to Americana.

VAN WYCK BROOKS

A Note on the Text

THIS EDITION *contains the text of each of the twenty-six issues of Poor Richard's Almanack published by Benjamin Franklin. For the most part, meteorological and astronomical material has been omitted, as well as a few factual articles to which Poor Richard contributed neither his wit nor his wisdom.*

The reader's attention is drawn to the Notes in the Appendix for (a) Poor Richard's use of astronomical and zodiacal symbols, (b) the reactions of some of his contemporaries to the early issues of Poor Richard, and (c) the sources of Franklin's borrowings. Also in the Appendix is an alphabetical list, with translations, of the aphorisms that he printed in various foreign languages. Notes printed at the foot of the page are Franklin's own.

Poor Richard occasionally repeats an aphorism — sometimes a few years later, sometimes only a few months later. In a very few instances (for reasons typographical) we have taken the similar liberty of transposing a proverb from its original month to another month of the same Almanack.

The texts in this edition have been scrupulously collated by Dr. Yvonne Noble with the rare originals in the collections of the following institutions, to whose directors the present publishers are happy to acknowledge their gratitude: American Philosophical Society, Franklin Institute, Historical Society of Pennsylvania, Library Company of Philadelphia, University of Pennsylvania Library, Rosenbach Foundation, New York Public Library, and Yale University Library.

The publishers particularly appreciate the kind cooperation given by Edwin Wolf II, Librarian, and Mrs. Joyce Graham, of the Library Company of Philadelphia; and Leonard W. Labaree, Editor, and Whitfield J. Bell, Jr., Associate Editor, "The Papers of Benjamin Franklin," published by Yale University Press.

BENJAMIN FRANKLIN:
POOR RICHARD's ALMANACKS

Illustrated by Norman Rockwell

Poor Richard's *Almanack, &c.*

Courteous READER,

I MIGHT in this place attempt to gain thy Favour, by declaring that I write Almanacks with no other View than that of the publick good; but in this I should not be sincere; and Men are now a-days too wise to be deceiv'd by Pretences how specious soever. The plain Truth of the Matter is, I am excessive poor, and my Wife, good Woman, is, I tell her, excessive proud; she cannot bear, she says, to sit spinning in her Shift of Tow, while I do nothing but gaze at the Stars; and has threatned more than once to burn all my Books and Rattling-Traps (as she calls my Instruments) if I do not make some profitable Use of them for the good of my Family. The Printer has offer'd me some considerable share of the Profits, and I have thus begun to comply with my Dame's desire.

Indeed this Motive would have had Force enough to have made me publish an Almanack many Years since, had it not been overpower'd by my Regard for my good Friend and Fellow-Student, Mr. *Titan Leeds*, whose Interest I was extreamly unwilling to hurt: But this Obstacle (I am far from speaking it with Pleasure) is soon to be removed, since inexorable Death, who was never known to respect Merit, has already

3

prepared the mortal Dart, the fatal Sister has already extended her destroying Shears, and that ingenious Man must soon be taken from us. He dies, by my Calculation[1] made at his Request, on *Oct.*17.1733. 3 ho. 29 m. *P.M.* at the very instant of the ♂ of ☉ and ☿: By his own Calculation he will survive till the 26th of the same Month. This small difference between us we have disputed whenever we have met these 9 Years past; but at length he is inclinable to agree with my Judgment; Which of us is most exact, a little Time will now determine. As therefore these Provinces may not longer expect to see any of his Performances after this Year, I think my self free to take up the Task, and request a share of the publick Encouragement, which I am the more apt to hope for on this Account, that the Buyer of my Almanack may consider himself, not only as purchasing an useful Utensil, but as performing an Act of Charity, to his poor

Friend and Servant

R. SAUNDERS.[2]

♄ *Saturn* diseas'd with Age, and left for dead;
Chang'd all his Gold to be involv'd in Lead.
♃ *Jove*, Juno leaves, and loves to take his Range;
From whom Man learns to love, and loves to change.
♂ is disarmed, and to ♀ gone,
Where *Vulcan's* Anvil must be struck upon.
That ☽ *Luna's* horn'd, it cannot well be said,
Since I ne'er heard that she was married.

🜨 JANUARY

More nice than wise.

Old Batchelor would have a Wife that's wise,
Fair, rich, and young, a Maiden for his Bed;
Not proud, nor churlish, but of faultless size;
A Country Houswife in the City bred.
   He's a nice Fool, and long in vain hath staid;
   He should bespeak her, there's none ready made.

Never spare the Parson's wine, nor the Baker's pudding.

Visits should be short, like a winters day,
Lest you're too troublesom hasten away.

A house without woman & Firelight, is like a body
without soul or sprite.

Kings & Bears often worry their keepers.

The ANATOMY *of* MAN'S BODY *as govern'd by the Twelve Constellations.*[3]

Here I sit naked, like some Fairy Elf,
My Seat a Pumpkin; I grudge no Man's Pelf;
Though I've no Bread nor Cheese upon my Shelf;
I'll tell thee gratis, when it safe is,
To purge, to bleed, or cut, thy Cattle, or —— thy self.

♈ *The Head and Face.*

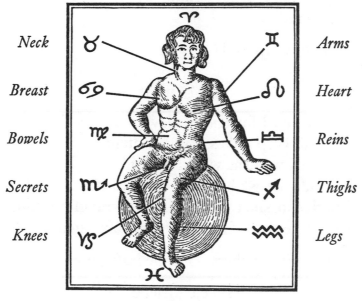

Neck	♉		♊	Arms
Breast	♋		♌	Heart
Bowels	♍		♎	Reins
Secrets	♏		♐	Thighs
Knees	♑		♒	Legs

♓ *The Feet.*

The Names and Characters of the Seven Planets.

♄ Saturn, ♃ Jupiter, ♂ Mars, ☉ Sol, ♀ Venus,
☿ Mercury, ☽ Luna, ☊ Dragons Head and ☋ Tail.

The Five Aspects. ☌ Conjunction, ✶ Sextile,
☍ Opposition, △ Trine, □ Quartile.

⚏ FEBRUARY

N. N. of B—s County, pray don't be angry with poor Richard.

Each Age of Men new Fashions doth invent;
  Things which are old, young Men do not esteem:
What pleas'd our Fathers, doth not us content;
  What flourish'd then, we out of fashion deem:
    And that's the reason, as I understand,
    Why *Prodigus* did sell his Father's Land.

Light purse, heavy heart.

He's a Fool that makes his Doctor his Heir.

Ne'er take a wife till thou hast a house (& a fire)
  to put her in.

He's gone, and forgot nothing but to say *Farewel*—
  to his creditors.

Love well, whip well.

⚏ MARCH

My Love and I for Kisses play'd,
She would keep stakes, I was content,
But when I won she would be paid;
This made me ask her what she meant:
    Quoth she, since you are in this wrangling vein,
    Here take your Kisses, give me mine again.

March many weathers. How he huffs, poor Fool!

        Let my respected friend *J.G.*
        Accept this humble verse of me.
          viz.
        Ingenious, learned, envy'd Youth,
        Go on as thou'st began;
        Even thy enemies take pride
        That thou'rt their countryman.

Hunger never saw bad bread.

🐾 APRIL

Kind Katharine to her husband kiss'd these words,
"Mine own sweet *Will*, how dearly I love thee!"
If true (quoth Will) the World no such affords.
And that its true I durst his warrant be;
 For ne'er heard I of Woman good or ill,
 But always loved best, her own sweet Will.

Beware of meat twice boil'd, & an old foe reconcil'd.

Great Talkers, little Doers.

A rich rogue, is like a fat hog, who never does good
 til as dead as a log.

Relation without friendship, friendship without power,
power without will, will without effect, effect without profit, &
profit without vertue, are not worth a farto.

👥 MAY

Mirth pleaseth some, to others 'tis offence,
Some commend plain conceit, some profound sense;
Some wish a witty Jest, some dislike that,
And most would have themselves they know not what.
 Then he that would please all, and himself too,
 Takes more in hand than he is like to do.

The favour of the Great is no inheritance.

Fools make feasts and wise men eat 'em.

Beware of the young Doctor & the old Barber.

He has chang'd his one ey'd horse for a blind one.

The poor have little, beggars none, the rich too much,
 enough not one.

Eat to live, and not live to eat.

March windy, and April rainy,
 makes *May* the pleasantest month of any.

JUNE

"Observe the daily circle of the sun,
  And the short year of each revolving moon:
  By them thou shalt foresee the following day,
  Nor shall a starry night thy hopes betray.
  When first the moon appears, if then she shrouds
  Her silver crescent, tip'd with sable clouds,
  Conclude she bodes a tempest on the main,
  And brews for fields impetuous floods of rain."

After 3 days men grow weary, of a wench, a guest,
  & weather rainy.

To lengthen thy Life, lessen thy Meals.

The proof of gold is fire, the proof of woman, gold;
  the proof of man, a woman.

After feasts made, the maker scratches his head.

JULY

"Ev'n while the reaper fills his greedy hands,
  And binds the golden sheafs in brittle bands,
  Oft have I seen a sudden storm arise
  From all the warring winds that sweep the skies:
  And oft whole sheets descend of slucy rain,
  Suck'd by the spungy clouds from off the main;
  The lofty skies at once come pouring down,
  The promis'd crop and golden labours drown."

Neither Shame nor Grace yet *Bob*.

Many estates are spent in the getting,
Since women for tea forsook spinning & knitting.

He that lies down with Dogs, shall rise up with fleas.

A fat kitchin, a lean Will.

Distrust & caution are the parents of security.

♌ AUGUST

"For us thro' 12 bright signs Apollo guides
  The year, and earth in sev'ral climes divides.
  Five girdles bind the skies, the torrid zone
  Glows with the passing and repassing sun.
  Far on the right and left, th' extreams of heav'n,
  To frosts and snows and bitter blasts are giv'n.
  Betwixt the midst and these, the Gods assign'd
  Two habitable seats for humane kind."

Take counsel in wine, but resolve afterwards in water.

He that drinks fast, pays slow.

Great famine when wolves eat wolves.

A good Wife lost is God's gift lost.

A taught horse, and a woman to teach, and teachers
  practising what they preach.

He is ill cloth'd, who is bare of Virtue.

Tongue double, brings trouble.

♍ SEPTEMBER

Death is a Fisherman, the world we see
His Fish-pond is, and we the Fishes be:
His Net some general Sickness; howe'er he
Is not so kind as other Fishers be;
For if they take one of the smaller Fry,
They throw him in again, he shall not die:
But Death is sure to kill all he can get,
And all is Fish with him that comes to Net.

Men & Melons are hard to know.

He's the best physician that knows the worthlessness
  of the most medicines.

There is no little enemy.

A fine genius in his own country, is like gold in the mine.

The heart of a fool is in his mouth, but the mouth
of a wise man is in his heart.

❧ OCTOBER

Time was my spouse and I could not agree,
Striving about superiority:
The text which saith that man and wife are one,
Was the chief argument we stood upon:
She held, they both one woman should become;
I held they should be man, and both but one.
Thus we contended daily, but the strife
Could not be ended, till both were one Wife.

The old Man has given all to his Son: O fool!
to undress thy self before thou art going to bed.

Cheese and salt meat, should be sparingly eat.

Doors and walls are fools paper.

Anoint a villain and he'll stab you, stab him & he'l
anoint you.

Keep your mouth wet, feet dry.

He has lost his Boots but sav'd his spurs.

❧ NOVEMBER

My neighbour *H——y* by his pleasing tongue,
Hath won a Girl that's rich, wise, fair and young;
The Match (he saith) is half concluded, he
Indeed is wondrous willing; but not she.
And reason good, for he has run thro' all
Almost the story of the Prodigal;
Yet swears he never with the hogs did dine;
That's true, for none would trust him with their swine.

Where bread is wanting, all's to be sold.

Nothing more like a Fool, than a drunken Man.

There is neither honour nor gain, got in dealing
   with a vil-lain.

The fool hath made a vow, I guess,
Never to let the Fire have peace.

Snowy winter, a plentiful harvest.

ᵭ DECEMBER

She that will eat her breakfast in her bed,
And spend the morn in dressing of her head,
And sit at dinner like a maiden bride,
And talk of nothing all day but of pride;
God in his mercy may do much to save her,
But what a case is he in that shall have her.

God works wonders now & then;
Behold! a Lawyer, an honest Man!

He that lives carnally, won't live eternally.

Innocence is its own Defence.

Time *eateth* all things, could old Poets say;
The Times are chang'd, our times *drink* all away.

Never mind it, she'l be sober after the Holidays.

The Benefit of going to LAW.

Dedicated to the Counties of K—t *&* H–n——rd–n.

Two Beggars travelling along,
   One blind, the other lame,
Pick'd up an Oyster on the Way
   To which they both laid claim:
The matter rose so high, that they
   Resolv'd to go to Law,
As often richer Fools have done,

Who quarrel for a Straw.
A Lawyer took it strait in hand,
Who knew his Business was,
To mind nor one nor t'other side,
But make the best o' th' Cause;
As always in the Law's the Case:
So he his Judgment gave,
And Lawyer-like he thus resolv'd
What each of them should have;
   Blind Plaintif, lame Defendant, share
   The Friendly Laws impartial Care,
   A Shell for him, a Shell for thee,
   The Middle is the Lawyer's Fee.

A Catalogue of the principal Kings and Princes in *Europe*, with the Time of their Births and Ages.

George II. King of *Great Britain, &c.*	Born 30 *Oct.* 1683	Age 50
Wilhelmina-Carolina, his Queen	1 *Mar.* 1685	48
Frederick, Prince of *Wales*	19 *Jan.* 1706	27
Charles 6. Emperor of *Germany*	1 *Oct.* 1685	48
Louis 15. King of *France*	15 *Feb.* 1710	23
Mary, Queen of *France*	23 *Jun.* 1703	30
Leopold I. Duke of *Lorain*	11 *Sept.* 1679	54
Philip 5. King of *Spain*	19 *Dec.* 1683	50
John 5. King of *Portugal*	22 *Oct.* 1689	44
Fred. W. King of *Prussia,* El. of *Brand.*	14 *Aug.* 1688	45
Fred. Augustus, King of *Poland*	12 *May* 1661	72
Frederick 4. King of *Denmark*	11 *Oct.* 1671	62
Frederick, King of *Sweden*	28 *Apr.* 1676	57
Charles Frederick, Duke of *Holstein*	14 *Apr.* 1700	33
Prince *Eugene* of *Savoy*	18 *Oct.* 1663	70
John Gaston, Grand Duke of *Tuscany*	24 *May* 1671	62
Poor Richard, an American Prince, without Subjects, his Wife being Viceroy over him,	23 *Oct.* 1684	49

Poor Richard's *Almanack*, &c.

Courteous READERS,

YOUR kind and charitable Assistance last Year, in purchasing so large an Impression of my Almanacks, has made my Circumstances much more easy in the World, and requires my grateful Acknowledgment. My Wife has been enabled to get a Pot of her own, and is no longer oblig'd to borrow one from a Neighbour; nor have we ever since been without something of our own to put in it. She has also got a pair of Shoes, two new Shifts, and a new warm Petticoat; and for my part, I have bought a second-hand Coat, so good, that I am now not asham'd to go to Town or be seen there. These Things have render'd her Temper so much more pacifick than it us'd to be, that I may say, I have slept more, and more quietly within this last Year, than in the three foregoing Years put together. Accept my hearty Thanks therefor, and my sincere Wishes for your Health and Prosperity.

In the Preface to my last Almanack, I foretold the Death of my dear old Friend and Fellow-Student, the learned and ingenious Mr. *Titan Leeds*, which was to be on the 17th of *October*, 1733, 3 h. 29 m. *P.M.* at the very Instant of the ♂ of ☉ and ☿. By his own Calculation he was to survive till the 26th of the same Month, and expire in the Time of the Eclipse, near 11 a clock, *A.M.* At which of these Times he died, or whether he be really yet dead, I cannot at this present Writing positively assure my Readers; forasmuch as a Disorder in my own Family demanded my Presence, and would not permit me as I had intended, to be with him in his last Moments, to receive his last Embrace, to close his Eyes, and do the Duty of a Friend in performing the last Offices to the Departed. Therefore it is that I cannot positively affirm whether he be dead or not; for the Stars only show to the Skilful, what will happen in the natural and universal Chain of Causes and Effects; but 'tis well known, that the Events which would otherwise certainly happen at certain Times in the Course of Nature, are sometimes set aside or postpon'd for wise and good Reasons, by the immediate particular Dispositions of Providence; which particular Dispositions the Stars can by no Means discover or foreshow. There is however, (and I cannot speak it without Sorrow) there is the strongest Probability that my dear Friend is *no more;* for there appears in his Name, as I am assured, an Almanack for the Year 1734, in which I am treated in a very gross and unhandsome Manner, in which I am called *a false Predicter, an Ignorant, a conceited Scribler, a Fool, and a Lyar.* Mr. *Leeds* was too well bred to use any Man so indecently and so scurrilously, and moreover his Esteem and Affection for me was extraordinary: So that it is to be feared that Pamphlet may be only a Contrivance of somebody or other, who hopes perhaps to sell two or three Year's Almanacks still, by the sole Force and Virtue of Mr *Leeds's* Name; but certainly, to put Words into the Mouth of a Gentleman and a Man of Letters, against his Friend, which the meanest and most scandalous of the People might be asham'd to utter even in a drunken Quarrel, is an unpardonable Injury to his Memory, and an Imposition upon the Publick.

Mr. *Leeds* was not only profoundly skilful in the useful Science he profess'd, but he was a Man of *exemplary Sobriety*, a most *sincere Friend*, and an *exact Performer of his Word*. These valuable Qualifications, with many others so much endear'd him to me, that although it should be so, that, contrary to all Probability, contrary to my Prediction and his own, he might possibly be yet alive, yet my Loss of Honour as a Prognosticator, cannot afford me so much Mortification, as his Life, Health and Safety would give me Joy and Satisfaction. I am,

> *Courteous and kind Reader,*
> *Your poor Friend and Servant,*

Octob. 30. 1733.   R. SAUNDERS.[4]

Good Women are like STARS in darkest Night,
Their Virtuous Actions shining as a Light
To guide their ignorant Sex, which oft times fall,
And falling oft, turns diabolical.
Good Women sure are Angels on the Earth,
Of those good Angels we have had a Dearth;
And therefore all you Men that have good Wives,
Respect their Virtues equal with your Lives.

JANUARY

From a cross Neighbour, and a sullen Wife,
A pointless Needle, and a broken Knife;
From Suretyship, and from an empty Purse,
A Smoaky Chimney and a jolting Horse;
From a dull Razor, and an aking Head,
From a bad Conscience and a buggy Bed;
A Blow upon the Elbow and the Knee,
From each of these, *Good L– –d deliver me.*

You cannot pluck roses without fear of thorns,
Nor enjoy a fair wife without danger of horns.

Without justice, courage is weak.

Many dishes many diseases.
Many medicines few cures.

Where carcasses are, eagles will gather,
And where good laws are, much people flock thither.

Would you live with ease,
Do what you ought, and not what you please.

FEBRUARY

What Death is, dost thou ask of me;
    Till dead I do not know;
Come to me when thou hear'st I'm dead;
    Then what 'tis I shall show.

Poor Richard: 1734

To die's to cease to be, it seems,
   So Learned *Seneca* did think;
But we've Philosophers of modern Date,
   Who say 'tis Death to cease to Drink.

Hot things, sharp things, sweet things, cold things
All rot the teeth, and make them look like old things.

Blame-all and *Praise-all* are two blockheads.

Be temperate in wine, in eating, girls, & sloth;
Or the Gout will seize you and plague you both.

⚘ MARCH

Some of our Sparks to *London* town do go
Fashions to see, and learn the World to know;
Who at Return have nought but these to show,
New Wig above, and new Disease below.
Thus the Jack Ass a Traveller once would be,
And roam'd abroad new Fashions for to see;
But home returned, Fashions he had none,
Only his Main and Tail were larger grown.

What pains our Justice takes his faults to hide,
With half that pains sure he might cure 'em quite.

In success be moderate.

Take this remark from *Richard* poor and lame,
Whate'er's begun in anger ends in shame.

What one relishes, nourishes.

No man e'er was glorious, who was not laborious.

⚘ APRIL

When Fortune fell asleep, and Hate did blind her,
Art, Fortune lost; and Ignorance did find her.
Since when, dull Ignorance with Fortune's Store
Hath been inrich'd, and Art hath still been poor.

16

Poets say Fortune's blind, and cannot see,
But certainly they must deceived be;
Else could it not most commonly fall out
That Fools should have and wise Men go without.

All things are easy to Industry,
All things difficult to *Sloth*.

If you ride a Horse, sit close and tight,
If you ride a Man, sit easy and light.

A new truth is a truth, an old error is an error,
Tho' *Clodpate* wont allow either.

> Don't think to hunt two hares with one dog.

> Fools multiply folly.

> Beauty & folly are old companions.

Better slip with foot than tongue.

> Hope of gain
> Lessens pain.

May

Wedlock, as old Men note, hath likened been,
Unto a publick Crowd or common Rout;
Where those that are without would fain get in,
And those that are within would fain get out.
Grief often treads upon the Heels of Pleasure,
Marry'd in Haste, we oft repent at Leisure;
Some by Experience find these Words misplac'd,
Marry'd at Leisure, they repent in Haste.

Where there's Marriage without Love,
   there will be Love without Marriage.

Lawyers, Preachers, and Tomtits Eggs,
   there are more of them hatch'd than come to perfection.

Be neither silly, nor cunning, but wise.

17

Neither a Fortress nor a Maidenhead will hold out long
   after they begin to parley.

Astrologers say,
This is a good Day,
To make Love in May.

Who pleasure gives,
Shall joy receive.

Be not sick too late, nor well too soon.

⚓ JUNE

When *Robin* now three Days had married been,
   And all his Friends and Neighbours gave him Joy;
This Question of his Wife he asked then,
   Why till her Marriage Day she prov'd so coy?
Indeed (said he) 'twas well thou didst not yield,
   For doubtless then my Purpose was to leave thee:
O, Sir, I once before was so beguil'd,
And was resolv'd the next should not deceive me.

All things are cheap to the saving, dear to the wasteful.

Would you persuade, speak of Interest, not of Reason.

Some men grow mad by studying much to know,
But who grows mad by studying good to grow.

Happy's the Wooing that's not long a doing.

Jack *Little* sow'd little, & little he'll reap.

⚓ JULY

A Lawyer being sick and extream ill
Was moved by his Friends to make his Will,
Which soon he did, gave all the Wealth he had
To frantic Persons, lunatick and mad;
And to his Friends this Reason did reveal
(That they might see with Equity he'd deal):

From Madmen's Hands I did my Wealth receive,
Therefore that Wealth to Madmen's Hands I leave.

There have been as great Souls unknown to fame
as any of the most famous.

Do good to thy Friend to keep him,
to thy enemy to gain him.

A good Man is seldom uneasy, an ill one never easie.

Teach your child to hold his tongue,
he'll learn fast enough to speak.

Drive thy Business! — let not it drive you.

Poor Richard: 1734

Don't value a man for the Quality he is of,
    but for the Qualities he possesses.

Bucephalus the Horse of *Alexand.*
    hath as lasting fame as his Master.

        Rain or Snow,
        To *Chili* go,
        You'll find it so,
        For ought we know.
        Time will show.

AUGUST

Some envious (speaking in their own Renown)
Say that my Book was not exactly done:
They wrong me; Yet, like Feasts I'd have my Books
Rather be pleasing to the Guests than Cooks.
    Ill thrives that hapless Family that shows
A Cock that's silent, and a Hen that crows:
I know not which lives more unnatural Lives,
Obeying Husbands, or commanding Wives.

Sam's Religion is like a *Chedder Cheese*, 'tis made
    of the *milk* of one & twenty Parishes.

Grief for a dead Wife, & a troublesome Guest,
Continues to the *threshold*, and there is at rest;
But I mean such wives as are none of the best.

As Charms are nonsense, Nonsense is a Charm.

He that cannot obey, cannot command.

An innocent *Plowman* is more worthy than a vicious *Prince.*

SEPTEMBER

S——l the Smith hath lately sworn and said,
That no Disease shall make him keep his Bed;
His reason is, I now begin to smell it,
He wants more Rum, and must be forc'd to sell it.

Nor less meant J——h when that Vow he made,
Than to give o'er his cousening Tapster's Trade,
Who, check'd for short and frothy Measure, swore
He never would from thenceforth fill Pot more.

He that is rich need not live sparingly,
    and he that can live sparingly need not be rich.

If you wou'd be reveng'd of your enemy, govern yourself.

A wicked Hero will turn his back to an innocent coward.

Laws like to *Cobwebs* catch small Flies,
Great ones break thro' before your eyes.

An Egg to day is better than a Hen to-morrow.

Drink Water, Put the Money in your Pocket,
    and leave the *Dry-bellyach* in the *Punchbowl.*

⚞ OCTOBER

Altho' thy Teacher act not as he preaches,
Yet ne'ertheless, if good, do what he teaches;
Good Counsel, failing Men may give; for why,
He that's aground knows where the Shoal doth lie.
My old Friend *Berryman*, oft, when alive,
Taught others Thrift; himself could never thrive:
Thus like the Whetstone, many Men are wont
To sharpen others while themselves are blunt.

The magistrate should obey the Laws,
    the People should obey the magistrate.

When 'tis fair be sure take your Great coat with you.

He does not possess Wealth, it possesses him.

Necessity has no Law; I know some Attorneys of the name.

Onions can make, ev'n Heirs and Widows weep.

Strange, that he who lives by Shifts,
    can seldom shift himself.

As sore places meet most rubs, proud folks
    meet most affronts.

    Button your breast,
    There's *Jack Norwest*.

❧ NOVEMBER

Dorothy would with *John* be married;
    Dorothy's wise, I trow:
But *John* by no means *Dorothy* will wed;
    John's the wiser of the two.
Those are my Verses which *Tom* reads;
    That is very well known:
But if in reading he makes 'em Nonsense,
    Then they are his own.

The thrifty maxim of the wary *Dutch*,
Is to save all the Money they can touch.

He that waits upon Fortune, is never sure of a Dinner.

A learned blockhead is a greater blockhead
    than an ignorant one.

Marry your Son when you will,
    but your Daughter when you can.

Avarice and Happiness never saw each other,
    how then shou'd they become acquainted.

❧ DECEMBER

By Mrs. Bridget Saunders, *my Dutchess, in Answer
to the* December *Verses of last Year*.

He that for sake of Drink neglects his Trade,
And spends each Night in Taverns till 'tis late,
And rises when the Sun is four hours high,
And ne'er regards his starving Family;
God in his Mercy may do much to save him.
But, woe to the poor Wife, whose Lot it is to have him.

Famine, Plague, War, and an unnumber'd throng
Of Guilt-avenging Ills, to Man belong;
Is't not enough Plagues, Wars, and Famines rise
To lash our crimes, but must our Wives be wise?

He that knows nothing of it, may by chance be a Prophet;
    while the wisest that is may happen to miss.

If you wou'd have Guests merry with your cheer,
Be so your self, or so at least appear.

Reader, farewel, all Happiness attend thee:
May each *New Year* better and richer find thee.

Of the E C L I P S E S, 1734

There will be but two: The first *April* 22, 18 min after 5 in the Morning; the second *Octob.* 15. 36 min. past 1 in the Afternoon. Both of the SUN; and both, like Mrs. ——*s*'s Modesty, and old Neighbour *Scrape-all*'s Money, *Invisible.* Or, like a certain Storekeeper late of—— County, *Not to be seen in these Parts.*

Since the Eclipses take up so little space, I have room to comply with the new Fashion, and propose a *Mathematical Question* to the *Sons of Art*; which perhaps is not more difficult to solve, nor of less Use when solved, than some of those that have been proposed by the ingenious Mr. *G——y.* It is this,

A certain rich Man had 100 *Orchards, in each Orchard was* 100 *Appletrees, under each Appletree was* 100 *Hogsties, in each Hogstie was* 100 *Sows, and each Sow had* 100 *Pigs. Question, How many Sow-Pigs were there among them?*

Note, *The Answer to this Question won't be accepted without the Solution.*

Felix quem faciunt aliena pericula cautum.

To such a height th'Expence of COURTS is gone,
That poor Men are redress'd—*till they're undone.*

William, your Cause is good, give me my Fee, and I'll defend it. But, alas! William is cast, the Verdict goes against him. *Give me another Fee, and I'll move the Court in Arrest of Judgment.* Then Sentence is confirmed. *T'other Fee, and I'll bring a Writ of Error.* But judgment is again confirm'd, and *Will* condemn'd to pay Costs. What shall we do now, Master, says William. *Why since it can't be helpt, there's no more to be said; pay the Knave his Money, and I'm satisfied.*

Of disposition they're most sweet,
Their Clients always kindly greet;
And tho' at Bar they rip old Sores,
And brawl and scold like drunken Wh——s,
Their Angers in a moment pass
Away at Night over a Glass;
Nay often laugh at the Occasion
Of their premeditated Passion.
O may you prosper as you treat us,
Until the D——l *sign your* Quietus.

Don't think to hunt two Hares with one Dog.

Poor Richard's *Almanack, &c.*

Courteous READER,

THIS is the third Time of my appearing in print, hitherto very much to my own Satisfaction, and, I have reason to hope, to the Satisfaction of the Publick also; for the Publick is generous, and has been very charitable and good to me. I should be ungrateful then, if I did not take every Opportunity of expressing my Gratitude; for *ingratum si dixeris, omnia dixeris*: I therefore return the Publick my most humble and hearty Thanks.

Whatever may be the Musick of the Spheres, how great soever the Harmony of the Stars, 'tis certain there is no Harmony among the Star-gazers; but they are perpetually growling and snarling at one another like strange Curs, or like some Men at their Wives: I had resolved to keep the Peace on my own part, and affront none of them; and I shall persist in that Resolution: But having receiv'd much Abuse from *Titan Leeds* deceas'd, (*Titan Leeds* when living would not have us'd me so!) I say, having receiv'd much Abuse from the Ghost of *Titan Leeds*, who pretends to be still living, and to write Almanacks in spight of me and my Predictions, I cannot help saying, that tho' I take it patiently, I take it very unkindly. And whatever he may pretend, 'tis undoubtedly true that

25

he is really defunct and dead. First because the Stars are seldom disappointed, never but in the Case of wise Men, *Sapiens dominabitur astris*, and they foreshow'd his Death at the Time I predicted it. Secondly, 'Twas requisite and necessary he should die punctually at that Time, for the Honour of Astrology, the Art professed both by him and his Father before him. Thirdly, 'Tis plain to every one that reads his two last Almanacks (for 1734 and 35) that they are not written with that *Life* his Performances use to be written with; the Wit is low and flat, the little Hints dull and spiritless, nothing smart in them but *Hudibras*'s Verses against Astrology at the Heads of the Months in the last, which no Astrologer but a *dead one* would have inserted, and no Man *living* would or could write such Stuff as the rest. But lastly, I shall convince him from his own Words, that he is dead, (*ex ore suo condemnatus est*) for in his Preface to his Almanack for 1734, he says, "*Saunders adds another* GROSS FALSHOOD *in his Almanack*, viz. *that by my own Calculation I shall* survive *until the* 26th *of the said Month October* 1733, *which is as* untrue *as the former*." Now if it be, as *Leeds* says, *untrue* and a *gross Falshood* that he surviv'd till the 26th of October 1733, then it is certainly *true* that he died *before* that Time: And if he died before that Time, he is dead now, to all Intents and Purposes, any thing he may say to the contrary notwithstanding. And at what Time before the 26th is it so likely he should die, as at the Time by me predicted, *viz*. the 17th of October aforesaid? But if some People will walk and be troublesome after Death, it may perhaps be born with a little, because it cannot well be avoided unless one would be at the Pains and Expence of laying them in the *Red Sea*; however, they should not presume too much upon the Liberty allow'd them; I know Confinement must needs be mighty irksome to the free Spirit of an Astronomer, and I am too compassionate to proceed suddenly to Extremities with it; nevertheless, tho' I resolve with Reluctance, I shall not long defer, if it does not speedily learn to treat its living Friends with better Manners. I am,

Courteous Reader,
Your obliged Friend and Servant,

R. SAUNDERS.

Octob. 30. 1734.

Says ♄ to ♂, Brother, when shall I see
Penn's People a scraping Acquaintance with thee?
Says ♂, only ♃ knows; but this I can tell,
They neglect me for *Hermes*, they love him too well.
O, if that be Case, says ♄, ne'er fear,
If they're tender of *Hermes*, and hold him so dear,
They'll solicit thy Help e'er I've finish'd my Round,
Using ♂ *Hermes'* Foes to deter or confound.

♒ JANUARY

The two or three Necessaries

Two or three Frolicks abroad in sweet *May*,
Two or three civil Things said by the way,
Two or three Languishes, two or three Sighs,
Two or three *Bless me's!* and *Let me die's!*
Two or three Squeezes and two or three Towzes
With 2 or 3 hundred Pound spent at their Houses
Can never fail cuckolding two or three Spouses.

Bad Commentators spoil the best of books
So God sends meat (they say) the devil Cooks.

Approve not of him who commends all you say.

By diligence and patience, the mouse bit in two the cable.

Full of courtesie, full of craft.

Look before, or you'll find yourself behind.

♓ FEBRUARY

Among the vain Pretenders of the Town,
Hibham of late is wondrous noted grown;
Hibham scarce reads, and is not worth a groat,
Yet with some high-flown Words and a fine Coat,
He struts and talks of Books, and of Estate,
And learned J——s he calls his Intimate.
The Mob admire! Thus mighty Impudence
Supplies the want of Learning, Wealth and Sense.

Poor Richard: 1735

A little House well fill'd, a little Field well till'd,
    and a little Wife well will'd, are great Riches.

Old Maids lead Apes there, where the old Batchelors
    are turn'd to Apes.

MARCH

There's many Men forget their proper Station,
And still are meddling with th' Administration
Of Government; that's wrong, and this is right,
And such a Law is out of Reason quite;
Thus spending too much Thought on State Affairs
The Business is neglected which is theirs.
So some fond Traveller gazing at the Stars
Slips in next Ditch and gets a dirty Arse.

Dyrro lynn y ddoeth e fydd ddoethach.

The poor man must walk to get meat for his stomach,
    the rich man to get a stomach to his meat.

He that goes far to marry,
        will either deceive or be deceived.

Eyes and Priests
Bear no Jests.

APRIL

William, because his Wife was something ill,
Uncertain in her Health, indifferent still,
He turn'd her out of Doors without reply:
I ask'd if he that Act could justifie.
*In Sickness and in Health, says he, I'm bound
To keep her; when she's worse or better found
I'll take her in again: And now you'll see,
She'll quickly either mend or end,* says he.

The Family of Fools is ancient.

Necessity never made a good bargain.

28

If Pride leads the Van, Beggary brings up the Rear.

There's many witty men whose brains can't fill their bellies.

Weighty Questions ask for deliberate Answers.

♊ M A Y

There's nought so silly, sure, as Vanity,
It self its chiefest End does still destroy.
To be commended still its Brains are racking
But who will give it what it's always taking?
Thou'rt fair 'tis true; and witty too, I know it;
And well-bred, *Sally*, for thy Manners show it;
But whilst thou mak'st Self-Praise thy only Care,
Thou'rt neither witty, nor well bred, nor fair.

Be slow in chusing a Friend, slower in changing.

Old *Hob* was lately married in the Night,
What needed Day, his fair young Wife is light.

Pain wastes the Body, Pleasures the Understanding.

The cunning man steals a horse, the wise man lets him alone.

When ♂ and ♀ in ♂ lie,
Then, Maids, whate'er is ask'd of you, deny.

♋ J U N E

When will the Miser's Chest be full enough?
When will he cease his Bags to cram and stuff?
All Day he labours and all Night contrives,
Providing as if he'd an hundred Lives.
While endless Care cuts short the common Span:
So have I seen with Dropsy swoln, a Man,
Drink and drink more, and still unsatisfi'd,
Drink till Drink drown'd him, yet he thirsty dy'd.

A Ship under sail and a big-bellied Woman,
Are the handsomest two things that can be seen common.

29

Keep thy shop, & thy shop will keep thee.

The King's cheese is half wasted in parings;
  but no matter, 'tis made of the peoples milk.

  Nothing but Money,
  Is sweeter than Honey.

Humility makes great men twice honourable.

❦ JULY

On Louis the XIV. *of* 𝕱rance.

Louis ('tis true, I own to you)
Paid Learned Men for Writing,
And valiant Men for Fighting;
Himself could neither write nor fight,
Nor make his People happy;
Yet Fools will prate, and call him *Great*,
Shame on their Noddles sappy.

Of learned Fools I have seen ten times ten,
Of unlearned wise men I have seen a hundred.

Three may keep a Secret, if two of them are dead.

Poverty wants some things, Luxury many things,
  Avarice all things.

A Lie stands on 1 leg, Truth on 2.

  What's given shines,
  What's receiv'd is rusty.

Sloth and Silence are a Fool's Virtues.

❧ AUGUST

Sam had the worst Wife that a Man could have,
Proud, Lazy, Sot, could neither get nor save,
Eternal Scold she was, and what is worse,
The D——l burn thee, was her common Curse.

30

Forbear, quoth *Sam*, that fruitless Curse so common,
He'll not hurt me who've married his Kinswoman.

There's small Revenge in Words, but Words
    may be greatly revenged.

Great wits jump (says the Poet) and hit his Head
    against the Post.

A man is never so ridiculous by those Qualities
    that are his own as by those that he affects to have.

Deny Self for Self's sake.

Thunder and Hail,
these Aspects seldom fail.

⚘ SEPTEMBER

Blind are the Sons of Men, few of the Kind
Know their *chief* Interest, or knowing, mind;
Most, far from following *what* they know is best,
Trifle in earnest, but mind *that* in jest.
So *Hal* the Fiddle tunes harmoniously,
While all is Discord in's Oeconomy.

Tim moderate fare and abstinence much prizes,
In publick, but in private gormandizes.

Ever since Follies have pleas'd, Fools have been able to divert.

It is better to take many Injuries than to give one.

Opportunity is the great Bawd.

    Wind and moist open weather,
    From these Aspects it I gather.

⚘ OCTOBER

Little Half-wits are wondrous pert, we find,
Scoffing and jeering on whole Womankind,
ALL false, ALL Whores, ALL this & that & t'other,

Poor Richard: 1735

Not one Exception left, ev'n for their Mother.
But Men of Wisdom and Experience know,
That there's no greater Happiness below
Than a good Wife affords; and such there's many,
For every Man has one, the best of any.

Early to bed and early to rise, makes a man healthy
   wealthy and wise.

To be humble to Superiors is Duty, to Equals Courtesy,
   to Inferiors Nobleness.

Here comes the Orator! with his Flood of Words,
   and his Drop of Reason.

❦ November

The Lying Habit is in some so strong,
To Truth they know not how to bend their Tongue;
And tho' sometimes their Ends Truth best would answer
Yet Lies come uppermost, do what they can, Sir,
Mendacio delights in telling News,
And that it may be such, himself doth use
To make it; but he now no longer need;
Let him tell Truth, it will be News indeed.

Sal laughs at every thing you say. Why?
   Because she has fine Teeth.

If what most men admire, they would despise,
'Twould look as if mankind were growing wise.

The Sun never repents of the good he does,
   nor does he ever demand a recompence.

An old young man, will be a young old man.

❧ December

'Tis not the Face with a delightful Air,
A rosy Cheek and lovely flowing Hair;
Nor sparkling Eyes to best Advantage set,

Nor all the Members rang'd in Alphabet,
Sweet in Proportion as the lovely Dies,
Which bring th' etherial Bow before our Eyes,
That can with Wisdom Approbation find,
Like pious Morals and an honest Mind;
By Virtue's living Laws from every Vice refin'd.

Some are weatherwise, some are otherwise.

Are you angry that others disappoint you?
   remember you cannot depend upon yourself.

One Mendfault is worth two Findfaults, but one Findfault
   is better than two Makefaults.

Reader, I wish thee Health, Wealth, Happiness,
And may kind Heaven thy Year's Industry bless.

Of the ECLIPSES, 1735

I shall not say much of the Signification of the Eclipses this Year, for in truth they do not signifie much; only I may observe by the way, that the first Eclipse of the Moon being celebrated in ≏ *Libra* or the *Ballance*, foreshews a Failure of Justice, where People judge in their own Cases. But in the following Year 1736, there will be six Eclipses, four of the Sun, and two of the Moon, which two Eclipses of the Moon will be both total, and portend great Revolutions in *Europe*, particularly in *Germany*; and some great and surprizing Events relating to these northern Colonies, of which I purpose to speak at large in my next.

The COURTS.

When Popery in *Britain* sway'd, I've read,
The 𝕷𝖆𝖜𝖞𝖊𝖗𝖘 fear'd they should be damn'd when dead,
Because they had no Saint to hand their Pray'rs,
And in Heav'n's Court take Care of their Affairs.
Therefore consulting, *Evanus* they sent
To *Rome* with a huge Purse, on this Intent
That to the Holy Father making known
Their woful Case, he might appoint them One.

Poor Richard: 1735

Being arriv'd, he offers his Complaint
In Language smooth, and humbly begs a Saint:
For why, says he, when others on Heav'n wou'd call, ⎞
Physicians, Seamen, Scholars, Tradesmen, all   ⎬
Have their own Saints, we *Lawyers* none at all. ⎠
The Pope was puzzel'd, never puzzel'd worse
For with pleas'd Eyes he saw the proffer'd Purse
But ne'er, in all his Knowledge or his Reading,
He'd met with one good Man that practis'd Pleading;
Who then should be the Saint? he could not tell.
At length the Thing was thus concluded well.
Within our City, says his Holiness,
There is one Church fill'd with the Images
Of all the Saints, with whom the Wall's surrounded,
Blindfold *Evanus*, lead him three times round it,
Then let him feel (*but give me first the Purse*)
And take the first he finds, for better or worse.
Round went *Evanus* till he came where stood
St. Michael with the Devil under's Foot;
And groping round, he seiz'd old Satan's Head,
This be our Saint, he cries: Amen, the Father said.
    But when they open'd poor Evanus' *Eyes,*
    Alack! he sunk with Shame and with Surprize!

Haste makes Waste.

Poor Richard's *Almanack, &c.*

Loving READERS,

YOUR kind Acceptance of my former Labours, has encouraged me to continue writing, tho' the general Approbation you have been so good as to favour me with, has excited the Envy of some, and drawn upon me the Malice of others. These Ill-willers of mine, despited at the great Reputation I gain'd by exactly predicting another Man's Death, have endeavour'd to deprive me of it all at once in the most effectual Manner by reporting that I my self was never alive. They say in short, *That there is no such a Man as I am*; and have spread this Notion so thoroughly in the Country, that I have been frequently told it to my Face by those that don't know me. This is not civil Treatment, to endeavour to deprive me of my very Being, and reduce me to a Non-entity in the Opinion of the publick. But so long as I know my self to walk about, eat, drink and sleep, I am satisfied that *there is really such a Man as I am*, whatever they may say to the contrary. And the World may be satisfied likewise; for if there were no such Man as I am, how is it possible I should appear publickly to hundreds of People, as I have done for several Years past, in print? I need not, indeed, have taken any Notice of so idle a Report, if it had not been for the sake of my Printer, to whom my Enemies are pleased to ascribe my Productions; and who it seems is as unwilling to father my Offspring, as I am to lose the Credit of it. Therefore to clear him entirely, as well as to vindicate my own Honour, I make this publick and serious Declaration, which I desire may be believed, to wit, *That what I have written heretofore and do now write, neither was nor is written by any other Man or Men, Person or Persons whatsoever.* Those who are not satisfied with this, must needs be very unreasonable.

My Performance for this Year follows; it submits itself, kind Reader, to thy Censure, but hopes for thy Candor, to forgive its Faults. It devotes itself entirely to thy Service, and will serve thee faithfully. And if it has the good Fortune to please its Master, 'tis Gratification enough for the Labour of

Poor

R. SAUNDERS.

Presumptuous Man! the Reason wouldst thou find
Why form'd so weak, so little, and so blind?
First, if thou canst, the harder reason guess
Why form'd no weaker, blinder, and no less?
Ask of thy Mother Earth, why Oaks are made,
Taller or stronger than the Weeds they shade?
Or ask of yonder argent Fields above,
Why JOVE's Satellites are less than JOVE?

JANUARY

Some have learnt many Tricks of sly Evasion,
Instead of Truth they use Equivocation,
And eke it out with mental Reservation,
Which to good Men is an Abomination.
Our Smith of late most wonderfully swore,
That whilst he breathed he would drink no more;
But since, I know his Meaning, for I think
He meant he would not breath whilst he did drink.

He is no clown that drives the plow,
    but he that doth clownish things.

If you know how to spend less than you get,
    you have the Philosophers-Stone.

The good Pay-master is Lord of another man's Purse.

Fish & Visitors stink in 3 days.

⚞ FEBRUARY

Sam's Wife provok'd him once; he broke her Crown,
The Surgeon's Bill amounted to Five Pound;
This Blow (she brags) *has cost my Husband dear,*
He'll ne'er strike more. Sam chanc'd to over-hear.
Therefore before his Wife the Bill he pays,
And to the Surgeon in her Hearing says:
Doctor, you charge Five Pound, here e'en take Ten,
My Wife may chance to want your Help again.

He that has neither fools, whores nor beggars among his
   kindred, is the son of a thunder gust.

Diligence is the Mother of Good-Luck.

He that lives upon Hope, dies farting.

Do not do that which you would not have known.

⚞ MARCH

Whate'er's desired, Knowledge, Fame, or Pelf,
Not one will change his Neighbour with himself.
The learn'd are happy Nature to explore,
The Fool is happy that he knows no more.
The Rich are happy in the Plenty given;
The Poor contents him with the Care of Heav'n.
Thus does some Comfort ev'ry State attend.
And Pride's bestow'd on all, a common Friend.

Never praise your Cyder, Horse, or Bedfellow.

Wealth is not his that has it, but his that enjoys it.

Tis easy to see, hard to foresee.

In a discreet man's mouth, a publick thing is private.

Poor Richard: 1736

⚘ APRIL

By nought is Man from Beast distinguished
More than by Knowledge in his learned Head.
Then Youth improve thy Time, but cautious see
That what thou learnest some how useful be.
Each Day improving, *Solon* waxed old;
For Time he knew was better far than Gold:
Fortune might give him Gold which would decay,
But Fortune cannot give him Yesterday.

Let thy maid-servant be faithful, strong, and homely.

Keep flax from fire, youth from gaming.

Bargaining has neither friends nor relations.

Admiration is the Daughter of Ignorance.

There's more old Drunkards than old Doctors.

⚘ MAY

Lalus who loves to hear himself discourse
   Keeps talking still as if he frantick were,
And tho' himself might no where hear a worse,
   Yet he no other but himself will hear.
Stop not his Mouth, if he be troublesome,
But stop his Ears, and then the Man is dumb.

She that paints her Face, thinks of her Tail.

Here comes Courage! that seiz'd the lion absent,
   and run away from the present mouse.

He that takes a wife, takes care.

Nor Eye in a letter, nor Hand in a purse,
   nor Ear in the secret of another.

He that buys by the penny, maintains not only himself,
   but other people.

⚓ JUNE

Things that are bitter, bitterrer than Gall
Physicians say are always physical:
Now Women's Tongues if into Powder beaten,
May in a Potion or a Pill be eaten,
And as there's nought more bitter, I do muse,
That Women's Tongues in Physick they ne'er use.
My self and others who lead restless Lives,
Would spare that bitter Member of our Wives.

If we have rain about the Change,
Let not my reader think it strange.

He that can have Patience, can have what he will.

Now I've a sheep and a cow, every body bids me good morrow.

God helps them that help themselves.

Why does the blind man's wife paint herself?

⚓ JULY

Who can charge *Ebrio* with Thirst of Wealth?
See he consumes his Money, Time and Health,
In drunken Frolicks which will all confound,
Neglects his Farm, forgets to till his Ground,
His Stock grows less that might be kept with ease;
In nought but Guts and Debts he finds Encrease.
In Town reels as if he'd shove down each Wall,
Yet Walls must stand, poor Soul, or he must fall.

None preaches better than the ant, and she says nothing.

The absent are never without fault,
    nor the present without excuse.

    If wind blows on you thro' a hole,
    Make your will and take care of your soul.

The rotten Apple spoils his Companion.

Poor Richard: 1736

❧ AUGUST

The Tongue was once a Servant to the Heart,
And what it gave she freely did impart;
But now Hypocrisy is grown so strong
The Heart's become a Servant to the Tongue.
Virtue we praise, but practice not her good,
(Athenian-like), we act not what we know,
As many Men do talk of *Robin Hood*
Who never did shoot Arrow in his Bow.

Don't throw stones at your neighbours,
    if your own windows are glass.

The excellency of hogs is fatness, of men virtue.

Good wives and good plantations are made by good husbands.

Pox take you, is no curse to some people.

He that sells upon trust, loses many friends,
    and always wants money.

Gifts burst rocks.

❧ SEPTEMBER

Briskcap, *thou'st little Judgment in thy Head,*
More than to dress thee, drink and go to Bed:
Yet thou shalt have the Wall, and the Way lead,
Since Logick wills that simple Things precede.

    Walking and meeting one not long ago,
I ask'd who 'twas, he said, he did not know.
I said, I know thee; so said he, I you;
But he that knows himself I never knew.

Force shites upon Reason's Back.

Lovers, Travellers, and Poets, will give money to be heard.

He that speaks much, is much mistaken.

Creditors have better memories than debtors.

Forewarn'd, forearm'd, unless in the case of Cuckolds,
who are often forearm'd before warn'd.

⚜ OCTOBER

Whimsical *Will* once fancy'd he was ill,
The Doctor's call'd, who thus examin'd *Will;*
How is your Appetite? O, as to that
I eat right heartily, you see I'm fat.
How is your Sleep anights? 'Tis sound and good;
I eat, drink, sleep as well as e'er I cou'd.
Well, says the Doctor, clapping on his Hat;
I'll give you something shall remove all that.

Three things are men most liable to be cheated in,
a Horse, a Wig, and a Wife.

He that lives well, is learned enough.

Poverty, Poetry, and new Titles of Honour,
make Men ridiculous.

He that scatters Thorns, let him not go barefoot.

There's none deceived but he that trusts.

⚜ NOVEMBER

When you are sick, what you like best is to be chosen for
a Medicine in the first Place; what Experience tells you is best,
is to be chosen in the second Place; what Reason (*i.e.* Theory)
says is best, is to be chosen in the last Place. But if you can get
Dr. *Inclination*, Dr. *Experience* and Dr. *Reason* to hold a Consultation together, they will give you the best Advice that can
be given.

God heals, and the Doctor takes the Fees.

If you desire many things, many things will seem but a few.

Mary's mouth costs her nothing,
for she never opens it but at others expence.

Receive before you write, but write before you pay.

I saw few die of Hunger, of Eating 100000.

☙ DECEMBER

☉ nearer the Earth in Winter than in Summer 15046 miles, (*his Lowness and short Appearance making Winter cold*) ☽ nearer in her *Perigeon* than *Apogeon*, 69512 miles: ♄ nearer 49868 miles; ♃ nearer 38613 miles: ♂ nearer 80608 miles: ♀ nearer 6209 miles: ☿ nearer 181427 miles. And yet ☿ is never distant from the ☉ a whole Sign, nor ♀ above two: You'll never find a ✶ ☉ ☿, nor a ☐ ☉ ♀.

Maids of *America*, who gave you bad teeth?
Answ. Hot Soupings & frozen Apples.

Marry your Daughter and eat fresh Fish betimes.

If God blesses a Man, his Bitch brings forth Pigs.

He that would live in peace & at ease,
Must not speak all he knows, nor judge all he sees.

Adieu.

Of the ECLIPSES, 1736.

There will be this Year six Eclipses, four of the Sun, and two of the Moon; those of the Moon both visible and total.

The first is a small Eclipse of the Sun, *March* the first, 35 minutes past 9 in the Morn. Scarcely visible in these Parts.

The second is an Eclipse of the Moon, *March* 15, beginning 30 minutes after 4 a Clock, *P. M.* the Moon being then beneath our Horizon, and rises totally dark, and continues so till 25 minutes after 7, and the Eclipse is not entirely ended till 20 minutes after 8. This Eclipse falls in *Libra*, or the Balance. Poor Germania! *Mene, mene, tekel upharsin!*

The Third is of the Sun, *March* 31. 30 minutes past 2 in the Morning. Invisible here.

The Fourth is of the Sun likewise, *Aug.* 25. 35 minutes after three in the Morning; no more to be seen than the former; the Sun at the Conjunction being under the Horizon.

The Fifth is of the Moon, *Sept.* 8. 18 minutes after 8 at Night; Beginning of total Darkness 18 min. after 9. Time of Emergence 57 min. after 10. End of the Eclipse at midnight.

The 6th and last, is of the Sun, *September* 23 at Noon: Invisible here tho' the Sun itself be visible. For there is this Difference between Eclipses of the Moon and of the Sun, *viz.* All Lunar Eclipses are universal, *i. e.* visible in all Parts of the Globe which have the Moon above their Horizon, and are every where of the same Magnitude: But Eclipses of the Sun do not appear the same in all Parts of the Earth where they are seen; being when total in some Places, only partial in others; and in other Places not seen at all, tho' neither Clouds nor Horizon prevent the Sight of the Sun it self.

As to the Effects of these two great Eclipses, suffer me to observe, that whoever studies the Eclipses of former Ages, and compares them with the great Events in the History of the Times and Years in which they happened (as every true Astrologer ought to do) shall find, that the Fall of the *Assyrian, Persian, Grecian* and *Roman* Monarchies, each of them, was remarkably preceded by great and total Eclipses of the Heavenly Bodies. Observations of this kind, join'd with the ancient and long-try'd Rules of our Art, (too tedious to repeat here) make me tremble for an Empire now in being. O *Christendom*! why art thou so fatally divided against thy self? O *Poland*! formerly the Bulwark of the Christian Faith, wilt thou become the Flood-gate to let in an Inundation of Infidelity? O mischievous *Crescent*! when shall we see thee at the Full, and rejoice at thy future Waning? May Heaven avert these presag'd Misfortunes, and confound the Designs of all wicked and impious Men!

COURTS.

For Gratitude there's none exceed 'em,
(Their Clients know this when they bleed 'em).
Since they who give most for their Laws,
Have most return'd, and carry th' Cause.
All know, except an arrant Tony,
That Right and Wrong's meer Ceremony.
It is enough that the Law Jargon,
Gives the best Bidder the best Bargain.

In my last Year's Almanack I mention'd, that the visible Eclipses of this Year, 1736, portended some great & surprizing Events relating to these Northern Colonies, of which I purposed this Year to speak at large. But as those Events are not to happen immediately this Year, I chuse rather, upon second Thought, to defer farther Mention of them, till the Publication of my Almanack for that Year in which they are to happen. However, that the Reader may not be entirely disappointed, here follow for his present Amusement a few

ENIGMATICAL PROPHECIES

Which they that do not understand, cannot well explain.

1. Before the middle of this Year, a Wind at N. East will arise, during which the *Water of the* Sea and Rivers will be in such a manner raised, that great part of the Towns of *Boston, Newport, New-York, Philadelphia*, the low Lands of *Maryland* and *Virginia*, and the Town of *Charlstown* in *South Carolina*, will be *under Water*. Happy will it be for the Sugar & Salt, standing in the Cellars of those Places, if there be tight Roofs and Cielings overhead; otherwise, without being a Conjurer, a Man may easily foretel that such Commodities will receive Damage.

2. About the middle of the Year, great Numbers of Vessels fully laden will be taken out of the Ports aforesaid, by a *Power* with which we are not now at War, and whose Forces shall not be *descried or seen* either coming or going. But in the End this may not be disadvantageous to those Places.

3. However, not long after, a visible Army of 20000 *Musketers* will land, some in *Virginia* & *Maryland*, and some in the lower Counties on both sides of *Delaware*, who will over-run the Country, and sorely annoy the Inhabitants: But the Air in this Climate will agree with them so ill towards Winter, that they will die in the beginning of cold Weather like rotten Sheep, and by Christmas the Inhabitans will get the better of them.

Note, *In my next Almanack these Enigmatical Prophecies will be explained.*

R.S.

1737

Poor Richard's Almanack, &c.

Courteous and Kind READER,

THIS is the fifth Time I have appear'd in Publick, chalking out the future Year for my honest Countrymen, and foretelling what shall, and what may, and what may not come to pass; in which I have the Pleasure to find that I have given general Satisfaction. Indeed, among the Multitude of our astrological Predictions, 'tis no wonder if some few fail; for, without any Defect in the Art itself, 'tis well known that a small Error, a single wrong Figure overseen in a Calculation, may occasion great Mistakes: But however we Almanack-makers may *miss it* in other things, I believe it will be generally allow'd *That we always hit the Day of the Month*, and that I suppose is esteem'd one of the most useful Things in an Almanack.

As to the Weather, if I were to fall into the Method my Brother J——n sometimes uses, and tell you, *Snow here or in New England,—Rain here or in South-Carolina,—Cold to the Northward,—Warm to the Southward*, and the like, whatever Errors I might commit, I should be something more secure of not being detected in them: But I consider, it will be of no Service to any body to know what Weather it is 1000 miles off, and therefore I always set down positively what Weather my Reader will have, be he where he will at the time. We modestly desire only the favourable Allowance of *a day or two before* and *a day or two after* the precise Day against which the Weather is set; and if it does not come to pass accordingly, let the Fault be laid upon the Printer, who, 'tis very like, may have transpos'd or misplac'd it, perhaps for the Conveniency of putting in his Holidays: And since, in spight of all I can say, People will give him great part of the Credit of making my Almanacks, 'tis but reasonable he should take some share of the Blame.

I must not omit here to thank the Publick for the gracious and kind Encouragement they have hitherto given me: But if the generous Purchaser of my Labours could see how often his *Fi'-pence* helps to light up the comfortable Fire, line the Pot, fill the Cup and make glad the Heart of a poor Man and an honest good old Woman, he would not think his Money ill laid out, tho' the Almanack of his

Friend and Servant

R. SAUNDERS

were one half blank Paper.

HINTS *for those that would be* Rich.

The use of Money is all the Advantage there is in having Money.

For 6*l.* a Year, you may have Use of 100*l.* if you are a Man of known Prudence and Honesty.

He that spends a Groat a day idly, spends idly above 6*l.* a year, which is the Price of using 100*l.*

He that wastes idly a Groat's worth of his Time per Day, one Day with another, wastes the Privilege of using 100*l.* each Day.

He that idly loses 5*s.* worth of time, loses 5*s.* and might as prudently throw 5*s.* in the River.

He that loses 5*s.* not only loses that Sum, but all the Advantage that might be made by turning it in Dealing, which by the time that a young Man becomes old, amounts to a comfortable Bag of Mony.

Again, He that sells upon Credit, asks a Price for what he sells, equivalent to the Principal and Interest of his Money for the Time he is like to be kept out of it: therefore

He that buys upon Credit, pays Interest for what he buys.

And he that pays ready Money, might let that Money out to use: so that

He that possesses any Thing he has bought, pays Interest for the Use of it.

Consider then, when you are tempted to buy any unnecessary Housholdstuff, or any superfluous thing, whether you will be willing to pay *Interest, and Interest upon Interest* for it as long as you live; and more if it grows worse by using.

Yet, in buying Goods, 'tis best to pay ready Money, because,

He that sells upon Credit, expects to lose 5 *per Cent.* by bad Debts; therefore he charges, on all he sells upon Credit, an Advance that shall make up that Deficiency.

Those who pay for what they buy upon Credit, pay their share of this Advance.

He that pays ready Money, escapes or may escape that Charge.

A Penny sav'd is Twopence clear, A pin a day is a Groat a Year. Save & have. Every little makes a mickle.

Light Purse, heavy Heart.

JANUARY

God offer'd to the Jews salvation
And 'twas refus'd by half the Nation:
Thus, (tho' 'tis Life's great Preservation)
Many oppose *inoculation.*
We're told by one of the black Robe
The Devil inoculated Job:
Suppose 'tis true, what he does tell;
Pray, Neighbours, *Did not Job do well?*

The greatest monarch on the proudest throne,
  is oblig'd to sit upon his own arse.

The Master piece of Man, is to live to the purpose.

He that steals the old man's supper, do's him no wrong.

FEBRUARY

The *Thracian* Infant, entring into Life,
Both Parents mourn for, both receive with Grief:
The *Thracian* Infant snatch'd by Death away,
Both Parents to the Grave with Joy convey.
This, *Greece* and *Rome*, you with Derision view;
This is meer *Thracian* Ignorance to you:
But if you weigh the Custom you despise,
This *Thracian* Ignorance may teach the wise.

A countryman between 2 Lawyers,
  is like a fish between two cats.

He that can take rest is greater than he that can take cities.

The miser's cheese is wholesomest.

Felix quem, &c.

MARCH

Doris, a Widow, past her Prime,
  Her Spouse long dead, her Wailing doubles;

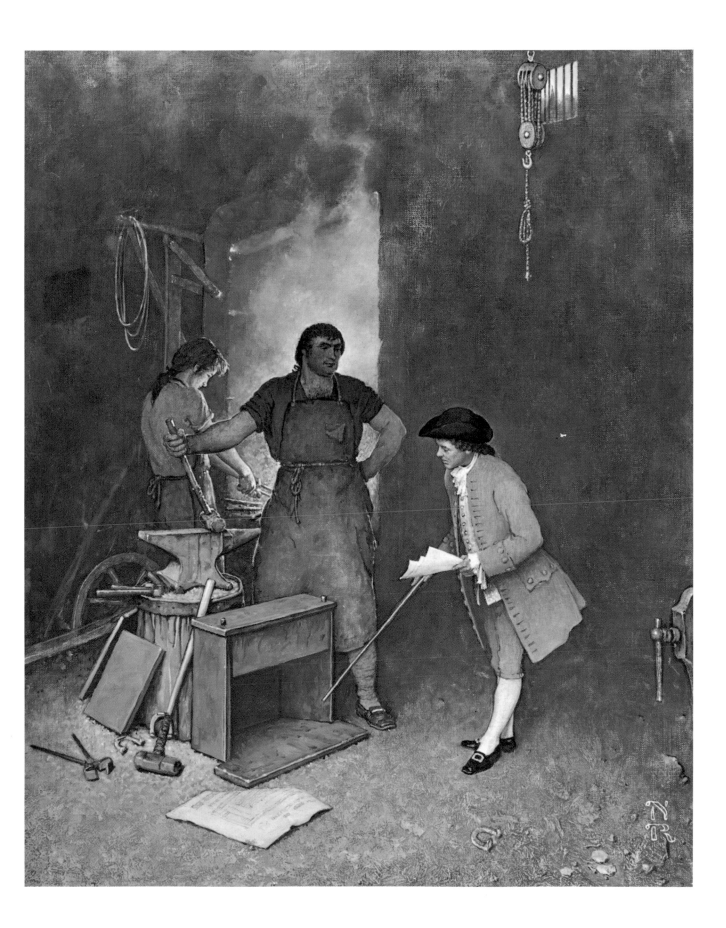

Her real Griefs increase by Time;
    What might abate, improves her Troubles.
Those Pangs her prudent Hopes supprest,
    Impatient now, she cannot smother,
How should the helpless Woman rest?
    One's gone; nor can she get another.

Love & lordship hate companions.

The nearest way to come at glory,
    is to do that for conscience which we do for glory.

There is much money given to be laught at,
    though the purchasers don't know it;
    witness *A's* fine horse, & *B's* fine house.

APRIL

A Nymph and a Swain to *Apollo* once pray'd;
The Swain had been jilted, the Nymph been betray'd
They came for to try if his Oracle knew
E'er a Nymph that was chast or a Swain that was true
Apollo stood mute, and had like t'have been pos'd;
At length he thus sagely the question disclos'd:
He alone may be true in whom none will confide,
And the nymph may be chast that has never been tryd.

He that can compose himself,
    is wiser than he that composes books.

Poor Dick, eats like a well man, and drinks like a sick.

After crosses and losses men grow humbler & wiser.

Love, Cough, & a Smoke, can't well be hid.

MAY

Rich *Gripe* does all his Thoughts & Cunning bend
T' encrease that Wealth he wants the Soul to spend:
Poor *Shifter* does his whole Contrivance set,
To spend that Wealth he wants the Sense to get.

How happy would appear to each his Fate,
Had *Gripe* his Humour, or he *Gripe's* Estate?
Kind Fate and Fortune, blend 'em if you can,
And of two *Wretches* make one happy Man.

Well done is better than well said.

   Fine linnen, girls and gold so bright.
   Chuse not to take by candle-light.

He that can travel well afoot, keeps a good horse.

There are no ugly Loves, nor handsome Prisons.

No better relation than a prudent & faithful Friend.

JUNE

   Boy, bring a Bowl of China here,
   Fill it with Water cool and clear:
   Decanter with Jamaica right,
   And Spoon of Silver clean and bright,
   Sugar twice-fin'd, in pieces cut,
   Knife, Sieve and Glass, in order put,
   Bring forth the fragrant Fruit, and then
   We're happy till the Clock strikes Ten.

A Traveller should have a hog's nose, deer's legs,
   and an ass's back.

At the working man's house hunger looks in
   but dares not enter.

A good Lawyer a bad Neighbour.

JULY

Impudent *Jack*, who now lives by his Shifts,
Borrowing of Driblets, boldly begging Gifts;
For Twenty Shillings lent him t'other day
(By one who ne'er expected he would pay)
On his Friend's Paper fain a Note wou'd write;

His Friend, as needless, did refuse it quite;
Paper was scarce, and 'twas too hard, it's true,
To part with Cash, and lose his Paper too.

    Certainlie these things agree,
    The Priest, the Lawyer, & Death all three:
    Death takes both the weak and the strong.
    The lawyer takes from both right and wrong,
    And the priest from living and dead has his Fee.

The worst wheel of the cart makes the most noise.

AUGUST

    On his Death-bed poor *Lubin* lies;
        His Spouse is in Despair;
    With frequent Sobs, and mutual Cries,
        They both express their Care.
    A diff'rent cause, says Parson *Sly*,
        The same Effect may give;
    Poor *Lubin* fears that he shall die;
        His Wife, that he may live.

Don't misinform your Doctor nor your Lawyer.

    I never saw an oft-transplanted tree,
    Nor yet an oft-removed family,
    That throve so well as those that settled be.

SEPTEMBER

To morrow you'll reform, you always cry;
In what far Country does this Morrow lie,
That 'tis so mighty long e'er it arrive?
Beyond the *Indies* does this Morrow live?
'Tis so far-fetch'd, this Morrow, that I fear,
'Twill be both very old, and very dear.
To-morrow I'll reform, the Fool does say:
To day it self's too late; the *Wise* did yesterday.

Three good meals a day is bad living.

Poor Richard: 1737

Let the letter stay for the Post, and not the Post for
the Letter.

Tis better leave for an enemy at one's death, than
beg of a friend in one's life.

To whom thy secret thou dost tell,
To him thy freedom thou dost sell.

❧ OCTOBER

On T. T. who destroy'd his Landlord's fine Wood.

Indulgent Nature to each kind bestows,
A secret Instinct to discern its Foes:
The Goose, a silly Bird, avoids the Fox;
Lambs fly from Wolves; & Sailors steer from rocks;
A Rogue the Gallows, as his Fate, foresees,
And bears the like Antipathy to Trees.

If you'd have a Servant that you like, serve your self.

He that pursues two Hares at once, does not catch one
and lets t'other go.

If you want a neat wife, chuse her on a Saturday.

If you have time don't wait for time.

❧ NOVEMBER

You say you'll spend Five hundred Pound
    The World and Men to know,
And take a Tour all *Europe* round,
    Improving as you go.
Dear *Sam*, in search of others sense,
    Discover not your own;
But wisely double the Expence
    That you may pass unknown.

Tell a miser he's rich, and a woman she's old,
    you'll get no money of one, nor kindness of t'other.

Don't go to the doctor with every distemper, nor to the
   lawyer with every quarrel, nor to the pot for every thirst.

DECEMBER

Women are Books, and Men the Readers be,
Who sometimes in those Books Erratas see;
Yet oft the Reader's raptur'd with each Line,
Fair Print and Paper fraught with Sense divine;
Tho' some neglectful seldom care to read,
And faithful Wives no more than Bibles heed.
Are Women Books? says *Hodge*, then would mine were
An *Almanack*, to change her every Year.

The Creditors are a superstitious sect,
   great observers of set days and times.

The noblest question in the world is,
   What Good may I do in it?

Nec sibi, sed toto, genitum se credere mundo.

Nothing so popular as GOODNESS.

Of the ECLIPSES, 1737.

There will be four Eclipses this Year, two of the Sun and two of the
Moon.

The first is a great and visible Eclipse of the Sun, *Feb.* 18. beginning at 8 h. 1 m. A.M. middle at 9 h. 11 m. end at 10 h. 20 m. Digits
eclipsed near nine, on the upper side of the Sun.

The second is of the Moon, *March* 5. at 10 h. 34 m. in the morning,
therefore invisible here.

The third is of the Sun, *Aug.* 14. at 7 h. 30 m. P.M. invisible also.

The fourth is a visible Defect of the Moon, *Aug.* 28. beginning 9 h.
40 m. P.M. the middle at 10 h. 51 m. End near midnight. Digits eclipsed
five & a quarter.

In my last, on the second Eclipse, which was of the Moon, *March*,
1736. celebrated in ♎ or *the Balance*, I hinted, *That Germany would be
weighed and found wanting.* The Course of the Year (I speak without

Boasting) has verified that Prediction; for that Empire now weighed in the *Balance of Europe*, is found to want two Kingdoms, to wit *Naples* & *Sicily*. May the Doubts I expressed concerning the Empire itself, prove groundless as to *Germany*, and be verified in the Turkish Dominion. *Tekel, Peres.*

In my last I published some *Enigmatical Prophecies*, which I did not expect any one would take for serious Predictions. The Explanation I promised, follows, *viz.*

1. The Water of the Sea and Rivers is raised in Vapours by the Sun, is form'd into Clouds in the Air, and thence descends in Rain. Now when there is Rain overhead, (which frequently happens when the Wind is at N.E.) the Cities and Places on the Earth below, are certainly *under Water*.

2. The Power with which *we were not then at War*, but which, it was said, would take many full laden Vessels out of our Ports before the End of the Year, is The WIND, whose Forces also *are not descried either coming or going.*

3. The Army which it was said would *land* in *Virginia, Maryland,* and the *Lower Counties* on *Delaware*, were not *Musketeers* with Guns on their Shoulders as some expected; but their Namesakes, in Pronunciation, tho' truly spelt *Moschitos*, arm'd only with a sharp Sting. Every one knows they are Fish before they fly, being bred in the Water; and therefore may properly be said *to land* before they become generally troublesome.

A WONDERFUL PROPHECY

For January 1737, *which consists entirely of odd Figures.*

E'er of this odd odd Year one Month has roll'd,
What Wonders, Reader, shall the World behold!
Four Kings with mighty Force shall *Albion's* Isle
Infest with Wars and Tumults for a while;
Then some shall unexpected Treasures gain,
While some mourn o'er an empty Purse in vain:
And many a christian's Heart shall ake for Fear,
When they the dreadful Sound of Trump shall hear.
Dead Bones shall then be tumbled up and down,
In every City and in every Town.

Poor Richard's Almanack, &c.

PREFACE by Mistress SAUNDERS

Dear READERS,

MY good Man set out last Week for *Potowmack*, to visit an old Stargazer of his Acquaintance, and see about a little Place for us to settle and end our Days on. He left the Copy of his Almanack seal'd up, and bid me send it to the Press. I suspected something, and therefore, as soon as he was gone, I open'd it, to see if he had not been flinging some of his old Skitts at me. Just as I thought, so it was. And truly, (for want of somewhat else to say, I suppose) he had put into his Preface, that his Wife *Bridget*—was this, and that, and t'other. —What a pease-cods! cannot I have a little Fault or two, but all the Country must see it in print! They have already been told, at one time that I am proud, another time that I am loud, and that I have got a new Petticoat, and abundance of such kind of stuff; and now, forsooth! all the World must know, that *Poor Dick's* Wife has lately taken a fancy to drink a little Tea now and then. A mighty matter, truly, to make a Song of! 'Tis true; I had a little Tea of a Present from the Printer last Year; and what, must a body throw it away? In short, I thought the Preface was not worth a printing, and so I fairly scratch'd it all out, and I believe you'll like our Almanack never the worse for it.

Upon looking over the Months, I see he has put in abundance of foul Weather this Year; and therefore I have scatter'd here and there, where I could find room, some *fair, pleasant, sunshiny*, &c. for the Good-Women to dry their Clothes in. If it does not come to pass according to my Desire, I have shown my Good-will, however; and I hope they'll take it in good part.

I had a Design to make some other Corrections; and particularly to change some of the Verses that I don't very well like; but I have just now unluckily broke my Spectacles; which obliges me to give it you as it is, and conclude

Your loving Friend,

BRIDGET SAUNDERS

Lo as a Giant strong, the lusty Sun
Multiply'd Rounds in one great Round doth run.
Twofold his Course, yet constant his Career
Changing the Day and finishing the Year.
Again when his descending Orb retires
And Earth perceives the Absence of his Fires
The Moon affords us her alternate Ray,
And with kind Beams distributes fainter Day.

JANUARY

Dick's Wife was sick, and pos'd the Doctor's Skill,
Who differ'd how to cure th' inveterate Ill.
Purging the one prescrib'd. No, quoth another,
That will do neither Good nor Harm, my Brother.
Bleeding's the only Way; 'twas quick reply'd,
That's certain Death;—But e'en let *Dick* decide.
Ise no great Skill, quo' Richard, *by the Rood;*
But I think Bleeding's like to do most good.

There are three faithful friends,
   an old wife, an old dog, and ready money.

Great talkers should be cropt, for they've no need of ears.

If you'd have your shoes last, put no nails in 'em.

Who has deceiv'd thee so oft as thy self?

☙ FEBRUARY

In Christendom we all are *Christians* now,
And thus I answer, if you ask me how;
Where with *Christ's Rule* our Lives will not comply,
We bend it like a Rule of Lead, say I;
Making it thus comply with what we be,
And only thus our Lives with th' Rule agree.
But from our Fathers we've the Name (perchance)
Ay, so our King is call'd *the King of France*.

Is there any thing Men take more pains about
than to render themselves unhappy?

Nothing brings more pain than too much pleasure; nothing
more bondage than too much liberty, (or libertinism).

Read much, but not many Books.

☙ MARCH

Jack's Wife was born in *Wiltshire*, brought up in *Cumberland*, led much of her Life in *Bedfordshire*, sent her Husband into *Huntingdonshire* in order to bring him into *Buckinghamshire*: But he took Courage in *Hartfordshire*, and carry'd her into *Staffordshire*, or else he might have liv'd and dy'd in *Shrewsbury*.

He that would have a short Lent,
Let him borrow Money to be repaid at Easter.

Write with the learned, pronounce with the vulgar.

Fly Pleasures, and they'll follow you.

Squirrel-like she covers her back with her tail.

APRIL

The old Gentry.

That all from Adam first begun,
    Since none but *Whiston* doubts,
And that his Son, and his Son's Son
    Were Plowmen, Clowns and Louts;
Here lies the only Difference now,
    Some shot off late, some soon;
Your Sires i'th' Morning left the Plow,
    And ours i'th' Afternoon.

Cæsar did not merit the triumphal Car,
    more than he that conquers himself.

Hast thou virtue? acquire also the graces & beauties of virtue.

Buy what thou hast no need of;
    and e'er long thou shalt sell thy necessaries.

If thou hast wit & learning, add to it Wisdom and Modesty.

MAY

A frugal Thought.

In an Acre of Land are 43560 square feet,
In 100 Acres are 4356000 square feet;
Twenty Pounds will buy 100 Acres of the Proprietor.
In 20*l*. are 4800 pence; by which divide the Number
    of Feet in 100 Acres; and you will find that one penny
    will buy 907 square Feet; or a Lot of 30 Feet square.
    —*Save your Pence.*

You may be more happy than Princes,
    if you will be more virtuous.

    If you wou'd not be forgotten
    As soon as you are dead and rotten,
    Either write things worth reading,
    or do things worth the writing.

Sell not virtue to purchase wealth, nor Liberty
  to purchase power.

⚓ JUNE

Epitaph on a talkative old Maid.

Beneath this silent Stone is laid,
A noisy antiquated Maid,
Who from her Cradle talk'd 'till Death,
And ne'er before was out of Breath.
Whither she's gone we cannot tell;
For, if she talks not, she's in Hell:
If she's in Heaven, she's there unblest,
Because she hates a Place of Rest.

Let thy vices die before thee.

Keep your eyes wide open before marriage,
  half shut afterwards.

The ancients tell us what is best;
  but we must learn of the moderns what is fittest.

⚓ JULY

One Month a Lawyer, thou the next wilt be
A grave Physician, and the third a Priest:
Chuse quickly one Profession of the three,
Marry'd to her thou may'st court the rest.
Resolve at once; deliberate no more;
Leap in, and stand not shiv'ring on the Shore.
On any one amiss thou can'st not fall:
Thou'lt end in nothing, if thou grasps at all.

'Tis less discredit to abridge petty charges,
  than to stoop to petty Gettings.

Since thou art not sure of a minute,
  throw not away an hour.

Since I cannot govern my own tongue, tho' within my own teeth, how can I hope to govern the tongues of others?

⚜ AUGUST

While faster than his costive Brain indites
Philo's quick Hand in flowing Nonsence writes,
His Case appears to me like honest *Teague*'s,
When he was run away with by his Legs.
Phæbus, give Philo o'er himself Command;
Quicken his Senses, or restrain his Hand;
Let him be kept from Paper, Pen and Ink;
So he may cease to write, and learn to think.

If you do what you should not,
    you must hear what you would not.

Defer not thy well-doing; be not like St. *George*,
    who is always a horseback, and never rides on.

Wish not so much to live long as to live well.

♏ SEPTEMBER

These Lines may be read backward or forward.

Joy, Mirth, Triumph, I do defie;
Destroy me Death, fain would I die:
Forlorn am I, Love is exil'd,
Scorn smiles thereat; Hope is beguil'd;
    Men banish'd bliss, in Woe must dwell,
    Then Joy, Mirth, Triumph all farewell.

As we must account for every idle word,
    so we must for every idle silence.

I have never seen the Philosopher's Stone that turns lead
    into Gold; but I have known the pursuit of it turn a Man's
    Gold into Lead.

Never intreat a servant to dwell with thee.

✵ October

A Doubtful Meaning:

The Female kind is counted ill:
And is indeed; The contrary;
No Man can find: That hurt they will:
But every where: Shew Charity;
To no Body: Malicious still;
In word or Deed: Believe you me.

Time is an herb that cures all Diseases.

Reading makes a full Man, Meditation a profound Man,
   discourse a clear Man.

If any man flatters me, I'll flatter him again;
   tho' he were my best Friend.

✵ November

A Monster in a Course of Vice grown old,
Leaves to his gaping Heir his ill-gain'd Gold;
The Preacher fee'd, strait are his Virtues shown;
And render'd lasting by the sculptur'd Stone.
If on the Stone or Sermon we rely,
Pity a Worth, like his, should ever die!
If Credit to his real Life we give,
Pity a Wretch like him, should ever live.

Wish a miser long life, and you wish him no good.

None but the well bred man knows how to confess a fault,
   or acknowledge himself in an error.

Drive thy business; let not that drive thee.

There is much difference between imitating a good man,
   and counterfeiting him.

Each year one vicious habit rooted out,
In time might make the worst Man good throughout.

❧ December

The Wiseman says, *It is a Wiseman's Part*
To keep his Tongue close Prisoner in his Heart.
If he then be a Fool whose Thought denies
There is a God, how desp'rately unwise,
How much more Fool is he whose Language shall
Proclaim in publick, *There's no God at all*:
What then are they, nay Fools in what degree
Whose Actions shall maintain't? *Such Fools are we.*

Wink at small faults; remember thou hast great ones.

Eat to please thyself, but dress to please others.

Search others for their virtues, thy self for thy vices.

Never spare the Parson's wine, nor Baker's Pudding.

Of the ECLIPSES, 1738.

There will be two, and both of the SUN.

The First on *Feb.* 7 at 1 afternoon, hardly visible here, but a great Eclipse in *Brasil, Peru, Paragua* and other southern Countries in *America*. And to the Astrologers of those Parts we leave it, to harangue on its terrible Effects.

The other on *August* 4. *A. M.* beginning at 4 h. 20 m. Middle at 5 h. 29 m. End at 6 h. 38 m. Digits Eclipsed 5 and three quarters on the north or upper Side. They that would see *Phœbus* with his Night-cap on this Morning, should be out of Bed before him to watch his Rising; and perhaps after all may be disappointed, by his intercepting Window-Curtains.

You will excuse me, dear Readers, that I afford you no Eclipses of the Moon this Year. The Truth is, I do not find they do you any Good. When there is one you are apt in observing it to expose yourselves too much and too long to the Night Air, whereby great Numbers of you catch Cold. Which was the Case last Year, to my very great Concern. However, if you will promise to take more Care of your selves, you shall have a fine one to stare at, the Year after next.

1739

Poor Richard's *Almanack, &c.*

Kind READER,

ENCOURAGED by thy former Generosity, I once more present thee with an Almanack, which is the 7th of my Publication.— While thou are putting Pence in my Pocket, and furnishing my Cottage with Necessaries, *Poor Dick* is not unmindful to do something for thy Benefit. The Stars are watch'd as narrowly as old *Bess* watch'd her Daughter, that thou mayst be acquainted with their Motions, and told a Tale of their Influences and Effects, which may do thee more good than a Dream of last Year's Snow.

Ignorant Men wonder how we Astrologers foretell the Weather so exactly, unless we deal with the old black Devil. Alas! 'tis as easy as pissing abed. For Instance; The Stargazer peeps at the Heavens thro' a long Glass: He sees perhaps *TAURUS*, or the great Bull, in a mighty Chase, stamping on the Floor of his House, swinging his Tail about, stretching out his Neck, and opening wide his Mouth. 'Tis natural from these Appearances to judge that this furious Bull is puffing, blowing, and roaring. Distance being consider'd, and Time allow'd for all this to come down, there you have Wind and Thunder. He spies perhaps *VIRGO* (or the Virgin); she turns her Head round as it were to see if any body observ'd her; then crouching down gently, with her Hands on her Knees, she looks wistfully for a while right forward. He judges rightly what she's about: And having calculated the Distance and allow'd Time for it's Falling, finds that next Spring we shall have a fine *April* shower. What can be more natural and easy than this? I might instance the like in many other particulars; but this may be sufficient to prevent our being taken for Conjurers. O the wonderful Knowledge to be found in the Stars! Even the smallest Things are written there, if you had but Skill to read. When my Brother *J—m—n* erected a Scheme to know which was best for his sick Horse, to sup a new-laid Egg, or a little Broth, he found that the Stars plainly gave their Verdict for Broth, and the Horse having sup'd his Broth; —— Now, what do you think became of that Horse? You shall know in my next.

Besides the usual Things expected in an Almanack, I hope the profess'd Teachers of Mankind will excuse my scattering here and there some instructive Hints in Matters of Morality and Religion. And be not thou disturbed, O grave and sober Reader, if among the many serious Sentences in my Book, thou findest me trifling now and then, and talking idly. In all the Dishes I have hitherto cook'd for thee, there is solid Meat enough for thy Money. There are Scraps from the Table of Wisdom, that will if well digested, yield strong Nourishment to thy Mind. But squeamish Stomachs cannot eat without Pickles; which 'tis true are good for nothing else, but they provoke an Appetite. The Vain Youth that reads my Almanack for the sake of an idle Joke, will perhaps meet with a serious Reflection, that he may ever after be the better for.

Some People observing the great Yearly Demand for my Almanack, imagine I must by this Time have become rich, and consequently ought to call myself *Poor Dick* no longer. But, the Case is this, When I first begun to publish, the Printer made a fair Agreement with me for my Copies, by Virtue of which he runs away with the greatest Part of the Profit.—However, much good may't do him; I do not grudge it him; he is a Man I have a great Regard for, and I wish his Profit ten times greater than it is. For I am, dear Reader, his, as well as thy

Affectionate Friend,

R. SAUNDERS.

Teague's *Criticism on the First of Genesis.*

Arra, now what shignifies the making the two great Lights
The shun to rule the Day, and the Mhoon to rule the Nights?
For the shun in the Day-time there ish no Ochashun;
Because we can she vhery whell all over the Nashun.
But for the Mhoons, they are very good in a dark Night.
Becaush, when we can't shee, they give us a Light.

JANUARY

Giles Jolt, as sleeping in his Cart he lay,
Some pilfring Villains stole his Team away;
Giles wakes and cries—What's here? a dickens, what?
Why, how now?—Am I *Giles?* or am I not?
If he, I've lost six Geldings, to my Smart;
If not,—odds buddikins, I've found a Cart.

> When Death puts out our Flame, the Snuff will tell,
> If we were Wax, or Tallow by the Smell.

At a great Pennyworth, pause a while.

> As to his Wife, *John* minds St. *Paul,* He's one
> That hath a Wife and is as if he'd none.

Kings and Bears often worry their Keepers.

FEBRUARY

Lord, if our Days be *few,* why do we spend,
And lavish them to such an evil End?
Or, why, if they be *evil,* do we wrong
Our selves and thee, in wishing them so long?
Our Days decrease, our evils still renew,
We make them *ill,* thou kindly mak'st them *few.*

If thou would'st live long, live well;
  for Folly and Wickedness shorten Life.

Trust thy self, and another shall not betray thee.

Prythee isn't Miss *Cloe's* a comical Case?
She lends out her Tail, and she borrows her Face.

MARCH

Thus with kind Words, 'squire *Edward* chear'd his Friend;
Dear *Dick*! thou on my Friendship mayst depend;
I know thy Fortune is but very scant;
But, be assur'd, I'll ne'er see *Dick* in Want.
Dick's soon confin'd—his Friend, no doubt, would free him:
—His Word he kept—in Want he ne'er would see him.

He that pays for Work before it's done,
    has but a pennyworth for twopence.

Historians relate, not so much what is done,
    as what they would have believed.

O Maltster! break that cheating Peck; 'tis plain,
When e'er you use it, you're a Knave in Grain.

Let thy Child's first Lesson be Obedience,
and the second will be what thou wilt.

APRIL

For's Country *Codrus* suffer'd by the Sword,
And, by his Death, his Country's Fame restor'd;
Cæsar into his Mother's Bosom bare
Fire, Sword, and all the Ills of civil War:
Codrus confirm'd his Country's wholesome Laws;
Cæsar in Blood still justify'd his Cause;
Yet following Kings ne'er 'dopted *Codrus'* Name,
But *Cæsar*, still, and *Emperor's* the same.

Doll learning *propria quæ maribus* without book,
Like *Nomen crescentis genitivo* doth look.

Grace thou thy House, and let not that grace thee.

Thou canst not joke an Enemy into a Friend;
but thou may'st a Friend into an Enemy.

Eyes & Priests
Bear no Jests.

MAY

Think, bright *Florella*, when you see
The constant Changes of the Year,
That nothing is from Ruin free,
And gayest Things must disappear.
Think of your Beauties in their bloom,
The Spring of sprightly Youth improve;
For cruel Age, alas, will come,
And then 'twill be too late to love.

He that falls in love with himself, will have no Rivals.

Let thy Child's first Lesson be Obedience,
and the second may be what thou wilt.

Blessed is he that expects nothing,
for he shall never be disappointed.

Rather go to bed supperless, than run in debt for a Breakfast.

JUNE

On his late Deafness.

Deaf, giddy, helpless, left alone,
To all my Friends a Burthen grown,
No more I hear a great Church-Bell,
Than if it rang out for my Knell:
At Thunder now no more I start,
Than at the whisp'ring of a F—t.
Nay, what's incredible, alack!
I hardly hear my *Bridget's* Clack.

Let thy Discontents be Secrets.

A Man of Knowledge like a rich Soil, feeds
If not a world of Corn, a world of Weeds.

An infallible Remedy for the *Tooth-ach*, viz. Wash the Root of an aching Tooth, in *Elder Vinegar*, and let it dry half an hour in the Sun; after which it will never ach more; *Probatum est.*

JULY

Says *George* to *William*, Neighbour, have a Care,
Touch not that Tree—'tis sacred to Despair;
Two Wives I had, but, ah! that Joy is past!
Who breath'd upon those fatal Boughs their last.
The best in all the Row, without Dispute,
Says *Will*—Wou'd mine but bear such precious Fruit!
When next you prune your Orchard, save for me,
(I have a Spouse) one Cyon of that Tree.

A modern Wit is one of *David's* Fools.

No Resolution of Repenting hereafter, can be sincere.

Pollio, who values nothing that's within,
Buys Books as men hunt Beavers,—for their Skin.

Honour thy Father and Mother, *i.e.* Live so as to be
an Honour to them tho' they are dead.

⚓ AUGUST

Ships sailing down *Delaware* Bay this Month, shall hear at ten Leagues Distance a confus'd rattling Noise, like a Shower of Hail on a Cake of Ice. Don't be frighted, good Passengers! The Sailors can inform you, that it's nothing but Lower County Teeth in the Ague. In a Southerly Wind you may hear it at *Philadelphia*. Witness *G. L. M. cum multis aliis.*

If thou injurest Conscience, it will have its Revenge on thee.

Hear no ill of a Friend, nor speak any of an Enemy.

Pay what you owe, and you'll know what's your own.

Be not niggardly of what costs thee nothing,
    as courtesy, counsel, & countenance.

Thirst after Desert, not Reward.

☙ SEPTEMBER

The Sun now clear, serene the golden Skies,
Where'er you go, as fast the Shadow flies;
A Cloud succeeds; the Sunshine now is o'er,
The fleeting Phantom fled, is seen no more;
With your bright Day, its Progress too does end:
See here vain Man! the Picture of thy Friend.

Beware of him that is slow to anger: He is angry
    for some thing, and will not be pleased for nothing.

No longer virtuous no longer free, is a Maxim as true
    with regard to a private Person as a Common-wealth.

When Man and Woman die, as Poets sung,
His Heart's the last part moves, her last, the tongue.

❧ OCTOBER

What Legions of Fables and whimsical Tales
Pass current for Gospel where Priestcraft prevails!

Poor Richard: 1739

Our Ancestors thus were most strangely deceiv'd,
What Stories and Nonsense for Truth they believ'd!
But we their wise Sons, who these Fables reject,
Ev'n Truth now-a-days, are too apt to suspect:
From believing too much, the right Faith we let fall;
So now we believe—'troth nothing at all.

Proclaim not all thou knowest, all thou owest,
    all thou hast, nor all thou canst.

Let our Fathers and Grandfathers be valued for
    their Goodness, ourselves for our own.

Industry need not wish.

Sin is not hurtful because it is forbidden
    but it is forbidden because it's hurtful.

*He that riseth late must trot all Day, and shall
scarce overtake his Business at Night.*

❧ NOVEMBER

Pinchall, possessing Heaps of Wealth,
    Lives miserably poor;
He says, 'tis to preserve his Health,
    But means by it, his Store.
Let *Freeman* but the Wretch invite
    To dine on Good-Cheer *gratis*,
Then he will gorge, like half-starv'd Wight,
    And cram his *Nunquam satis*.

Nor is a Duty beneficial because it is commanded,
    but it is commanded, because it's beneficial.

A——, they say, has Wit; for what?
For writing?————No; For writing not.

George came to the Crown without striking a Blow.
Ah! quoth the Pretender, would I could do so.·

❧ DECEMBER

In Travel, Pilgrims oft do ask, to know
What *Miles* they've gone, and what they have to go:
Their Way is tedious and their Limbs opprest,
And their Desire is to be at rest.
In Life's more tedious Journey, Man delays
T'enquire out the Number of his Days:
He cares, not he, how slow his Hours spend,
The Journey's better than the Journey's End.

O Lazy-Bones! Dost thou think God would have given thee
    Arms and Legs, if he had not design'd thou should'st
    use them.

A Cure for Poetry,
    Seven wealthy Towns contend for *Homer*, dead,
    Thro' which the living *Homer* beg'd his Bread.

Great Beauty, great strength, & great Riches, are
    really & truly of no great Use; a right Heart exceeds all.

On the LAW.

Nigh Neighbour to the Squire, poor *Sam* complain'd
Of frequent Wrongs, but no Amends he gain'd.
Each Day his Gates thrown down, his Fences broke,
And injur'd still the more, the more he spoke;
At last, resolv'd his potent Foe to awe,
A Suit against him he began in Law;
Nine happy Terms thro' all the Forms he run,
Obtain'd his Cause—had Costs—and was undone.

A True PROGNOSTICATION, for 1739.

Courteous Readers,

Having consider'd the infinite Abuses arising from the false Prognostications published among you, made under the shadow of a Pot of Drink, or so, I have here calculated one of the most sure and unerring that ever was seen in black and white, as hereafter you'll find. For doubtless it is a heinous, foul & crying Sin, to deceive the poor gaping World, greedy of the Knowledge of Futurity, as we Americans all are.

Take Notice by the by, that having been at a great deal of pains in the Calculation, if you don't believe every Syllable, Jot & Tittle of it, you do me a great deal of wrong; for which either here or elsewhere, you may chance to be claw'd off with a Vengeance.—A good Cowskin, Crabtree or Bulls pizzle may be plentifully bestow'd on your outward Man. You may snuff up your Noses as much as you please, 'tis all one for that.

Well however, come, snite your Noses my little Children; and you old doating Father Grey-Beards, pull out your best Eyes, on wi' your Barnacles, and carefully observe every Scruple of what I'm going to tell you.

Of the GOLDEN NUMBER.

The Golden Number, *non est inventus.* I cannot find it this Year by any Calculation I have made. I must content myself with a Number of Copper. No matter, go on.

Of the ECLIPSES *this Year.*

There are so many invisible Eclipses this Year, that I fear, not unjustly, our Pockets will suffer Inanition, be full empty, and our Feeling at a Loss. During the first visible Eclipse *Saturn* is retrograde: For which Reason the Crabs will go sidelong, and the Ropemakers backward. The Belly will wag before, and the A——— shall sit down first. *Mercury* will have his share in these Affairs, and so confound the Speech of People, that when a *Pensilvanian* would say PANTHER, he shall say PAINTER. When a *New-Yorker* thinks to say (THIS) he shall say (DISS) and the People in *New-England* and *Cape-May* will not be able to say (COW) for their Lives, but will be forc'd to say (KEOW) by a certain involuntary Twist in the Root of their Tongues. No *Connecticut-Man* nor *Marylander* will be able to open his Mouth this Year, but (SIR) shall be the first or last Syllable he pronounces, and sometimes both. Brutes shall speak in many Places, and there will be above seven and twenty irregular Verbs made this Year, if Grammar don't interpose. Who can help these Misfortunes!

Of the DISEASES *this Year.*

This Year the Stone-blind shall see but very little; the Deaf shall hear but poorly; and the Dumb shan't speak very plain. And it's much, if my Dame *Bridget* talks at all this Year. Whole Flocks, Herds and Droves of Sheep, Swine and Oxen, Cocks and Hens, Ducks and Drakes, Geese and Ganders shall go to Pot; but the Mortality will not be altogether so great among Cats, Dogs and Horses. As for old Age, 'twill be incurable this Year, because of the Years past. And towards the Fall some People will be seiz'd with an unaccountable Inclination to roast and eat their own Ears: Should this be call'd Madness, Doctors? I think not.—But the worst Disease of all will be a certain most horrid, dreadful, malignant, catching, perverse and odious Malady, almost epidemical, insomuch that many shall run Mad upon it; I quake for very Fear when I think on't; for I assure you very few will escape this Disease; which is called by the learned Albumazar *Lacko'mony.*

Of the FRUITS *of the* EARTH.

I find that this will be a plentiful Year of all manner of good Things, to those who have enough; but the Orange Trees in *Greenland* will go near to fare the worse for the Cold. As for Oats, they'll be a great Help to Horses. I dare say there won't be much more Bacon than Swine. *Mercury* somewhat threatens our Parsley-beds, yet Parsly will be to be had for Money. Hemp will grow faster than the Children of this Age, and some will find there's but too much on't. As for Corn, Fruit, Cyder and Turnips, there never was such Plenty as will be now; if poor Folks may have their Wish.

Of the CONDITION *of some* Countries.

I foresee an universal *Drought* this Year thro' all the Northern Colonies. Hence there will be *dry* Rice in *Carolina, dry* Tobacco in *Virginia* and *Maryland, dry* Bread in *Pennsylvania* and *New-York;* and, in *New-England, dry* Fish & *dry* Doctrine. *Dry* Throats there will be every-where; but then how pleasant it will be to drink cool Cyder! tho' some will tell you nothing is more contrary to Thirst. I believe it; and indeed, *Contraria, contrariis curantur.*

R. SAUNDERS.

He's the best Physician that knows the Worthlessness of most Medicines.

Poor Richard's *Almanack, &c.*

Courteous READER,

YOU may remember that in my first Almanack, published for the Year 1733, I predicted the Death of my dear Friend *Titan Leeds*, Philomat. to happen that Year on the 17th Day of *October*, 3 h. 29 m. *P. M.* The good Man it seems, died accordingly: But *W. B.* and *A.B.*[4a] have continued to publish Almanacks in his Name ever since; asserting for some Years that he was still living; At length when the Truth could no longer be conceal'd from the World, they confess his Death in their Almanack for 1739, but pretend that he died not till last Year, and that before his Departure he had furnished them with Calculations for 7 Years to come. Ah, *My Friends*, these are poor Shifts and thin Disguises; of which indeed I should have taken little or no Notice, if you had not at the same time accus'd me as a false Predictor; an Aspersion that the more affects me, as my whole Livelyhood depends on a contrary Character.

But to put this Matter beyond Dispute, I shall acquaint the World with a Fact, as strange and surprizing as it is true; being as follows, *viz.*

On the 4th Instant, towards midnight, as I sat in my little Study writing this Preface, I fell fast asleep; and continued in that Condition

75

for some time, without dreaming any thing, to my Knowledge. On awaking, I found lying before me the following letter, *viz.*

Dear Friend SAUNDERS,

My Respect for you continues even in this separate State, and I am griev'd to see the Aspersions thrown on you by the Malevolence of avaricious Publishers of Almanacks, who envy your Success. They say your Prediction of my Death in 1733 *was false, and they pretend that I remained alive many Years after. But I do hereby certify, that I did actually die at that time, precisely at the Hour you mention'd, with a Variation only of* 5 min. 53 sec. *which must be allow'd to be no great matter in such Cases. And I do farther declare that I furnish'd them with no Calculations of the Planets Motions, &c. seven Years after my Death, as they are pleased to give out: so that the Stuff they publish as an Almanack in my Name is no more mine than 'tis yours.*

You will wonder perhaps, how this Paper comes written on your Table. You must know that no separate Spirits are under any Confinement till after the final Settlement of all Accounts. In the meantime we wander where we please, visit our old Friends, observe their Actions, enter sometimes into their Imaginations, and give them Hints waking or sleeping that may be of Advantage to them. Finding you asleep, I entred your left Nostril, ascended into your Brain, found out where the Ends of those Nerves were fastned that move your right Hand and Fingers, by the Help of which I am now writing unknown to you; but when you open your Eyes, you will see that the Hand written is mine, tho' wrote with yours.

The People of this Infidel Age, perhaps, will hardly believe this Story. But you may give them these three Signs by which they shall be convinc'd of the Truth of it. About the middle of June *next, J. J————n, Philomat, shall be openly reconciled to the* Church of Rome, *and give all his Goods and Chattles to the Chappel, being perverted by a certain* Country School-master.[4b] *On the* 7th *of* September *following my old Friend* W. B————t *shall be sober* 9 *Hours, to the Astonishment of all his Neighbours: And about the same time* W. B. *and* A. B. *will publish another Almanack in my Name, in spight of Truth and Common-Sense.*

As I can see much clearer into Futurity, since I got free from the dark Prison of Flesh, in which I was continually molested and almost blinded with Fogs arising from Tiff, and the Smoke of burnt Drams; I shall in kindness to you, frequently give you Informations of things to come, for the Improvement of your Almanack: being Dear Dick,

Your affectionate Friend,

T. LEEDS.

For my own part I am convinc'd that the above Letter is genuine. If the Reader doubts of it, let him carefully observe the three Signs; and if they do not actually come to pass, believe as he pleases.

I am his humble Friend,

R. SAUNDERS.

Of ECLIPSES *for* 1740.

There will be Six Eclipses this Year . . . . Some of these Eclipses foreshow great Grief and many Tears among the soft Sex this Year; whether for the Breaking of their Crockery Ware, the Loss of their Loves, or in Repentance for their Sins, I shall not say; tho' I must own I think there will be a great deal of the latter in the Case. War we shall hear but too much of (for all Christians have not yet learn'd to *love one another*) and, I doubt, of some ineffectual Treaties of Peace. I pray Heav'n defend these Colonies from every Enemy; and give them, Bread enough, Peace enough, Money enough, and plenty of good Cyder.

🐟 JANUARY

My sickly Spouse, with many a Sigh
Once told me,—*Dicky*, I shall die:
I griev'd, but recollected strait,
'Twas bootless to contend with Fate:
So Resignation to Heav'ns Will
Prepar'd me for succeeding Ill;
'Twas well it did; for, on my Life,
'Twas Heav'n's Will to spare my Wife.

To bear other Peoples Afflictions, every one
has Courage enough, and to spare.

77

No wonder *Tom* grows fat, th' unwieldy Sinner
Makes his whole Life but one continual Dinner.

An empty Bag cannot stand upright.

⇚ February

While the good Priest with eyes devoutly clos'd
Left on the book the marriage fee expos'd,
The new made bridegroom his occasion spies,
And pleas'd, repockets up the shining prize:
Yet not so safe, but Mr. *Surplice* views
The Frolick, and demands his pilfer'd dues.
No, quoth the man, good Doctor, I'll nonsuit y',
A plain default, I found you off your Duty?
More carefully the holy book survey;
Your Rule is, you should *watch* as well as *pray*.

Happy that nation, fortunate that age,
  whose history is not diverting.

What is a butterfly? At best
He's but a caterpiller drest,
The gaudy Fop's his picture just.

None are deceived but they that confide.

An empty Bag cannot stand upright.

🐏 MARCH

When *Pharoah*'s Sins provok'd th' Almighty's hand
To pour his Wrath upon the guilty Land;
A tenfold Plague the great Avenger shed;
The King offended, and the Nation bled.
Had'st thou, unaided, *Feria*, but been sent
Vial elect, for *Pharoah*'s Punishment,
Thro' what a various Curse the Wretch had run,
He more than Heaven's ten Plagues had felt in one.

    An open Foe may prove a curse;
    But a pretended friend is worse.

    A wolf eats sheep but now and then,
    Ten Thousands are devour'd by Men.

    Man's tongue is soft, and bone doth lack;
    Yet a stroke therewith may break a man's back.

🐂 APRIL

    Says *Roger* to his Wife, my dear;
    The strangest piece of News I hear!
    A Law, 'tis said, will quickly pass,
    To purge the matrimonial Class;
    Cuckolds, if any such we have here
    Must to a Man be thrown i'th' River.
    She smiling cry'd, My dear, you seem
    Surpriz'd! *Pray han't you learn'd to swim?*

Many a Meal is lost for want of meat.

    To all apparent Beauties blind
    Each Blemish strikes an envious Mind.

    The Poor have little, Beggars none;
    the Rich too much, enough not one.

Tricks and Trechery are the Practice of Fools,
    that have not Wit enough to be honest.

✴ MAY

A Carrier ev'ry Night and Morn,
Would see his Horses eat their Corn:
This sunk the Hostler's Vails, 'tis true;
But then his Horses had their Due.
Were we so cautious in all Cases,
Small Gain would rise from greater Places.

There are lazy Minds as well as lazy Bodies.

Who says Jack is not generous? he is always fond of giving,
and cares not for receiving.—What? Why; Advice.

✴ JUNE

How weak, how vain is human Pride!
Dares Man upon himself confide?
The Wretch who glories in his Gain,
Amasses Heaps on Heaps in vain.
Can those (when tortur'd by Disease)
Chear our sick Heart, or purchase Ease?
Can those prolong one Gasp of Breath,
Or calm the troubled Hour of Death?

The Man who with undaunted toils,
sails unknown seas to unknown soils,
With various wonders feasts his Sight:
What stranger wonders does he write?

Fear not Death; for the sooner we die,
the longer shall we be immortal.

✴ JULY

The Monarch of long regal Line,
Was rais'd from Dust as frail as mine:
Can he pour Health into his Veins,
Or cool the Fever's restless Pains?
Can he (worn down in Nature's Course)

New-brace his feeble Nerves with Force?
Can he (how vain is mortal Pow'r!)
Stretch Life beyond the destin'd Hour?

Those who in quarrels interpose,
Must often wipe a bloody nose.

Promises may get thee Friends, but Nonperformance
    will turn them into Enemies.

In other men we faults can spy,
And blame the mote that dims their eye;
Each little speck and blemish find;
To our own stronger errors blind.

AUGUST

The Man of pure and simple Heart
Thro' Life disdains a double part;
He never needs the screen of Lies
His inward Bosom to disguise.
In vain malicious Tongues assail,
Let Envy snarl, let Slander rail,
From Virtue's shield (secure from Wound)
Their blunted venom'd shafts rebound.

When you speak to a man, look on his eyes;
    when he speaks to thee, look on his mouth.

Jane, why those tears? why droops your head?
Is then your other husband dead?
Or doth a worse disgrace betide?
Hath no one since his death apply'd?

Observe all men; thy self most.

SEPTEMBER

We frequently misplace *Esteem*
By judging Men by what they seem.
With partial Eyes we're apt to see

The Man of noble Pedigree.
To Birth, Wealth, Power we should allow
Precedence, and our lowest Bow:
In that is due Distinction shown:
Esteem is Virtue's Right alone.

Thou hadst better eat salt with the Philosophers of *Greece*,
    than sugar with the Courtiers of *Italy*.

Seek Virtue, and, of that possest,
To Providence, resign the rest.

Marry above thy match, and thou'lt get a Master.

Fear to do ill, and you need fear nought else.

OCTOBER

What's Beauty? Call ye that your own,
A Flow'r that fades as soon as blown!
Those Eyes of so divine a Ray,
What are they? Mould'ring, mortal Clay.
Those Features cast in heav'nly Mould,
Shall like my coarser Earth, grow old;
Like common Grass, the fairest Flow'r
Must feel the hoary Season's Pow'r.

He makes a Foe who makes a jest.

    Can grave and formal pass for wise,
    When Men the solemn Owl despise?

    Some are justly laught at for keeping their Money
foolishly, others for spending it idly: He is the greatest
fool that lays it out in a purchase of repentance.

NOVEMBER

Old *Socrates* was obstinately Good,
Virtuous by force, *by* Inclination lewd.
When secret Movements drew his Soul aside,
He quell'd his Lust, and stemm'd the swelling Tide;

Sustain'd by Reason still, unmov'd he stood,
And steady bore against th' opposing Flood.
He durst correct what Nature form'd amiss,
And forc'd unwilling Virtue to be his.

Who knows a fool, must know his brother;
For one will recommend another.

Avoid dishonest Gain: No price
Can recompence the Pangs of Vice.

When befriended, remember it:
When you befriend, forget it.

Great souls with gen'rous pity melt;
Which coward tyrants never felt.

DECEMBER

O blessed Season! lov'd by Saints and Sinners,
For long Devotions, or for longer Dinners;
More grateful still to those who deal in Books,
Now not with Readers, but with Pastry-Cooks:
Learn'd Works, despis'd by those to Merit blind,
By these well weigh'd, their certain Value find.
Bless'd Lot of Paper, falsely called *Waste*,
To bear those Cates, which Authors seldom taste.

Employ thy time well, if thou meanest to gain leisure.

A Flatterer never seems absurd:
The Flatter'd always take his Word.

Lend Money to an Enemy, and thou'lt gain him,
to a Friend and thou'lt lose him.

Neither praise nor dispraise, till seven Christmasses be over.

COURTS.

I know you Lawyers can, with Ease,
Twist Words and Meanings as you please;

That Language, by your Skill made pliant,
Will bend to favour ev'ry Client;
That 'tis the Fee directs the Sense
To make out either Side's Pretence:
When you peruse the clearest Case,
You see it with a double Face,
For Scepticism's your Profession;
You hold there's Doubt in all Expression.
    Hence is the Bar with Fees supply'd.
Hence Eloquence takes either Side.
Your Hand would have but paultry gleaning;
Could every Man express his Meaning.
Who dares presume to pen a Deed,
Unless you previously are fee'd?
'Tis drawn, and, *to augment the Cost*,
In dull Prolixity engrost:
And now we're well secur'd by Law,
'Till the next Brother find a Flaw.

*You can bear your own Faults,
and why not a Fault in your Wife?*

Poor Richard's *Almanack, &c.*

❧ J A N U A R Y 4c

Your homely Face, *Flippanta*, you disguise
With Patches, numerous as *Argus'* Eyes:
I own that Patching's requisite for you;
For more we're pleas'd, if less your Face we view:
Yet I advise, if my Advice you'd ask,
Wear but one Patch;—but be that Patch a Mask.

Enjoy the present hour, be mindful of the past;
And neither fear nor wish the Approaches of the last.

Learn of the skilful: He that teaches himself,
hath a fool for his master.

❧ F E B R U A R Y

The cringing Train of Pow'r, survey;
What Creatures are so low as they!
With what obsequiousness they bend!
To what vile Actions condescend!
Their Rise is on their Meanness built,
And Flatt'ry is their smallest Guilt.

Best is the Tongue that feels the rein;—
He that talks much, must talk in vain;
We from the wordy Torrent fly:
Who listens to the chattering Pye?

Think *Cato* sees thee.

No Wood without Bark.

MARCH

Enrag'd was *Buckram*, when his Wife he beat,
That she'd so often *lousy Knave*, repeat.
At length he seiz'd and drag'd her to the Well,
I'll cool thy Tongue, or I'll thy Courage quell.
Ducking, thy Case, poor *Buckram*, little mends;
She had her Lesson at her Fingers Ends.
Sows'd over head, her Arms she raises high;
And *cracking* Nails the Want of *Tongue* supply.

Monkeys warm with envious spite,
Their most obliging FRIENDS will bite;—
And, fond to copy human Ways,
Practise new Mischiefs all their days.

Joke went out, and brought home his fellow,
and they two began a quarrel.

APRIL

Rash Mortals, e'er you take a Wife,
Contrive your Pile to last for Life:
On Sense and Worth your Passion found,
By DECENCY cemented round;
Let Prudence with Good-Nature strive
To keep Esteem and Love alive;
Then, come old Age when e'er it will,
Your *Friendship* shall continue still.

Let thy discontents be thy Secrets;—if the world
knows them, 'twill despise *thee* and increase *them*.

E'er you remark another's Sin,
Bid your own Conscience look within.

Anger and Folly walk cheek by-jole;
Repentance treads on both their Heels.

🐟 MAY

Fair *Decency*, celestial Maid,
Descend from Heav'n to Beauty's Aid:
Tho' Beauty may beget Desire,
'Tis thou must fan the Lover's Fire:
For, Beauty, like supreme Dominion,
Is best supported by Opinion:
If *Decency* bring no Supplies,
Opinion falls and Beauty dies.

Turn Turk *Tim*, and renounce thy Faith
in Words as well as Actions:
Is it worse to follow *Mahomet* than the Devil?

Don't overload Gratitude; if you do, she'll kick.

Be always asham'd to catch thy self idle.

🦗 JUNE

When painful *Colin* in his Grave was laid,
His mournful Wife this Lamentation made;
I've lost, alas! (poor Wretch, what must I do?)
The best of Friends, and best of Husbands too.
Thus of all Joy and Happiness bereft;
And with the Charge of ten poor Children left;
A greater Grief no Woman sure can know.
Who (with ten Children)—who will have me now?

Where yet was ever found the Mother,
Who'd change her booby for another?

At 20 years of age the Will reigns; at 30 the Wit;
at 40 the Judgment.

Christianity commands us to pass by Injuries;
   Policy, to let them pass by us.

❧ JULY

Nature expects Mankind should share
The Duties of the publick Care.
Who's born for Sloth? To some we find
The Plough share's annual Toil assign'd;
Some at the sounding Anvil glow;
Some the swift Sliding Shuttle throw;
Some, studious of the Wind and Tide,
From Pole to Pole our Commerce guide.

Lying rides upon Debt's back.

They who have nothing to be troubled at,
   will be troubled at nothing.

   Wife from thy Spouse each blemish hide
   More than from all the World beside:
   Let *Decency* be all thy Pride.

❧ AUGUST

Some (taught by Industry) impart
With Hands and Feet the Works of Art;
While some, of Genius more refin'd,
With Head and Tongue assist Mankind:
Each aiming at one common End
Proves to the whole a needful Friend.
Thus, born each other's useful Aid,
By Turns are Obligations paid.

Nick's Passions grow fat and hearty;
   his Understanding looks consumptive!

   If evils come not, then our fears are vain:
   And if they do, Fear but augments the pain.

Rob not for burnt offerings.

If you would keep your Secret from an enemy,
  tell it not to a friend.

❧ SEPTEMBER

The Monarch, when his Table's spread,
To th' Farmer is oblig'd for Bread;
And when in all his Glory drest,
Owes to the Loom his royal Vest:
Do not the Mason's Toil and Care
Protect him from th' inclement Air?
Does not the Cutler's Art supply
The Ornament that guards his Thigh?

[*Cont'd Oct.*

Bess brags she 'as *Beauty*, and can prove the same:
As how? why thus, Sir, 'tis her *puppy*'s name.

Up, Sluggard, and waste not life;
  in the grave will be sleeping enough.

Well done, is twice done.

Clearly spoken, Mr. Fog! You explain English by Greek.

❧ OCTOBER

All these, in Duty, to the Throne
Their common Obligations own.
'Tis he (his own and People's Cause)
Protects their Properties and Laws:
Thus they their honest Toil employ,
And with Content the Fruits enjoy
In every Rank, or great or small,
'Tis INDUSTRY supports us all.

Formio bewails his Sins with the same heart,
As Friends do Friends when they're about to part.
Believe it *Formio* will not entertain,
One chearful Thought till they do meet again.

Honours change Manners.

❧ November

Syl. dreamt that bury'd in his fellow Clay,
Close by a common Beggar's Side he lay:
And, as so mean a Neighbour shock'd his Pride
Thus, like a Corpse of consequence, he cry'd:
Scoundrel, begone; and henceforth touch me not:
More manners learn; and, at a distance, rot.
How! Scoundrel! in a haughtier Tone cry'd he;
Proud Lump of Dirt, I scorn thy Words and thee;
Here all are equal; now thy Case is mine;
This is my Rotting Place, and that is thine.

Jack eating rotten cheese, did say,
Like *Sampson* I my thousands slay;
I vow, quoth *Roger*, so you do,
And with the self-same weapon too.

There are no fools so troublesome as those that have wit.

Quarrels never could last long,
If on one side only lay the wrong.

❧ December

On a Bee, stifled in Honey,

From Flow'r to Flow'r, with eager Pains,
    See the poor busy Lab'rer fly!
When all that from her Toil she gains
    Is, in the Sweets she hoards, to die.
'Tis thus, would Man the Truth believe,
    With Life's soft Sweets, each fav'rite Joy:
If we taste wisely, they relieve;
    But if we plunge too deep, destroy.

Let no Pleasure tempt thee, no Profit allure thee, no
Ambition corrupt thee, no Example sway thee, no Persuasion
move thee, to do any thing which thou knowest to be Evil; So
shalt thou always live jollily: for a good Conscience is a continual Christmas. Adieu.

COURTS.

He that by Injury is griev'd,
And goes to Law to be reliev'd,
Is sillier than a sottish Chouse,
Who when a Thief has robb'd his House,
Applies himself to cunning Men
To help him to his Goods again:
When, all he can expect to gain,
Is but to squander more in vain.
For Lawyers, lest the Bear Defendant,
And Plaintiff Dog should make an End on't,
Do stave and tail with Writs of Error,
Reverse of Judgment and Demurrer,
To let them breath a-while, and then
Cry *Whoop*, and set them on again:
Until, with subtil cobweb Cheats,
They're catch'd in knotted Law, like Nets,
In which, when once they are embrangl'd,
The more they stir the more they're tangl'd:
For while their Purses can dispute,
There's no End of th' immortal Suit.

Hud.[5]

If you would have a faithful Servant, serve yourself.

1742

Poor Richard's *Almanack, &c.*

Courteous READER,

THIS is the ninth Year of my Endeavours to serve thee in the Capacity of a Calendar-Writer. The Encouragement I have met with must be ascrib'd, in a great Measure, to your Charity, excited by the open honest Declaration I made of my Poverty at my first Appearance. This my Brother *Philomaths* could, without being Conjurers, discover; and *Poor Richard*'s Success, has produced ye a *Poor Will*, and a *Poor Robin*; and no doubt *Poor John*, &c. will follow, and we shall all be *in Name* what some Folks say we are already *in Fact*, A Parcel of *poor Almanack Makers*. During the Course of these nine Years, what Buffetings have I not sustained! The Fraternity have been all in Arms. Honest *Titan*, deceas'd, was rais'd, and made to abuse his old Friend. Both Authors and Printers were angry. Hard names, and many, were bestow'd on me. *They deny'd me to be the Author of my own Works;* declar'd there never was any such Person; asserted that I was dead 60 Years ago; prognosticated my Death to happen within a Twelvemonth: with many other malicious Inconsistences, the Effects of blind Passion, Envy at my Success; and a vain Hope of depriving me (dear Reader) of thy wonted Countenance and Favour.—*Who knows him?* they cry: *Where does he live?*—But what is that to them? If I delight in a private Life, have they any Right to drag me out of my Retirement? I have good Reasons for concealing the Place of my Abode. 'Tis time for an old Man, as I am, to think of preparing for his great Remove. The perpetual Teasing of both Neighbours and Strangers, to calculate Nativities, give Judgment on Schemes, erect Figures, discover Thieves, detect Horse-Stealers, describe the Route of Run-aways and stray'd Cattle; The Croud of Visitors with a 1000 trifling Questions; *Will my Ship return safe? Will my Mare win the Race? Will her next Colt be a Pacer? When will my Wife die? Who shall be my Husband, and HOW LONG first? When is the best time to cut Hair, trim Cocks, or sow sallad?* These and the like Impertinences I have now neither Taste nor Leisure for. I have had enough of 'em. All that these angry Folks can say, will never provoke me to tell them where I live. I would eat my Nails first.

My last Adversary is *J. J——n,* Philomat. who *declares and protests* (in his Preface, 1741) that the *false Prophecy put in my Almanack, concerning him, the Year before, is altogether* false and untrue: *and that I am one of Baal's false Prophets.* This *false, false Prophecy* he speaks of, related to his Reconciliation with the Church of *Rome*; which, notwithstanding his Declaring and Protesting, is, I fear, too true. Two Things in his elegiac Verses confirm me in this Suspicion. He calls the First of *November* by the Name of *All Hallows Day.* Reader: does not this smell of Popery? Does it in the least savour of the pure Language of Friends? But the plainest Thing is; his Adoration of Saints, which he confesses to be his Practice, in these Words, page 4.

> *When any Trouble did me befal,*
> *To my dear* Mary *then I would call:*

Did he think the whole World were so stupid as not to take Notice of this? So ignorant as not to know, that all Catholicks pay the highest Regard to the *Virgin-Mary?* Ah! Friend *John,* We must allow you to be a Poet, but you are certainly no Protestant. I could heartily wish your Religion were as good as your Verses.

RICHARD SAUNDERS.[6]

Poor Richard: 1742

☙ JANUARY

Foot, Horse and Waggons, now cross Rivers, dry,
And Ships unmov'd, the boistrous Winds defy,
In frozen Climes: when all conceal'd from Sight,
The pleasing Objects that to Verse invite;
The Hills, the Dales, and the delightful Woods,
The flowry Plains, and Silver-streaming Floods,
By Snow disguis'd, in bright Confusion lie,
And with one dazling Waste fatigue the Eye.

Strange! that a Man who has wit enough to write a Satyr;
should have folly enough to publish it.

He that hath a Trade, hath an Estate.

Have you somewhat to do to-morrow; do it to-day.

*A Man may, if he know not how to save, keep his Nose
to the Grindstone, and die not worth a Groat at last.*

⪺ FEBRUARY

James ne'er will be prefer'd; he cannot bow
And cringe beneath a supercilious Brow;
He cannot fawn, his stubborn Soul recoils
At Baseness, and his Blood too highly boils.
A Courtier must be supple, full of Guile,
Must learn to praise, to flatter, to revile
The Good, the Bad; an Enemy, a Friend;
To give false Hopes, and on false Hopes depend.

No workman without tools,
No Lawyer without Fools,
Can live by their Rules.

The painful Preacher, like a candle bright,
Consumes himself in giving others Light.

Speak and speed: the close mouth catches no flies.

⪻ MARCH

As honest *Hodge* the Farmer sow'd his Field,
Chear'd with the Hope of future Gain 'twould yield,
Two upstart Jacks in Office, proud and vain,
Come riding by, and thus insult the Swain.
You drudge, and sweat, and labour here, Old Boy,
But we the Fruit of your hard Toil enjoy.
Belike you may, *quoth Hodge*, and but your Due,
For, Gentlemen, 'tis *HEMP* I'm sowing now.

Visit your Aunt, but not every Day;
   and call at your Brother's, but not every night.

Bis dat, qui cito dat.

Money and good Manners make the Gentleman.

Late Children, early Orphans.

Ben beats his Pate, and fancy wit will come;
But he may knock, there's no body at home.

95

Poor Richard: 1742

APRIL

The Winter spent, *Joe* feels the Poet's Fire,
The Sun advances, and the Fogs retire:
The genial Spring unbinds the frozen Earth,
Dawns on the Trees, and gives the Prim-rose Birth.
Loos'd from their Friendly Harbours, once again,
Our floating Forts assemble on the Main;
The Voice of War the gallant Soldier wakes;
And weeping *Cloe* parting Kisses takes.

The good Spinner hath a large Shift.

Tom, vain's your Pains; They all will fail:
Ne'er was good Arrow made of a Sow's Tail.

MAY

What knowing Judgment, or what Piercing Eye,
Can *MAN*'s mysterious Maze of Falshood try?
Intriguing *MAN*, of a suspicious Mind,
MAN only knows the Cunning of his Kind;
With equal Wit can counter-work his Foes,
And Art with Art, and Fraud with Fraud oppose.
Then heed ye FAIR, e'er you their Cunning prove,
And think of Treach'ry, while they talk of LOVE.

Empty Freebooters, cover'd with Scorn:
They went out for Wealth, & come ragged and torn,
As the Ram went for Wool, and was sent back shorn.

Ill Customs & bad Advice are seldom forgotten.

He that sows thorns, should not go barefoot.

JUNE

Sometimes a Man speaks Truth without Design,
As late it happen'd with a Friend of mine.
Two reverend Preachers talking, one declar'd,

That to preach twice each Sunday was full hard.
To you, perhaps (says t'other) *for I suppose,*
That all Men don't with the same Ease compose:
But I, desiring still my Flock to profit,
Preach twice each Sunday, and make nothing of it.

Reniego de grillos, aunque sean d'oro.

Men meet, mountains never.

When Knaves fall out, honest Men get their goods:
When Priests dispute, we come at the Truth.

❦ JULY

Man only from himself can suffer Wrong;
His Reason fails as his Desires grow strong:
Hence, wanting Ballast, and too full of Sail,
He lies expos'd to every rising Gale.
From Youth to Age, for *Happiness* he's bound;
He splits on Rocks, or runs his Bark aground;
Or, wide of Land a desart Ocean views,
And, to the last, the flying Port pursues.

Kate would have *Thomas*, no one blame her can:
Tom won't have *Kate*, and who can blame the Man?

A large train makes a light Purse.

Death takes no bribes.

One good Husband is worth two good Wives; for the
scarcer things are the more they're valued.

⚖ AUGUST

The Busy-Man's Picture.

BUSINESS, thou Plague and Pleasure of my Life,
Thou charming Mistress, thou vexatious Wife;
Thou Enemy, thou Friend, to Joy, to Grief,

Thou bring'st me all, and bring'st me no Relief,
Thou bitter, sweet, thou pleasing, teazing Thing,
Thou Bee, that with thy Honey wears a Sting;
Some Respite, prithee do, yet do not give,
I cannot with thee, nor without thee live.

He that riseth late, must trot all day,
  and shall scarce overtake his business at night.

He that speaks ill of the Mare, will buy her.

You may drive a gift without a gimblet.

Eat few Suppers, and you'll need few Medicines.

♎ SEPTEMBER

The Reverse.

Studious of Ease, and fond of humble Things,
Below the Smiles, below the Frowns of Kings:
Thanks to my Stars, I prize the Sweets of Life,
No sleepless Nights I count, no Days of Strife.
I rest, I wake, I drink, I sometimes love,
I read, I write, I settle, or I rove;
Content to live, content to die unknown,
Lord of myself, accountable to none.

You will be careful, if you are wise;
How you touch Men's Religion, or Credit, or Eyes.

After Fish,
Milk do not wish.

Heb Dduw heb ddim, a Duw a digon.

They who have nothing to trouble them,
  will be troubled at nothing.

♏ OCTOBER

On him true HAPPINESS shall wait
Who shunning noisy Pomp and State

Those *little* Blessings of the *Great*,
    Consults the Golden Mean.
In prosp'rous Gales with Care he steers,
Nor adverse Winds, dejected, fears,
In ev'ry Turn of Fortune bears
    A Face and Mind serene.

Against Diseases here, the strongest Fence,
Is the defensive Virtue, Abstinence.

Fient de chien, & marc d'argent,
Seront tout un au jour du jugement.

If thou dost ill, the joy fades, not the pains;
If well, the pain doth fade, the joy remains.

NOVEMBER

Celia's rich Side-board seldom sees the Light,
Clean is her Kitchen, and her Spits are bright;
Her Knives and Spoons, all rang'd in even Rows,
No Hands molest, nor Fingers discompose:
A curious Jack, hung up to please the Eye,
Forever still, whose Flyers never fly:
Her Plates unsully'd, shining on the Shelf;
For *Celia* dresses nothing,—*but herself.*

To err is human, to repent divine, to persist devilish.

Money & Man a mutual Friendship show:
Man makes *false* Money, Money makes Man so.

Industry pays Debts, Despair encreases them.

Bright as the day and as the morning fair,
Such *Cloe* is, & common as the air.

DECEMBER

Among the Divines there has been much Debate,
Concerning the World in its ancient Estate;
Some say 'twas once good, but now is grown bad,

Some say 'tis reform'd of the Faults it once had:
I say, 'tis the best World, this that we now live in,
Either to lend, or to spend, or to give in;
But to borrow, to beg, or to get a Man's own,
It is the worst World that ever was known.

Here comes *Glib-tongue*: who can out-flatter a Dedication;
   and lie, like ten Epitaphs.

Hope and a Red-Rag, are Baits for Men and Mackrel.

With the old Almanack and the old Year,
Leave thy old Vices, tho' ever so dear.

COURTS.

Honest Men often go to Law for their Right; when Wise
Men would sit down with the Wrong, supposing the first Loss
least. In some Countries the Course of the Courts is so tedious,
and the Expence so high, that the Remedy, *Justice*, is worse
than, *Injustice*, the Disease. In my Travels I once saw a Sign
call'd *The Two Men at Law*; One of them was painted on one
Side, in a melancholy Posture, all in Rags, with this Scroll, *I
have lost my Cause*. The other was drawn capering for Joy, on
the other Side, with these Words, *I have gain'd my Suit*; but
he was stark naked.

Rules of Health and long Life, and to preserve from Malignant Fevers, and Sickness in General.

Eat and drink such an exact Quantity as the Constitution of thy
Body allows of, in reference to the Services of the Mind.
   They that study much, ought not to eat so much as those that work
hard, their Digestion being not so good.
   The exact Quantity and Quality being found out, is to be kept to
constantly.
   Excess in all other Things whatever, as well as in Meat and Drink,
is also to be avoided.
   Youth, Age, and Sick require a different Quantity.

And so do those of contrary Complexions; for that which is too much for a flegmatick Man, is not sufficient for a Cholerick.

The Measure of Food ought to be (as much as possibly may be) exactly proportionate to the Quality and Condition of the Stomach, because the Stomach digests it.

That Quantity that is sufficient, the Stomach can perfectly concoct and digest, and it sufficeth the due Nourishment of the Body.

A greater Quantity of some things may be eaten than of others, some being of lighter Digestion than others.

The Difficulty lies, in finding out an exact Measure; but eat for Necessity, not Pleasure, for Lust knows not where Necessity ends.

Wouldst thou enjoy a long Life, a healthy Body, and a vigorous Mind, and be acquainted also with the wonderful Works of God? labour in the first place to bring thy Appetite into Subjection to Reason.

Rules to find out a fit Measure of Meat and Drink.

If thou eatest so much as makes thee unfit for Study, or other Business, thou exceedest the due Measure.

If thou art dull and heavy after Meat, it's a sign thou hast exceeded the due Measure; for Meat and Drink ought to refresh the Body, and make it chearful, and not to dull and oppress it.

If thou findest these ill Symptoms, consider whether too much Meat, or too much Drink occasions it, or both, and abate by little and little, till thou findest the Inconveniency removed.

Keep out of the Sight of Feasts and Banquets as much as may be; for 'tis more difficult to refrain good Cheer, when it's present, than from the Desire of it when it is away; the like you may observe in the Objects of all the other Senses.

If a Man casually exceeds, let him fast the next Meal, and all may be well again, provided it be not too often done; as if he exceed at Dinner, let him refrain a Supper, &c.

A temperate Diet frees from Diseases; such are seldom ill, but if they are surprised with Sickness, they bear it better, and recover sooner; for most Distempers have their Original from Repletion.

Use now and then a little Exercise a quarter of an Hour before Meals, as to swing a Weight, or swing your Arms about with a small Weight in each Hand; to leap, or the like, for that stirs the Muscles of the Breast.

A temperate Diet arms the Body against all external Accidents; so that they are not easily hurt by Heat, Cold, or Labour; if they at any time should be prejudiced, they are more easily cured, either of Wounds, Dislocations or Bruises.

But when malignant Fevers are rife in the Country or City where thou dwelst, 'tis adviseable to eat and drink more freely, by Way of Prevention; for those are Diseases that are not caused by Repletion, and seldom attack Full-feeders.

A sober Diet makes a Man die without Pain; it maintains the Senses in Vigour; it mitigates the Violence of the Passions and Affections. It preserves the Memory, it helps the Understanding, it allays the Heat of Lust; it brings a Man to a Consideration of his latter End; it makes the Body a fit Tabernacle for the Lord to dwell in; which makes us happy in this World, and eternally happy in the World to come, through Jesus Christ our Lord and Saviour.

Fools make Feasts and wise Men eat them!

1743

Poor Richard's *Almanack, &c.*

Friendly READER,

BECAUSE I would have every Man make Advantage of the Blessings of Providence, and few are acquainted with the Method of making Wine of the Grapes which grow wild in our Woods, I do here present them with a few easy Directions, drawn from some Years Experience, which, if they will follow, they may furnish themselves with a wholesome sprightly Claret, which will keep for several Years, and is not inferior to that which passeth for *French* Claret.

Begin to gather Grapes from the 10th of *September* (the ripest first) to the last of *October*, and having clear'd them of Spider webs, and dead Leaves, put them into a large Molosses- or Rum-Hogshead; after having washed it well, and knock'd one Head out, fix it upon the other Head, on a Stand, or Blocks in the Cellar, if you have any, if not, in the warmest Part of the House, about 2 Feet from the Ground; as the Grapes sink, put up more, for 3 or 4 Days; after which, get into the Hogshead bare-leg'd, and tread them down until the Juice works up about your Legs, which will be in less than half an Hour; then get out, and turn the Bottom ones up, and tread them again, a Quarter of an Hour; this will be sufficient to get out the good Juice; more pressing wou'd burst the unripe Fruit, and give it an ill Taste. This done, cover the Hogshead close with a thick Blanket, and if you have no Cellar, and the Weather proves Cold, with two.

In this Manner you must let it take its first Ferment, for 4 or 5 Days it will work furiously; when the Ferment abates, which you will know by its making less Noise, make a Spile-hole within six Inches of the Bottom, and twice a Day draw some in a Glass. When it looks as clear as Rock-water, draw it off into a clean, rather than new Cask, proportioning it to the Contents of the Hogshead or Wine*Vat; that is, if the Hogshead holds twenty Bushels of Grapes, Stems and all, the Cask must at least, hold 20 Gallons, for they will yield a Gallon per Bushel. Your Juice or† Must thus drawn from the Vat, proceed to the second Ferment.

You must reserve in Jugs or Bottles, 1 Gallon or 5 Quarts of the Must to every 20 Gallons you have to work; which you will use according to the following Directions.

Place your Cask, which must be chock full, with the Bung up, and open twice every Day, Morning and Night; feed your Cask with the reserved Must; two Spoonfuls at a time will suffice, clearing the Bung, after you feed it, with your Finger or a Spoon, of the Grape-Stones and other Filth which the Ferment will throw up; you must continue feeding it thus until *Christmas*, when you may bung it up, and it will be fit for Use or to be rack'd into clean Casks or Bottles, by *February*.

N. B. Gather the Grapes after the Dew is off, and in all dry Seasons. Let not the Children come at the Must, it will scour them severely. If you make Wine for Sale, or to go beyond Sea, one quarter Part must be distill'd, and the Brandy put into the three Quarters remaining. One Bushel of Grapes, heap Measure, as you gather them from the Vine, will make at least a Gallon of Wine, if good, five Quarts.

These Directions are not design'd for those who are skill'd in making Wine, but for those who have hitherto had no Acquaintance with that Art.

---

* Vat *or* Fatt, *a Name for the Vessel, in which you tread the Grapes, and in which the* Must *takes its first Ferment.*

† Must *is a Name for the Juice of the Vine before it is fermented, afterwards 'tis called Wine.*

JANUARY

On the FLORIDA WAR.

From *Georgia* t' *Augustine* the General goes;
From *Augustine* to *Georgia* come our Foes;
Hardy from *Charlestown* to *St. Simons* hies,
Again from thence to *Charlestown* back he flies.
Forth from *St. Simons* then the *Spaniards* creep;
Say Children, Is not this your Play, *Bo Peep?*

How few there are who have courage enough to own
their Faults, or resolution enough to mend them!

Men differ daily, about things which are subject to Sense,
is it likely then they should agree about things invisible.

Wars bring Scars.

Poor Richard: 1743

FEBRUARY

Democritus, dear Droll, revisit Earth;
And with our Follies glut thy heighten'd Mirth:
Sad *Heraclitus*, serious Wretch, return;
In louder Grief, our greater Crimes to mourn
Between you both, I unconcern'd stand by:
Hurt, can I laugh? and honest, need I cry.

Mark with what insolence and pride,
Blown *Bufo* takes his haughty stride;
As if no toad was toad beside.

Ill Company is like a dog who dirts those most,
    that he loves best.

MARCH

From bad Health, bad Conscience, & Parties dull Strife,
From an insolent Friend, & a termagant Wife,
From the Kindred of such (on one Side or t'other)
Who most wisely delight in plaguing each other;
From the Wretch who can cant, while he Mischief designs,
From old rotten Mills, bank'd Meadows & Mines;
From Curses like these if kind Heav'n defends me,
I'll never complain of the Fortune it sends me.

In prosperous fortunes be modest and wise,
The greatest may fall, and the lowest may rise:
But insolent People that fall in disgrace,
Are wretched and no body pities their Case.

Le sage entend à demi mot.

Sorrow is dry.

APRIL

A Parrot is for Prating priz'd,
But prattling Women are despis'd;
She who attacks another's Honour

Draws every living Thing upon her.
Think, Madam, when you stretch your Lungs,
That all your Neighbours too have Tongues;
One Slander fifty will beget;
The World with Interest pays the Debt.

The World is full of fools and faint hearts, and yet every one has courage enough to bear the misfortunes, and wisdom enough to manage the Affairs of his neighbour.

Beware, beware! he'll cheat 'ithout scruple, who can without fear.

MAY

The Snows are gone, and genial Spring once more
New clothes the Meads with Grass, the Trees with Leaves;
And the proud Rivers that disdain'd a Shore
Within their Banks now roll their lessen'd Waves.
Nature seems all renew'd, youthful and gay,
Ev'n Luna doth her monthly Loss supply;
But Years and Hours that whirl our Time away,
Describe our State, and tell us *we must die.*

The D——l wipes his B——ch with poor Folks Pride.

Content and Riches seldom meet together,
Riches take thou, contentment I had rather.

Speak with contempt of none, from slave to king,
The meanest Bee hath, and will use, a sting.

JUNE

*Every Man for himself, &*c.

A Town fear'd a Siege, and held Consultation,
What was the best Method of Fortification:
A grave skilful Mason declar'd his Opinion,
That nothing but Stone could secure the Dominion.
A Carpenter said, Tho' that was well spoke,
Yet he'd rather advise to defend it with Oak.

Poor Richard: 1743

A Tanner much wiser than both these together,
Cry'd, *Try what you please, but nothing's like Leather.*

The church the state, and the poor, are 3 daughters
which we should maintain, but not portion off.

A achwyno heb achos; gwneler achos iddo.

A little well-gotten will do us more good,
Than lordships and scepters by Rapine and Blood.

❦ July

Friend *Col* and I, both full of Whim,
To shun each other oft' agree;
For I'm not Beau enough for him;
And he's too much a Beau for me.
Then let us from each other fly
And Arm-in-arm no more appear;
That I may ne'er offend your Eye;
That you may ne'er offend my Ear.

Borgen macht sorgen.

Let all Men know thee, but no man know thee
thoroughly: Men freely ford that see the shallows.

'Tis easy to frame a good bold resolution;
But hard is the Task that concerns execution.

Cold & cunning come from the north:
but cunning sans wisdom is nothing worth.

❦ August

On buying a BIBLE.

'Tis but a Folly to rejoice, or boast,
How small a Price thy well-bought Purchase cost.
Until thy Death, thou shalt not fully know
Whether it was a Pennyworth, or no;
And, at that time, believe me, 'twill appear
Extreamly cheap, or else extreamly dear.

'Tis vain to repine,
Tho' a learned Divine
Will die at nine.

A noddo duw, ry noddir.

Ah simple Man! when a boy two precious jewels were given thee,
Time, and good Advice; one thou hast lost, and the other thrown away.

Na funno i hûn.
Na wnaid i ûn.

❧ SEPTEMBER

Good Death, said a Woman, for once be so kind
To take me, and leave my dear Husband behind,
But when Death appear'd with a sour Grimace,
The Woman was dash'd at his thin hatchet Face;
So she made him a Courts'y, and modestly sed,
If you come for my Husband, he lies there in Bed.

Dick told his spouse, he durst be bold to swear,
Whate'er she pray'd for, Heav'n would thwart her pray'r:
Indeed! says *Nell*, 'tis what I'm pleas'd to hear;
For now I'll pray for your long life, my dear.

The sleeping Fox catches no poultry. Up! up!

❧ OCTOBER

A Musketo just starv'd, in a sorry Condition,
Pretended to be a most skilful Musician;
He comes to a Bee-hive, and there he would stay,
To teach the Bees Children to sing *Sol la fa*.
The Bees told him plainly the Way of their Nation,
Was breeding up Youth in some honest Vocation;
Lest not bearing Labour, they should not be fed,
And then curse their Parents for being high bred.

Came you from Court? for in your Mien,
A self-important air is seen.

If you'd be wealthy, think of saving, more than of getting: The *Indies* have not made *Spain* rich, because her Outgoes equal her Incomes.

Tugend bestehet wen alles vergehet.

❧ NOVEMBER

A Year of Wonders now behold!
Britons despising *Gallic* Gold!
A Year that stops the *Spanish* Plunders!
A Year that they must be Refunders!
A Year that sets our Troops a marching!
A Year secures our Ships from Searching!
A Year that Charity's extended!
A Year that *Whig* and *Tory*'s blended!
Amazing Year! that we're defended!

Hear what *Jack Spaniard* says,
    Con todo el Mundo Guerra,
    Y Paz con Ingalatierra.

If you'd have it done, Go: If not, send.

Many a long dispute among Divines may be thus abridg'd,
    It is so: It is not so, It is so; It is not so.

❧ DECEMBER

Inclement Winter rages o'er the Plains,
Incrusts the Earth and binds the Floods in Chains.
Is the Globe mov'd? or does our Country roll,
In nearer Latitude to th' artic Pole?
The Fate of *Lapland* and its Cold we bear,
Yet want the Fur, the Sledge and harness'd Deer:
To punish Guilt, do angry Stars combine
Conjunct or Opposite, Quartile or Trine?

Experience keeps a dear school, yet Fools will learn
    in no other.

Felix quem faciunt aliena pericula cautum.

How many observe Christ's Birth-day! How few,
    his Precepts! O! 'tis easier to keep Holidays
    than Commandments.

Once on a Time it by Chance came to pass,
That a Man and his Son were leading an Ass.
Cries a Passenger, Neighbour, you're shrewdly put to't,
To lead an Ass empty, and trudge it on foot.
Nay, quoth the old Fellow, if Folk do so mind us
I'll e'en climb the Ass, and Boy mount behind us:
But as they jogg'd on, they were laught at and hiss'd,
What, two booby Lubbers on one sorry Beast!
This is such a Figure as never was known;
'Tis a Sign that the Ass is none of your own.
Then down gets the Boy, and walks by the Side,
Till another cries, What, you old Fool must you ride?
When you see the poor Child that's weakly and young
Forc'd thro' thick and thin to trudge it along.
Then down gets the Father, and up gets the Son;
If this cannot please them we ne'er shall have done.
They had not gone far, but a Woman cries out,
O you young graceless Imp, you'll be hang'd, no doubt!
Must you ride an Ass, and your Father that's grey
E'en foot it, and pick out the best of his Way?
So now to please all they but one Trick lack,
And that was to carry the Ass a pick-pack:
But when that was try'd, it appear'd such a Jest,
It occasion'd more Laughter by half than the rest.
Thus he who'd please all, and their Good-liking gain,
Shows a deal Good-Nature, but labours in vain.

COURTS.

A Person threatning to go to Law, was dissuaded from it
by his Friend, who desired him to *consider*, for the Law was
chargeable. I don't care, reply'd the other, I will not consider,

I'll go to Law. Right, said his Friend, for if you go to law, I am sure you don't consider.

A Farmer once made a Complaint to a Judge,
My Bull, if it please you, Sir, owing a Grudge,
Belike to one of your good Worship's Cattle,
Has slain him out-right in a mortal Battle:
I'm sorry at heart because of the Action,
And want to know how must be made Satisfaction.
Why, you must give me your Bull, that's plain
Says the Judge, or pay me the Price of the Slain.
But I have mistaken the Case, Sir, says *John*,
The dead Bull I talk of, & please you, 's my own:
And yours is the Beast that the Mischief has done.
The Judge soon replies with a serious Face:
Say you so; then this Accident *alters the Case*.

*Now I have a Sheep and a Cow, every Body
bids me Good-morrow.*

Poor Richard's *Almanack, &c.*

Courteous READER,

THIS is the Twelfth Year that I have in this Way laboured for the Benefit —— of Whom? —— of the Publick, if you'll be so good-natured as to believe it; if not, e'en take the naked Truth, 'twas for the Benefit of my own dear self; not forgetting in the mean time, our gracious Consort and Dutchess the peaceful, quiet, silent Lady *Bridget*. But whether my Labours have been of any Service to the Publick or not, the Publick I must acknowledge has been of Service to me; I have lived Comfortably by its Benevolent Encouragement; and I hope I shall always bear a grateful Sense of its continued Favour.

My Adversary *J—n J————n* has indeed made an Attempt to *outshine* me, by pretending to penetrate *a Year deeper* into Futurity; and giving his Readers *gratis* in his Almanack for 1743 an Eclipse of the Year 1744, to be beforehand with me: His Words are, "The first Day of *April* next Year 1744, there will be a GREAT ECLIPSE of the Sun; it begins about an Hour before Sunset. It being in the Sign Aries, the House of Mars, and in the 7th, shows Heat, Difference and Animosities between Persons of the highest Rank and Quality," *&c.* I am very glad, for the Sake of these Persons of Rank and Quality, that there is *no manner of Truth* in this Prediction: They may, if they please, live in

Love and Peace. And I caution his Readers (they are but few, indeed, and so the Matter's the less) not to give themselves any Trouble about observing this imaginary Great Eclipse; for they may stare till they're blind without seeing the least Sign of it. I might, on this Occasion, return Mr. *J———n* the Name of *Baal's false Prophet* he gave me some Years ago in his Wrath, on Account of my Predicting his Reconciliation with the *Church of Rome*, (tho' he seems now to have given up that Point) but I think such Language between old Men and Scholars unbecoming; and I leave him to settle the Affair with the Buyers of his Almanack as well as he can, who perhaps will not take it very kindly, that he has done what in him lay (by sending them out to gaze at an invisible Eclipse on the first of *April*) to make *April Fools* of them all. His old thread bare Excuse which he repeats Year after Year about the *Weather*, "That no Man can be infallible therein, by Reason of the many contrary Causes happening at or near the same-time, and the Unconstancy of the Summer Showers and Gusts," *&c.* will hardly serve him in the Affair of *Eclipses*; and I know not where he'll get another.

I have made no Alteration in my usual Method, except adding the Rising and Setting of the Planets, and the Lunar Conjunctions. Those who are so disposed, may thereby very readily learn to know the Planets, and distinguish them from each other.

I am, dear Reader,

Thy obliged Friend,

R. SAUNDERS.

The COUNTRY MAN.

Happy the Man whose Wish and Care
   A few paternal Acres bound,
Content to breathe his native Air,
   In his own Ground.

Whose Herds with Milk, whose Fields with Bread,
   Whose Flocks supply him with Attire,
Whose Trees in Summer yield him Shade,
   In Winter Fire.

Blest, who can unconcernedly find
   Hours, Days and Years slide soft away,
In Health of Body, Peace of Mind,
     Quiet by Day,

Sound Sleep by Night; Study and Ease
   Together mixt; sweet Recreation;
And Innocence which most does please
     with Meditation.

Thus let me live, unseen, unknown,
   Thus unlamented let me die,
Steal from the World, and not a Stone
     Tell where I lie.

JANUARY

   Biblis does Solitude admire,
   A wond'rous Lover of the Dark;
   Each Night puts out her Chamber-Fire,
   And just keeps in a *single Spark*;
   'Till four she keeps herself alive,
   Warm'd by her Piety, no doubt;
   Then, tir'd with kneeling, just at five,
   She sighs—and lets that Spark *go out*.

He that drinks his Cyder alone,
   let him catch his Horse alone.

Who is strong? He that can conquer his bad Habits.

Who is rich? He that rejoices in his Portion.

FEBRUARY

Our youthful Preacher see, intent on Fame;
Warm to gain Souls?—No, 'tis to gain a Name.
Behold his Hands display'd, his Body rais'd;
With what a Zeal he labours—to be prais'd.
Touch'd with each Weakness which he does arraign,

With Vanity he talks against the Vain;
With Ostentation does to Meekness guide;
Proud of his Periods form'd to strike at Pride.

He that has not got a Wife, is not yet a compleat Man.

MARCH

Without Repentance none to Heav'n can go,
Yet what Repentance is few seem to know:
'Tis not to cry out *Mercy*, or to sit
    And droop, or to confess that thou hast fail'd;
'Tis to bewail the Sins thou didst commit,
    And not commit those Sins thou hast bewail'd.
He that *bewails* and not *forsakes* them too,
Confesses rather what he *means to do*.

What you would seem to be, be really.

If you'd lose a troublesome Visitor, lend him Money.

Tart Words make no Friends: a spoonful of honey
    will catch more flies than a Gallon of Vinegar.

APRIL

With what a perfect World-revolving Power
Were first the unweildy Planets launch'd along
Th' illimitable Void! Thus to remain
Amid the Flux of many thousand Years,
That oft has swept the busy Race of Men,
And all their labour'd Monuments away:
Unresting, changeless, matchless, in their Course;
To Night and Day, with the delightful Round
Of Seasons, faithful, not eccentric once:
So pois'd, and perfect is the vast Machine!

    Dine with little, sup with less:
    Do better still; sleep supperless.

Industry, Perseverance, & Frugality, make Fortune yield.

✽ MAY

Irus tho' wanting Gold and Lands,
    Lives chearful, easy, and content;
Corvus, unbless'd, with twenty Hands
    Employ'd to count his yearly Rent.
Sages in Wisdom! tell me which
    Of these you think possesses more!
One with his Poverty is rich,
    And one with all his Wealth is poor.

I'll warrant ye, goes before *Rashness*;
  Who'd-a-tho't it? comes sneaking after.

Prayers and Provender hinder no Journey.

Make haste slowly.

✽ JUNE

Of all the Causes which conspire to blind
Man's erring Judgment, and misguide the Mind,
What the weak Head with strongest Biass rules,
Is *Pride*, that never-failing Vice of Fools.
Whatever Nature has in Worth deny'd,
She gives in large Recruits of needful Pride;
For as in Bodies, thus in Souls we find
What wants in Blood & Spirits, swell'd with Wind.

Hear *Reason*, or she'll make you feel her.

Give me yesterday's Bread, this Day's Flesh,
  and last Year's Cyder.

✽ JULY

All-conq'ring HEAT, oh intermit thy Wrath!
And on my throbbing Temples potent thus
Beam not so hard! Incessant still you flow,
And still another fervent Flood succeeds,

Pour'd on the Head profuse. In vain I sigh,
And restless turn, and look around for night;
Night is far off; and hotter Hours approach.
Who can endure! – – – –

God heals, and the Doctor takes the Fees.

Sloth (like Rust) consumes faster than Labour wears:
   the used Key is always bright.

Light Gains heavy Purses.

AUGUST

Would Men but follow what the Sex advise,
All things would prosper, all the World grow wise.
'Twas by *Rebecca*'s Aid that *Jacob* won
His Father's Blessing from an elder Son.
Abusive *Nabal* ow'd his forfeit Life
To the wise Conduct of a prudent Wife.
At *Hester*'s Suit, the persecuting Sword
Was sheath'd, and *Israel* liv'd to bless the Lord.

Keep thou from the Opportunity,
   and God will keep thee from the Sin.

Where there's no Law, there's no Bread.

As Pride increases, Fortune declines.

SEPTEMBER

All other Goods by Fortune's Hand are giv'n,
A WIFE is the peculiar Gift of Heav'n.
Vain Fortune's Favours, never at a Stay,
Like empty Shadows, pass, and glide away;
One solid Comfort, our eternal Wife,
Abundantly supplies us all our Life:
This Blessing lasts (if those that try say true)
As long as Heart can wish—and longer too.

Drive thy Business, or it will drive thee.

A full Belly is the Mother of all Evil.

The same man cannot be both Friend and Flatterer.

He who multiplies Riches multiplies Cares.

An old Man in a House is a good Sign.

❧ OCTOBER

Be Niggard's of *Advice* on no Pretence;
For the worst Avarice is that of Sense.
Yet 'tis not all, your Counsel's free and true;
Blunt Truths more Mischief than nice Falshoods do.
Men must be taught as if you taught them not,
And Things unknown propos'd as Things forgot;
Without *Good Breeding* Truth is disapprov'd
That only makes superior Sense belov'd.

Those who are fear'd, are hated.

The Things which hurt, instruct.

The Eye of a Master, will do more Work than his Hand.

A soft Tongue may strike hard.

❧ NOVEMBER

Sylvia while young, with ev'ry Grace adorn'd,
Each blooming Youth, and fondest Lover scorn'd:
In Years at length arriv'd at Fifty-nine,
She feels Love's Passion as her Charms decline:
    —Thus Oaks a hundred Winters old
        Just as they now expire,
    Turn Touchwood, doated, grey and old,
        And at each SPARK take Fire.—

If you'd be belov'd, make yourself amiable.

A true Friend is the best Possession.

Fear God, and your Enemies will fear you.

Poor Richard: 1744

❧ DECEMBER

This World's an Inn, all Travellers are we;
And this World's Goods th' Accommodations be.
Our Life is nothing but a Winter's Day;
Some only break their *Fast*, and so away.
Others stay Dinner, and depart full fed.
The deepest Age but *sups* and goes to bed.
He's most in Debt that lingers out the Day;
Who dies betimes has less and less to pay.

Epitaph on a Scolding Wife by her Husband.
Here my poor *Bridget*'s Corps doth lie, she is at rest,
   —and so am I.

COURTS.

Two trav'ling Beggars, (I've forgot their Name)
An Oister found to which they both laid Claim.
Warm the Dispute! At length to Law they'd go,
As richer Fools for Trifles often do.
The Cause two Petty-foggers undertake,
Resolving right or wrong some Gain to make.
They jangle till the Court this Judgment gave,
Determining what every one should have.
    Blind Plaintiff, lame Defendant, share
    The friendly Law's impartial Care:
    A Shell for him, a Shell for thee;
    The MIDDLE'S *Bench and Lawyer's Fee.*

Great Talkers should be cropp'd,
for they have no need of ears.

Poor Richard's *Almanack, &c.*

Courteous READER,

FOR the Benefit of the Publick, and my own Profit, I have performed this my thirteenth annual Labour, which I hope will be as acceptable as the former.

The rising and setting of the Planets, and their Conjunctions with the Moon, I have continued; whereby those who are unacquainted with those heavenly Bodies, may soon learn to distinguish them from the fixed Stars, by observing the following Directions.

All those glittering Stars (except five) which we see in the Firmament of Heaven, are called fixed Stars, because they keep the same Distance from one another, and from the Ecliptic; they rise and set on the same Points of the Horizon, and appear like so many lucid Points fixed to the celestial Firmament. The other five have a particular and different Motion, for which Reason they have not always the same Distance from one another; and therefore they have been called wandering Stars or Planets, *viz. Saturn* ♄, Jupiter ♃, *Mars* ♂, *Venus* ♀, and *Mercury* ☿, and these may be distinguished from the fixed Stars by their not twinkling. The brightest of the five is *Venus*, which appears the biggest; and when this glorious Star appears, and goes before the Sun, it is called *Phosphorus*, or the Morning Star, and *Hesperus*, or the Evening-Star, when it follows the Sun. *Jupiter* appears almost as big as *Venus*, but not so bright. *Mars* may be easily known from the rest of the Planets, because it appears red like a hot Iron or burning Coal, and twinkles a little. *Saturn*, in Appearance, is less than *Mars*, and of a pale Colour, *Mercury* is so near the Sun, that it is seldom seen.

Against the 6th Day of *January* you may see ♂ rise 10 35, which signifies the Planet *Mars* rises 35 Minutes after 10 o'Clock at Night, when that Planet may be seen to appear in the East. Also against the 10th Day of *January* you will find ♀ sets 7 13, which shows *Venus* sets 13 Minutes after 7 o'Clock at Night. If you look towards the West that Evening, you may see that beautiful Star till the Time of its setting. Again, on the 18th Day of the same Month, you will find ♄ rise 9 18, which shews that *Saturn* rises 18 Minutes after 9 at Night.

Or the Planets may be known by observing them at the Time of their Conjunctions with the Moon, *viz.* against the 14 Day of *January* are inserted these Characters, ♂ ☽ ♄, which shews there will be a Conjunction of the Moon and *Saturn* on that Day. If you look out about 5 o'Clock in the Morning, you will see *Saturn* very near the Moon. The like is to be observed at any other time by the rising and setting of the Planets, and their Conjunctions with the Moon; by which Method they may be distinctly known from the fixed Stars.

I have nothing further to add at present, but my hearty Wishes for your Welfare, both temporal and spiritual, and Thanks for all your past Favours, being,

Dear Reader,

Thy obliged Friend,

R. SAUNDERS.

Go, wond'rous Creature! mount where Science guides,
Go measure Earth, weigh Air, and state the Tides;
Shew by what Laws the wand'ring Planets stray,
Correct old Time, and teach the Sun his Way.
Go soar with Plato to th' empyreal Sphere,
To the *first* Good, *first* Perfect, and *first* Fair;
Or tread the mazy Round his Follow'rs trod,
And, quitting Sense, called *imitating God,*

As Eastern Priests in giddy Circles run,
And turn their Heads to imitate the *Sun*.
Go teach Eternal Wisdom how to rule,—
Then drop into thyself, and be a Fool.

☙ JANUARY

I give and I devise (old Euclio said,
And sigh'd) "My Lands and Tenements to Ned."
Your Money, Sir? My Money, Sir! what all?
"Why—if I must—(then wept) I give it *Paul*"
The Mannor, Sir? "The Mannor! hold, he cry'd,
"Not that – – – I cannot part with that" – – – and dy'd.

Beware of little Expences,
    a small Leak will sink a great Ship.

Wars bring scars.

A light purse is a heavy Curse.

As often as we do good, we sacrifice.

Help, Hands; For I have no Lands.

☙ FEBRUARY

Self Love but serves the virtuous Mind to wake,
As the small Pebble stirs the peaceful Lake;
The Centre mov'd, a Circle strait succeeds,
Another still, and still another spreads,
Friend, Parent, Neighbour, first it will embrace,
His Country next, and next all human Race;
Wide and more wide, th' o'erflowings of the Mind
Take every Creature in of every Kind.

It's common for Men to give pretended Reasons
    instead of one real one.

Poor Richard: 1745

MARCH

Fame but from Death a Villian's Name can save,
As Justice tears his Body from the Grave;
When what t' oblivion better were resign'd
Is hung on high to poison half Mankind.
All Fame is foreign but of *true Desert*,
Plays round the Head, but comes not to the Heart.
One *Self-approving Hour* whole Years outweighs
Of stupid Starers, and of loud Huzza's.

Vanity backbites more than *Malice*.

He's a Fool that cannot conceal his Wisdom.

Great spenders are bad lenders.

All blood is alike ancient.

APRIL

'Tis not for Mortals always to be blest:
But him the least the dull and painful Hours
Of Life oppress, whom sober SENSE conducts,
And VIRTUE, thro' this Labyrinth we tread.
Virtue and Sense are one; and, trust me, he
Who has not Virtue, is not truly wise.

You may talk too much on the best of subjects.

A Man without ceremony has need of great merit in its place.

No gains without pains.

MAY

VIRTUE, (for meer GOOD-NATURE, is a Fool)
Is Sense and Spirit, with HUMANITY;
'Tis sometimes angry, and its Frown confounds;
'Tis ev'n vindictive, but in Vengeance just.
Knaves fain would laugh at it; some great Ones dare;

But at his Heart, the most undaunted Son
Of Fortune, dreads its Name and awful Charms.

Had I revenged wrong, I had not worn my skirts so long.

Graft good Fruit all, or graft not at all.

JUNE

Unhappy *Italy*! whose alter'd State
Has felt the worst Severity of Fate;
Not that *Barbarian* Bands her *Fasces* broke,
And bow'd her haughty Neck beneath her Yoke;
Nor that her Palaces to Earth are thrown,
Her Cities desart, and her Fields unsown;
But that her ancient Spirit is decay'd,
That sacred Wisdom from her Bounds is fled.
That there the Source of Science flows no more,
Whence its rich Streams supply'd the World before.

Idleness is the greatest Prodigality.

Old young and old long.

Punch-coal, cut-candle, and set brand on end,
is neither good house-wife, nor good house-wife's friend.

At this Season 'tis no wonder
if we have clouds, hail, rain and thunder.

JULY

Hot from the Field, indulge not yet your Limbs
In wish'd Repose, nor court the fanning Gale,
Nor taste the Spring. O! by the sacred Tears
Of Widows, Orphans, Mothers, Sisters, Sires,
Forbear! – – – – No other Pestilence has driven
Such Myriads o'er th' irremeable Deep.

He who buys had need have 100 Eyes,
  but one's enough for him that sells the Stuff.

There are no fools so troublesome as those that have wit.

AUGUST

Has God, thou Fool! work'd solely for thy Good,
Thy Joy, thy Pastime, thy Attire, thy Food?
Who for thy Table feeds the wanton Fawn,
For him as kindly spread the flow'ry Lawn.
Is it for thee the Lark descends and sings?
Joy tunes his Voice, Joy elevates his Wings.
Is it for thee the Mock-bird pours his Throat?
Loves of his own, and Raptures, swell the note.

Many complain of their Memory, few of their Judgment.

One Man may be more cunning than another,
    but not more cunning than every body else.

SEPTEMBER

The bounding Steed you pompously bestride,
Shares with his Lord the Pleasure and the Pride.
Is thine alone the Seed that strows the Plain?
The Birds of Heav'n shall vindicate their Grain.
Thine the full Harvest of the golden Year?
Part pays, and justly, the deserving Steer.
The Hog that plows not, nor obeys thy Call,
Lives on the Labours of this Lord of all.

To God we owe fear and love; to our neighbours justice
    and charity; to our selves prudence and sobriety.

Fools make feasts and wise men eat them.

Light heel'd mothers make leaden-heel'd daughters.

OCTOBER

For Forms of Government let Fools contest,
Whate'er is best administer'd is best;
For Modes of Faith let graceless Zealots fight,

His can't be wrong, whose Life is in the right:
All must be false, that thwart this one great End,
And all of God, that bless Mankind, or mend.

The good or ill hap of a good or ill life,
is the good or ill choice of a good or ill wife.

'Tis easier to prevent bad habits than to break them.

❧ November

Fair Summer's gone, and Nature's Charms decay.
See gloomy Clouds obscure the chearful Day!
Now hung with Pearls the dropping Trees appear,
Their faded Honours scatter'd here and there.
Behold the Groves that shine with silver Frost,
Their Beauty wither'd, and their Verdure lost.
Sharp *Boreas* blows, and Nature feels Decay,
Time conquers all and we must Time obey.

Every Man has Assurance enough to boast of his honesty,
few of their Understanding.

Interest which blinds some People, enlightens others.

❧ December

These Blessings, Reader, may Heav'n grant to thee;
A faithful Friend, equal in Love's degree;
Land fruitful, never conscious of the Curse,
A liberal Heart and never-failing Purse;
A smiling Conscience, a contented mind;
A temp'rate Knowledge with true Wisdom join'd;
A Life as long as fair, and when expir'd,
A kindly Death, unfear'd as undesir'd.

An ounce of wit that is bought,
Is worth a pound that is taught.

He that resolves to mend hereafter,
resolves not to mend now.

COURTS.

The Christian Doctrine teaches to believe
It's every Christian's Duty, to forgive.
Could we forgive as fast as Men offend
The LAWS slow Progresses would quickly end.
Revenge of past Offences is the Cause
Why peaceful Minds consented to have Laws.
Yet Plaintiffs and Defendants much mistake
Their Cure, and their Diseases lasting make;
For to be reconcil'd, and to comply,
Would prove their cheap and shortest Remedy.

Many a long Dispute may be thus abridged:
It is so. It is not so. It is so. It is not so.

1746

Poor Richard's *Almanack, &c.*

PREFACE.

Who is *Poor Richard*? People oft enquire,
Where lives? What is he?—never yet the nigher.
Somewhat to ease your Curiositie,
Take these slight Sketches of my Dame and me.
   Thanks to kind Readers and a careful Wife,
With Plenty bless'd, I lead an easy Life;
My Business Writing; hers to drain the Mead,
Or crown the barren Hill with useful Shade;
In the smooth Glebe to see the Plowshare worn,
And fill the Granary with needful Corn.
Press nectarous Cyder from my loaded Trees,
Print the sweet Butter, turn the drying Cheese.
Some Books we read, tho' few there are that hit
The happy Point where Wisdom joins with Wit;
That set fair Virtue naked to our View,
And teach us what is *decent*, what is *true*.
The Friend sincere, and honest Man, with Joy
Treating or treated oft our Time employ.
Our Table neat, Meals temperate; and our Door
Op'ning spontaneous to the bashful Poor.

Free from the bitter Rage of Party Zeal,
All those we love who seek the publick Weal.
Nor blindly follow Superstition's Lore,
Which cheats deluded Mankind o'er and o'er.
Not over righteous, quite beyond the Rule,
Conscience perplext by every canting Tool.
Nor yet when Folly hides the dubious Line,
Where Good and Bad their blended Colours join;
Rush indiscreetly down the dangerous Steep,
And plunge uncertain in the darksome Deep.
Cautious, if right; if wrong resolv'd to part
The Inmate Snake that folds about the Heart.
Observe the *Mean*, the *Motive* and the *End*;
Mending our selves, or striving still to mend.
Our Souls sincere, our Purpose fair and free,
Without Vain Glory or Hypocrisy:
Thanful if well; if ill, we kiss the Rod;
Resign with Hope, and put our Trust in GOD.

JANUARY

Nothing exceeds in Ridicule, no doubt,
A Fool *in* Fashion, but a Fool that's *out*;
His Passion for Absurdity's so strong
He cannot bear a Rival in the Wrong.
Tho' wrong the Mode, comply; more Sense is shewn
In wearing others Follies than your own.
If what is out of Fashion most you prize,
Methinks you should endeavour to be wise.

When the Well's dry, we know the Worth of Water.

He that whines for Glass without G
Take away L and that's he.

FEBRUARY

Man's rich with little, were his Judgment true,
Nature is frugal, and her Wants are few;

Those few Wants answer'd, bring sincere Delights,
But Fools create themselves new Appetites.
Fancy and Pride seek Things at vast Expence,
Which relish not to *Reason* nor to *Sense*
Like Cats in Airpumps, to subsist we strive
On Joys too thin to keep the Soul alive.

A good Wife & Health, is a Man's best Wealth.

A quarrelsome Man has no good Neighbours.

MARCH

O sacred *Solitude*! divine Retreat!
Choice of the Prudent! Envy of the Great!
By thy pure Stream, or in thy waving Shade,
We court fair Wisdom, that celestial Maid:
The genuine Offspring of her lov'd Embrace,
(Strangers on Earth) are Innocence and Peace.
There blest with Health, with Business unperplext,
This Life we relish, and ensure the next.

Wide will wear, but Narrow will tear.

Silks and Sattins put out the Kitchen Fire.

Vice knows she's ugly, so puts on her Mask.

APRIL

Zara resembles *Ætna* crown'd with Snows,
Without she freezes, and within she glows;
Twice e'er the Sun descends, with Zeal inspir'd,
From the vain Converse of the World retir'd,
She reads the Psalms and Chapters of the Day,
In – – – – some leud Novel, new Romance, or Play.
Thus gloomy *Zara*, with a solemn Grace,
Deceives Mankind, and *hides* behind her *Face*.

All Mankind are beholden to him that is kind to the Good.

131

Women & Wine, Game & Deceit,
Make the Wealth small and the Wants great.

It's the easiest Thing in the World for a Man to deceive
himself.

✿ MAY

Pleasures are few, and fewer we enjoy;
Pleasure like *Quicksilver*, is bright and *coy*;
We strive to grasp it with our utmost skill,
Still it eludes us, and it glitters still.
If seiz'd at last, compute your mighty Gains,
What is it but rank Poison in your Veins.

A Plowman on his Legs is higher than a Gentleman
on his Knees.

Virtue and Happiness are Mother and Daughter.

The generous Mind least regards money,
and yet most feels the Want of it.

For one poor Man there are an hundred indigent.

✿ JUNE

What's Man's Reward for all his Care and Toil?
But *One*; a female Friend's endearing Smile:
A tender Smile, our Sorrow's only Balm,
And in Life's Tempest the sad Sailor's Calm.
How have I seen a gentle Nymph draw nigh,
Peace in her Air, Persuasion in her Eye;
Victorious Tenderness, it all o'ercame,
Husbands look'd mild, and Savages grew tame.

Dost thou love Life? then do not squander Time;
for that's the Stuff Life is made of.

Good Sense is a Thing all need, few have,
and none think they want.

❧ JULY

Who taught the rapid Winds to fly so fast,
Or shakes the Centre with his Western Blast?
Who from the Skies can a whole Deluge pour?
Who strikes thro' Nature, with the solemn Roar
Of dreadful *Thunder*, points it where to fall,
And in fierce Light'ning wraps the flying Ball?
Not he who trembles at the darted Fires,
Falls at the Sound, and in the Flash expires.

What's proper, is becoming: See the Blacksmith
  with his white Silk Apron!

The Tongue is ever turning to the aching Tooth.

Want of Care does us more Damage than
  Want of Knowledge.

❧ AUGUST

Can Gold calm *Passion*, or make *Reason* shine;
Can we dig *Peace* or *Wisdom* from the Mine?
Wisdom to Gold prefer, for 'tis much less
To make our *Fortune*, than our *Happiness*.
That Happiness which Great Ones often see,
With Rage and Wonder, in a low Degree,
Themselves unblest. The Poor are *only* poor;
But what are they who *droop* amid their Store?

Take Courage, Mortal; Death can't banish thee out of the
  Universe.

The Sting of a Reproach, is the Truth of it.

Do me the Favour to deny me at once.

❧ SEPTEMBER

Can Wealth give Happiness? look round and see,
What gay Distress! What splendid Misery!

Poor Richard: 1746

Whatever Fortune lavishly can pour,
The Mind annihilates, and calls for more.
Wealth is a Cheat, believe not what it says;
Greatly it promises, but never pays.
Misers may startle, but they shall be told,
That Wealth is Bankrupt, and *insolvent* Gold.

The most exquisite Folly is made of Wisdom spun too fine.

A life of leisure, and a life of laziness, are two things.

October

Some Ladies are too beauteous to be wed,
For where's the Man that's worthy of their Bed?
If no Disease reduce her Pride before,
Lavinia will be ravisht at threescore.
Then she submits to venture in the Dark,
And nothing, now, is wanting – – – – but her Spark.

Mad Kings and mad Bulls,
    are not to be held by treaties & packthread.

Changing Countries or Beds,
    cures neither a bad Manager, nor a Fever.

November

There are, who, tossing on the Bed of *Vice*,
For *Flattery's* Opiate give the highest Price;
Yet from the saving Hand of *Friendship* turn,
Her Med'cines dread, her generous Offers spurn.
Deserted *Greatness*! who but pities thee?
By Crowds encompass'd, thou no *Friend* canst see.
Or should kind *Truth* invade thy tender Ear,
We pity still, for thou no Truth canst bear.

A true great Man will neither trample on a Worm,
    nor sneak to an Emperor.

Ni ffyddra llaw dyn, er gwneithr da idd ei hûn.

December

What's Female Beauty, but an Air divine,
Thro' which the Mind's all gentle Graces shine?
They, like the Sun, irradiate all between;
The Body *charms*, because the Soul is *seen*.
Hence, Men are often Captives of a Face,
They know not why, of no peculiar Grace.
Some Forms tho' bright, no mortal Man can *bear*;
Some, none *resist*, tho' not exceeding fair.

Tim and his Handsaw are good in their Place,
Tho' not fit for preaching or shaving a face.

Half-Hospitality opens his Doors
   and shuts up his Countenance.

COURTS.

From Earth to Heav'n when *Justice* fled,
The Laws decided in her Stead;
From Heav'n to Earth should she return,
Lawyers might beg, and Lawbooks burn.

A good Wife and Health, is a Man's best Wealth.

1747

Poor Richard's *Almanack, &c.*

Courteous READER,

THIS is the 15th Time I have entertain'd thee with my annual Productions; I hope to thy Profit as well as mine. For besides the astronomical Calculations, and other Things usually contain'd in Almanacks, which have their daily Use indeed while the Year continues, but then become of no Value, I have constantly interspers'd *moral* Sentences, *prudent* Maxims, and *wise* Sayings, many of them containing *much good Sense* in *very few* Words, and therefore apt to leave *strong* and *lasting* Impressions on the Memory of young Persons, whereby they may receive Benefit as long as they live, when both Almanack and Almanack-maker have been long thrown by and forgotten. If I now and then insert a Joke or two, that seem to have little in them, my Apology is, that such may have their Use, since perhaps for their Sake light airy Minds peruse the rest, and so are struck by somewhat of more Weight and Moment. The Verses on the Heads of the Months are also generally design'd to have the same Tendency. I need not tell thee that not many of them are of my own Making. If thou hast any Judgment in Poetry, thou wilt easily discern the Workman from the Bungler. I know as well as thee, that I am no *Poet born*; and it is a Trade I never learnt, nor indeed could learn. *If I make Verses, 'tis in Spight—Of Nature and my Stars I write.* Why then should I give my Readers *bad Lines* of my

136

own, when *good Ones* of other People's are so plenty? 'Tis methinks a poor Excuse for the bad Entertainment of Guests, that the Food we set before them, tho' coarse and ordinary, is *of one's own Raising, off one's own Plantation*, &c. when there is Plenty of what is ten times better, to be had in the Market.—On the contrary, I assure ye, my Friends, that I have procur'd the best I could for ye, and *much Good may't do ye.*

I cannot omit this Opportunity of making honourable Mention of the late deceased Ornament and Head of our Profession, Mr. JACOB TAYLOR, who for upwards of 40 Years (with some few Intermissions only) supply'd the good People of this and the neighbouring Colonies, with the most compleat Ephemeris and most accurate Calculations that have hitherto appear'd in *America.* – – – – He was an ingenious Mathematician, as well as an expert and skilful Astronomer; and moreover, no mean Philosopher. But what is more than all, He was a PIOUS and an HONEST Man. *Requiescat in pace.*

I am thy poor Friend, to serve thee,

R. SAUNDERS.

JANUARY

To show the Strength, and Infamy of Pride,
By all 'tis follow'd, and by all deny'd.
What Numbers are there, which at once pursue
Praise, and the Glory to contemn it too?
To praise himself *Vincenna* knows a Shame,
And therefore lays a Stratagem for Fame;
Makes his Approach in Modesty's Disguise,
To win Applause, and takes it by Surprize.

Strive to be the *greatest* Man in your Country, and you may be disappointed; Strive to be the *best*, and you may succeed: He may well win the race that runs by himself.

FEBRUARY

See *Wealth* and *Pow'r*! Say, what can be more great?
Nothing – – – – but *Merit* in a low Estate.
To Virtue's humblest Son let none prefer

Vice, tho' a *Cræsus* or a Conqueror.
Shall Men, like Figures, pass for high, or base,
Slight, or important, only by their *Place*?
Titles are Marks of honest Men, and Wise;
The Fool, or Knave that wears a Title, lies.

'Tis a strange Forest that has no rotten Wood in't
And a strange Kindred that all are good in't.

None know the unfortunate, and the fortunate
    do not know themselves.

MARCH

Celestial PATIENCE! How dost thou defeat
The Foe's proud Menace, and elude his Hate?
While *Passion* takes his Part, betrays our Peace;
To Death and Torture swells each slight Disgrace;
By not opposing, Thou dost Ill destroy,
And wear thy conquer'd Sorrows into Joy.

There's a time to wink as well as to see.

Honest *Tom*! you may trust him with a house-full of
    untold Milstones.

There is no Man so bad, but he secretly respects the Good.

APRIL

RELIGION's Force divine is best display'd,
In a Desertion of all human Aid:
To succour in Extreams is her Delight,
And cheer the Heart when Terror strikes the Sight.
We, disbelieving our own Senses, gaze,
And wonder what a Mortal's Heart can raise,
To smile in Anguish, triumph in his Grief,
And comfort those who come to bring Relief.

When there's more Malice shown than Matter:
On the Writer falls the satyr.

✸ MAY

Girls, mark my Words; and know, for Men of Sense
Your strongest Charms are native Innocence.
Shun all deceiving Arts; the Heart that's gain'd
By Craft alone, can ne'er be long retain'd.
Arts on the Mind, like Paint upon the Face,
Fright him, that's worth your Love, from your Embrace.
In simple Manners all the Secret lies.
Be kind and virtuous, you'll be blest and wise.

Courage would fight, but *Discretion* won't let him.

Delicate *Dick*! whisper'd the Proclamation.

Cornelius ought to be *Tacitus*.

✸ JUNE

O, form'd Heav'n's Dictates nobly to rehearse,
PREACHER DIVINE! accept the grateful Verse.
Thou hast the Power, the harden'd Heart to warm,
To grieve, to raise, to terrify, to charm;
To fix the Soul on God, to teach the Mind
To know the Dignity of Human Kind;
By stricter Rules well-govern'd Life to scan,
And practise o'er the Angel in the Man.

Pride and the *Gout*, are seldom cur'd throughout.

We are not so sensible of the greatest Health
as of the least Sickness.

A good Example is the best sermon.

✸ JULY

Men drop so fast, ere Life's mid Stage we tread,
Few know so many Friends *alive* as *dead*;
Yet, as *immortal*, in our uphill Chace,
We press coy Fortune with unslacken'd Pace;

Our ardent Labours for the Toy we seek,
Join Night to Day, and Sunday to the Week,
Our very Joys are anxious, and expire
Between *Satiety* and fierce *Desire*.

A Father's a Treasure; a Brother's a Comfort;
   a Friend is both.

Despair ruins some, Presumption many.

A quiet Conscience sleeps in Thunder,
but Rest and Guilt live far asunder.

⚓ AUGUST

A *decent Competence* we fully taste;
It strikes our *Sense*, and gives a constant Feast:
More, we perceive by Dint of *Thought* alone;
The Rich must *labour* to possess *their own*,
To feel their great Abundance; and request
Their humble Friends to *help* them to be blest;
To *see* their Treasures, *hear* their Glory told,
And *aid* the wretched Impotence of Gold.
                      [*Cont'd Sept.*

He that won't be counsell'd, can't be help'd.

Craft must be at charge for clothes,
   but *Truth* can go naked.

Write Injuries in Dust, Benefits in Marble.

⚖ SEPTEMBER

But some, good Souls, and touch'd with Warmth divine,
Give *Gold* a *Price*, and teach its *Beams* to *shine*;
All *hoarded* Treasures they repute a Load,
Nor think their Wealth *their own* till well bestow'd.
Grand *Reservoirs* of public Happiness,
Thro' *secret* Streams diffusively they bless;
And while their Bounties glide conceal'd from View,
Relieve our *Wants*, and *spare* our *Blushes* too.

What is Serving God? 'Tis doing Good to Man.

What maintains one Vice would bring up two Children.

Many have been ruin'd by buying good pennyworths.

✺ OCTOBER

One to destroy, is Murder by the Law,
And Gibbets keep the lifted Hand in Awe.
To murder Thousands, takes a specious Name,
War's glorious Art, and gives immortal Fame.
O great Alliance! O divine Renown!
With Death and Pestilence to share the Crown!
When Men extol a wild Destroyer's Name,
Earth's Builder and Preserver they blaspheme.

Better is a little with content than much with contention.

A Slip of the Foot you may soon recover:
But a Slip of the Tongue you may never get over.

What signifies your Patience, if you can't find it
when you want it.

✺ NOVEMBER

I envy none their Pageantry and Show;
I envy none the Gilding of their Woe.
Give me, indulgent Heav'n, with Mind serene,
And guiltless Heart, to range the Sylvan Scene.
No splendid Poverty, no smiling Care,
No well-bred Hate, or servile Grandeur there.
There pleasing Objects useful Thought suggest,
The Sense is ravish'd, and the Soul is blest;
On every Thorn delightful Wisdom grows,
In every Rill a sweet Instruction flows.

Time enough, always proves *little enough*.

It is wise not to seek a Secret, and Honest not to reveal it.

A Mob's a Monster; Heads enough, but no Brains.

The Devil sweetens Poison with Honey.

☙ DECEMBER

Old Age *will* come, Disease may come before,
Fifteen is full as mortal as *Threescore*.
Thy Fortune and thy Charms may soon decay;
But grant these *Fugitives* prolong their Stay;
Their Basis totters, their Foundation shakes,
Life that supports them, in a Moment breaks:
Then, *wrought* into the Soul, let Virtue shine,
The *Ground* eternal, as the *Work* divine.

He that cannot bear with other People's Passions,
    cannot govern his own.

He that by the Plow would thrive,
himself must either hold or drive.

I know not which lives more unnatural Lives,
Obeying Husbands, or commanding Wives.

Poor Richard's *Almanack, &c.*

Kind READER,

THE favourable Reception my annual Labours have met with from the Publick these 15 Years past, has engaged me in Gratitude to endeavour some Improvement of my Almanack. And since my Friend *Taylor* is no more, whose *Ephemerides* so long and so agreeably serv'd and entertain'd these Provinces, I have taken the Liberty to imitate his well-known Method, and give two Pages for each Month; which affords me Room for several valuable Additions, as will best appear on Inspection and Comparison with former Almanacks. Yet I have not so far follow'd his Method, as not to continue my own where I thought it preferable; and thus my Book is increas'd to a Size beyond his, and contains much more Matter.[7]

> *Hail Night serene! thro' Thee where'er we turn*
> *Our wond'ring Eyes, Heav'n's Lamps profusely burn;*
> *And Stars unnumber'd all the Sky adorn.*
> *But lo!—what's that I see appear?*
> *It seems far off a pointed flame;*
> *From Earthwards too the shining Meteor came:*
> *How swift it climbs th' etherial Space!*
> *And now it traverses each Sphere,*
> *And seems some knowing Mind, familiar to the Place.*

143

Dame, hand my Glass, the longest, strait prepare;—
'Tis He—'tis TAYLOR's Soul, that travels there.
O stay! thou happy Spirit, stay,
And lead me on thro' all th' unbeaten Wilds of Day;
Where Planets in pure Streams of Ether driven,
Swim thro' the blue Expanse of Heav'n.
There let me, thy Companion, stray
From Orb to Orb, and now behold
Unnumber'd Suns, all Seas of molten Gold,
And trace each Comet's wand'ring Way.—

Souse down into Prose again, my Muse; for Poetry's no more thy Element, than Air is that of the Flying-Fish; whose Flights, like thine, are therefore always short and heavy.—

We complain sometimes of hard Winters in this Country; but our Winters will appear as Summers, when compar'd with those that some of our Countrymen undergo in the most Northern *British* Colony on this Continent, which is that upon *Churchill* River, in *Hudson's Bay,* Lat. 58d. 56m. Long, from *London* 94d. 50m. West. Captain *Middleton,* a Member of the *Royal Society,* who had made many Voyages thither, and winter'd there 1741-2, when he was in Search of the *North-West* Passage to the *South-Sea,* gives an Account of it to that Society, from which I have extracted these Particulars, *viz.*

The Hares, Rabbits, Foxes, and Partridges, in *September* and the Beginning of *October,* change their Colour to a snowy White, and continue white till the following Spring.

The Lakes and standing Waters, which are not above 10 or 12 Feet deep, are frozen to the Ground in Winter, and the Fishes therein all perish. Yet in Rivers near the Sea, and Lakes of a greater Depth than 10 or 12 Feet, Fishes are caught all the Winter, by cutting Holes thro' the Ice, and therein putting Lines and Hooks. As soon as the Fish are brought into the open Air, they instantly freeze stiff.

Beef, Pork, Mutton, and Venison, kill'd in the Beginning of the Winter, are preserved by the Frost for 6 or 7 Months, entirely free from Putrefaction. Likewise Geese, Partridges, and other Fowls, kill'd at the same Time, and kept with their Feathers on and Guts in, are preserv'd by the Frost, and prove good Eating. All Kinds of Fish are preserv'd in the same Manner.

In large Lakes and Rivers, the Ice is sometimes broken by imprison'd Vapours; and the Rocks, Trees, Joists, and Rafters of our Buildings, are burst with a Noise not less terrible than the firing of many Guns together. The Rocks which are split by the Frost, are heaved up in great Heaps, leaving large Cavities behind. If Beer or Water be left even in Copper Pots by the Bed-side, the Pots will be split before Morning. Bottles of strong Beer, Brandy, strong Brine, Spirits of Wine, set out in the open Air for 3 or 4 Hours, freeze to solid Ice. The Frost is never out of the Ground, how deep is not certain; but on digging 10 or 12 Feet down in the two Summer Months, it has been found hard frozen.

All the Water they use for Cooking, Brewing, &c. is melted Snow and Ice; no Spring is yet found free from freezing, tho' dug ever so deep down.—All Waters inland, are frozen fast by the Beginning of *October*, and continue so to the Middle of *May*.

The Walls of the Houses are of Stone, two Feet thick; the Windows very small, with thick wooden Shutters, which are close shut 18 Hours every Day in Winter. In the Cellars they put their Wines, Brandies, &c. Four large Fires are made every Day, in great Stoves to Warm the Rooms: As soon as the Wood is burnt down to a Coal, the Tops of the Chimnies are close stopped, with an Iron Cover; this keeps the Heat in, but almost stifles the People. And notwithstanding this, in 4 or 5 Hours after the Fire is out, the Inside of the Walls and Bed-places will be 2 or 3 Inches thick with Ice, which is every Morning cut away with a Hatchet. Three or four Times a Day, Iron Shot, of 24 Pounds Weight, are made red hot, and hung up in the Windows of their Apartments, to moderate the Air that comes in at Crevices; yet this, with a Fire kept burning the greatest Part of 24 Hours, will not prevent Beer, Wine, Ink, &c. from Freezing.

For their Winter Dress, a Man makes use of three Pair of Socks, of coarse Blanketting, or Duffeld, for the Feet, with a Pair of Deerskin Shoes over them; two Pair of thick *English* Stockings, and a Pair of Cloth Stockings upon them; Breeches lined with Flannel; two or three *English* Jackets, and a Fur, or Leather Gown over them; a large Beaver Cap, double, to come over the Face and Shoulders, and a Cloth of Blanketting under the Chin; with Yarn Gloves, and a large Pair of Beaver Mittins, hanging down from the Shoulders before, to put the Hands in, reaching up as high as the Elbows. Yet notwithstanding this warm Clothing, those that stir Abroad when any Wind blows from the Northward, are sometimes dreadfully frozen; some have their Hands, Arms, and Face blistered and froze in a terrible Manner, the Skin coming off soon after they enter a warm House, and some lose their Toes. And keeping House, or lying-in for the Cure of these Disorders, brings on the Scurvy, which many die of, and few are free from; nothing preventing it but Exercise and stirring Abroad.

The Fogs and Mists, brought by northerly Winds in Winter, appear visible to the naked Eye to be Icicles innumerable, as small as fine Hairs, and pointed as sharp as Needles. These Icicles lodge in their Clothes, and if their Faces and Hands are uncover'd, presently raise Blisters as white as a Linnen Cloth, and as hard as Horn. Yet if they immediately turn their Back to the Weather, and can bear a Hand out of the Mitten, and with it rub the blister'd Part for a small Time, they sometimes bring the Skin to its former State; if not, they make the best of their Way to a Fire, bathe the Part in hot Water, and thereby dissipate the Humours raised by the frozen Air; otherwise the Skin wou'd be off in a short Time, with much hot, serous, watry Matter, coming from under along with the Skin; and this happens to some almost every Time they go Abroad, for 5 or 6 Months in the Winter, so extreme cold is the Air, when the Wind blows any Thing strong. – – – – Thus far Captain *Middleton*. And now, my tender Reader, thou that shudderest when the Wind blows a little at N-West, and criest, *'Tis extrrrrream cohohold! 'Tis terrrrrible cohold!* what dost thou think of removing to that delightful Country? Or dost thou not rather chuse to stay in *Pennsylvania*, thanking God that *He has caused thy Lines to fall in pleasant Places.*

> *I am,*
> *Thy Friend to serve thee,*
>
> R. SAUNDERS.

❧ JANUARY

Luke, on his dying Bed, embrac'd his Wife,
And begg'd one Favour: Swear, my dearest Life,
Swear, if you love me, never more to wed,
Nor take a second Husband to your Bed.
Anne dropt a Tear. You know, my dear, says she,
Your least Desires have still been Laws to me;

But from this Oath, I beg you'd me excuse;
For I'm already promis'd to *J—n H—s.*

Robbers must exalted be,
Small ones on the Gallow-Tree,
While greater ones ascend to Thrones,
But what is that to thee or me?

Lost Time is never found again.

On the 16th Day of this Month, *Anno* 1707, the Union Act pass'd in *Scotland.*

On the 19th of this Month, *Anno* 1493, was born the famous Astronomer *Copernicus*, to whom we owe the Invention, or rather the Revival (it being taught by *Pythagoras* near 2000 Years before) of that now generally receiv'd System of the World which bears his Name, and supposes the Sun in the Center, this Earth a Planet revolving round it in 365 Days, 6 Hours, *&c.* and that Day and Night are caused by the Turning of the Earth on its own Axis once round in 24 h. *&c.* The *Ptolomean* System, which prevail'd before *Copernicus*, suppos'd the Earth to be fix'd, and that the Sun went round it daily. Mr. *Whiston*, a modern Astronomer, says, the Sun is 230,000 times bigger than the Earth, and 81 Millions of Miles distant from it: That vast Body must then have mov'd more than 480 Millions of Miles in 24 h. A prodigious Journey round this little Spot! How much more natural is *Copernicus*'s Scheme! – – – – *Ptolomy* is compar'd to a whimsical Cook, who, instead of Turning his Meat in Roasting, should fix That, and contrive to have his whole Fire, Kitchen and all, whirling continually round it.

❧ FEBRUARY

Don't after foreign Food and Cloathing roam,
But learn to eat and wear what's rais'd at Home.
Kind Nature suits each Clime with what it wants,
Sufficient to subsist th' Inhabitants.
Observing this, we less impair our Health,
And by this Rule we more increase our Wealth:
Our Minds a great Advantage also gain,
And more sedate and uncorrupt remain.

To lead a virtuous Life, my Friends, and get
to Heaven in Season,
You've just so much more Need of *Faith*, as
you have less of *Reason*.

To avoid Pleurisies, *&c.* in cool Weather; Fevers, Fluxes,
&c. in hot; beware of *Over-Eating and Over-Heating*.

On the 4th day of this month, *Anno* 1710, was born *Lewis* the 15th, present king of *France*, called his *most christian* majesty. He bids fair to be as great a mischief-maker as his grandfather; or, in the language of poets and orators, a *Hero*. There are three great destroyers of mankind, *Plague, Famine*, and *Hero*. Plague and Famine destroy your persons only, and leave your goods to your Heirs; but Hero, when he comes, takes life and goods together; his business and glory it is, to destroy man and the works of man.

> *In horrid grandeur haughty* Hero *reigns,*
> *And thrives on mankind's miseries and pains.*
> *What slaughter'd hosts! What cities in a blaze!*
> *What wasted countries! and what crimson seas!*
> *What orphans tears his impious bowl o'erflows;*
> *And cries of kingdoms lull him to repose.*

Hero, therefore, is the worst of the three; and thence *David*, who understood well the effects of heroism, when he had his choice, wisely pitch'd on *Plague* as the milder mischief.

MARCH

The Sun, whose unexhausted Light
   Does Life and Heat to Earth convey;
The Moon, who, Regent of the Night,
   Shines with delegated Ray;
The Stars, which constant seem to Sight,
   And Stars that regularly stray:
All these God's plastick Will from Nothing brought,
Assign'd their Stations, and their Courses taught.

The Heathens when they dy'd, went to Bed without a Candle.

Knaves & Nettles are akin; stroak 'em kindly,
 yet they'll sting.

On the 20th of this month, 1727, died the prince of astronomers and philosophers, sir *Isaac Newton*, aged 85 years: Who, as *Thomson* expresses it, *Trac'd the boundless works of God, from laws sublimely simple.*

What were his raptures then! how pure! how strong!
And what the triumphs of old Greece *and* Rome,
By his diminish'd, but the pride of boys
In some small fray victorious! when instead
Of shatter'd parcels of this earth usurp'd
By violence unmanly, and sore deeds
Of cruelty and blood; Nature *herself*
Stood all-subdu'd by him, and open laid
Her every latent glory to his view.[8]

Mr. *Pope*'s epitaph on sir *Isaac Newton*, is justly admired for its conciseness, strength, boldness, and sublimity:

Nature and nature's laws lay hid in night;
God said, Let NEWTON be, *and all was light.*

APRIL

On EDUCATION all our Lives depend;
And few to that, too few, with Care attend:
Soon as Mamma permits her darling Joy
To quit her Knee, and trusts at School her Boy,
O, touch him not, whate'er he does is right,
His Spirit's tender, tho' his Parts are bright.
Thus all the Bad he can, he learns at School,
Does what he will, and grows a lusty Fool.

Life with Fools consists in Drinking;
With the wise Man, Living's Thinking.

Eilen thut selten gut.

On the 25th of this month, *Anno* 1599, was OLIVER CROMWELL born, the son of a private gentleman, but became the conqueror and protector (some say the tyrant) of three great kingdoms. His son *Richard* succeeded him, but being of an easy peaceable disposition, he soon descended from that lofty station, and became a private man, living, unmolested, to a good old age; for he died not till about the latter end of queen *Anne*'s reign, at his lodgings in *Lombard-street*, where he had lived many years unknown, and seen great changes in government, and violent struggles for that, which, by experience, he knew could afford no solid happiness.

Oliver was once about to remove to *New-England*, his goods being on ship-board; but somewhat alter'd his mind. There he would doubtless have risen to be a *Select Man*, perhaps a *Governor*; and then might have had 100 bushels of *Indian* corn *per Annum*, the salary of a governor of that then small colony in those days.

> *Great* Julius *on the mountains bred,*
> *A flock, perhaps, or herd had led;*
> *He that the world subdu'd, had been*
> *But the best wrestler on the green.*
>
> WALLER.[9]

🏵 MAY

> Read much; the Mind, which never can be still,
> If not intent on Good, is prone to Ill.
> And where bright Thoughts, or Reas'nings just you find,
> Repose them careful in your inmost Mind.
> To deck his *Chloe*'s Bosom thus the Swain
> With pleasing Toil surveys th' enamel'd Plain,
> With Care selects each fragrant flow'r he meets,
> And forms one Garland of their mingled sweets.

Sell-cheap kept Shop on *Goodwin Sands,*
   and yet had Store of Custom.

Liberality is not giving much but giving wisely.

Finikin *Dick*, curs'd with nice Taste,
Ne'er meets with good dinner, half starv'd at a feast.

JUNE

Of all the Charms the Female Sex desire,
That Lovers doat on, and that Friends admire,
Those most deserve your Wish that longest last,
Not like the Bloom of Beauty, quickly past;
VIRTUE the Chief: This Men and Angels prize,
Above the finest Shape and brightest Eyes.
By this alone, untainted Joys we find,
As large and as immortal as the Mind.

Alas that Heroes ever were made!
The *Plague*, and the *Hero*, are both of a Trade!
Yet the Plague spares our Goods which the Heroe does not;
So a Plague takes such Heroes and let their Fames rot.

Q. P. D.

A philosophic Thought.

I pluck'd this morn these beauteous flow'rs,
Emblem of my fleeting hours;
'Tis thus, said I, my life-time flies,
So it blooms, and so it dies.
And, lo! how soon they steal away,
Wither'd e'er the noon of day.
Adieu! well-pleas'd my end I see,
Gently taught philosophy:
Fragrance and ornament alive,
Physic after death they give.
Let me, throughout my little stay,
Be as useful and as gay;
My close as early let me meet,
So my odour be as sweet.

The 19th of this month, 1719, died the celebrated *Joseph Addison*, Esq; aged 47, whose writings have contributed more to the improvement of the minds of the *British* nation, and polishing their manners, than those of any other *English* pen whatever.

❦ JULY

When great *Augustus* rul'd the World and *Rome*,
The Cloth he wore was spun and wove at Home,
His EMPRESS ply'd the Distaff and the Loom.
Old England's Laws the proudest beauty name,
When single, *Spinster*, and when married, *Dame*.
For *Housewifery* is Woman's noblest Fame.
The Wisest houshold Cares to Women yield,
A large, an useful, and a grateful Field.

To Friend, Lawyer, Doctor, tell plain your whole Case;
Nor think on bad Matters to put a good Face:
How can they advise, if they see but a Part?
'Tis very ill driving black Hogs in the dark.

On the 1st of this month *Anno* 1690, was fought the memorable battle of the *Boyne*, in *Ireland*; when God crown'd our great deliverer, King WILLIAM, with success and victory. He was one of the right sort of *Heroes*. Your *true* hero fights to *preserve*, and not to *destroy*, the lives, liberties, and estates, of his people. His neighbours also, and all that are oppress'd, share his cares and his protection. But this sort is thin sown, and comes up thinner. *Hercules* was one, among the ancients; and our glorious BILLY, of *Cumberland*, another among the moderns; God bless him! I might have mention'd, in the month of *April*, his happy victory over the rebels; who, with the united assistance of the kings of *France* and *Spain*, the *Pope* and the *Devil*, threatened destruction to our religion and liberties; but had all their schemes defeated by this battle. The sacred names of *justice* and *religion* were made use of as the cloaks of that invasion, wicked as it was. A pretended prince was to be restor'd to his *rights*, forsooth; and we were all to be converted to the *Catholick* faith! *Strada* says, that when the duke of *Parma* heard of the defeat of the *Spanish Armada*, in 1588 (which by the way happen'd the 21st of this same month) he said very piously, *That it was an enterprize so well concerted, as nothing could have disappointed but the* sins *of the people of* England. It seems they were unworthy so great a blessing. And he makes this further reflection on queen *Elizabeth*'s proclaiming a thanksgiving: *Mistaken woman! Blind nation!* says he, *to return thanks for the greatest* misfortune *that could have befallen them! For had that enterprize suc-ceeded, they would all have been converted to the true Catholick Faith.* The *most christian* king, and his *catholick* majesty, and his *Holiness*, and the sham *defender of the faith*, (Fine titles all!) have now an opportunity of making the same pious reflections.

⚜ AUGUST

To make the cleanly Kitchen send up Food,
Not costly vain, but plentifully Good.
To bid the Cellar's Fountain never fail,
Of sparkling Cyder, or of well-brew'd Ale;
To buy, to pay, to blame, or to approve,
Within, without, below-stairs, and above;
To shine in every Corner, like the Sun,
Still working every where, or looking on.

Suspicion may be no Fault,
    but shewing it may be a great one.

He that's secure is not safe.

The second Vice is Lying; the first is Running in Debt.

The Muses love the Morning.

Muschitoes, or *Musketoes*, a little venomous fly, so light, that perhaps 50 of them, before they've fill'd their bellies, scarce weigh a grain, yet each has all the parts necessary to life, motion, digestion, generation, &c. as veins, arteries, muscles, &c. each has in his little body room for the five senses of seeing, hearing, feeling, smelling, tasting: How inconceivably small must their organs be! How inexpressibly fine the workmanship! And yet there are little animals discovered by the microscope, to whom a *Musketo* is an *Elephant*! – – – – In a scarce summer any citizen may provide Musketoes sufficient for his own family, by leaving tubs of rain-water uncover'd in his yard; for in such water they lay their eggs, which when hatch'd, become first little fish, afterwards put forth legs and wings, leave the water, and fly into your windows. *Probatum est*.

☙ SEPTEMBER

One glorious Scene of Action still behind,
The Fair that likes it is secure to find;
Cordials and Med'cines *gratis* to dispense,
A beauteous Instrument of Providence;
Plaisters, and Salves, and Sores, to understand,
The Surgeon's Art befits a tender Hand:
To friendless Pain unhop'd-for Ease to give,
And bid the Hungry eat, and Sickly live.

Two Faults of one a Fool will make;
He half repairs, that owns *&* does forsake.

Harry Smatter, has a Mouth for every Matter.

When you're good to others, you are best to yourself.

On the first of this month, *Anno*, 1733, *Stanislaus*, originally a private gentleman of *Poland*, was chosen the *second time* king of that nation. The power of *Charles* XII. of *Sweden*, caused his first election, that of *Louis* XV. of *France*, his second. But neither of them could keep him on the throne; for PROVIDENCE, often opposite to the wills of princes, reduc'd him to the condition of a private gentleman again.

On the 2d of this month, *Anno*, 1666, began the fire of *London*, which reduc'd to ashes 13,200 houses and 89 churches: Near ten times as much building as *Philadelphia*!

The great ART of succeeding in CONVERSATION (saith Mons. *St. Evremond*) is, To admire little, to hear much, *always* to distrust our own reason, and *sometimes* that of our friends; never to pretend to wit; but to make that of others appear as much as possibly we can; to hearken to what is said, and to answer to the purpose.

Ut jam nunc dicat jam nunc debentia dici.

Observe, the precept is *hear much*, not *speak much*. *Herbert*, the poet, says,

— — — — a well-bred guest,
Will no more talk all *than* eat all *the feast.*

And, *When you do speak*, says another, *speak to the purpose; Or else to what purpose do you speak?* Observe the present disposition of the company; and

> *Let what you say the converse suit,*
> *Not say things merely 'cause they're good.*
> *For if you thus intrude your sense,*
> *It then becomes impertinence:*
> *Your salt is good, we may agree,*
> *But pray don't salt our Punch and Tea.*

❧ OCTOBER

And thus, if we may credit Fame's Report,
The best and fairest in the *Gallic* Court,
An Hour sometimes in Hospitals employ,
To give the dying Wretch a Glimpse of Joy;
T' attend the Crouds that hopeless Pangs endure,
And soothe the Anguish which they cannot cure;
To clothe the Bare, and give the Empty Food;
As bright as Guardian Angels, and as good.

Half Wits talk much but say little.

If *Jack's* in love, he's no judge of *Jill's* Beauty.

Most Fools think they are only ignorant.

On the 14th of this month, *Anno* 1644, was born WILLIAM PENN, the great founder of this Province; who prudently and benevolently sought success to himself by no other means, than securing the *liberty*, and endeavouring the *happiness* of his people. Let no envious mind grudge his posterity, those advantages which arise to them from the wisdom and goodness of their ancestor; and to which their own merit, as well as the laws, give them an additional title.

On the 28th, *Anno* 1704, died the famous *John Locke*, Esq; the *Newton* of the *Microcosm*: For, as *Thomson* says,

> *He made the whole* internal world *his own.*

His book on the *Human Understanding*, shows it. *Microcosm*, honest reader, is a hard word, and, they say, signifies the *little world*, man being so called, as containing within himself the four elements of the *greater*, &c. &c. I here explain *Greek* to thee by *English*, which, I think, is rather a more intelligible way, than explaining *English* by *Greek*, as a certain writer does, who gravely tells us, *Man is rightly called* a little world, *because he is a* Microcosm.

On the 29th, *Anno* 1618, was the famous sir *Walter Rawleigh* beheaded; to the eternal shame of the attorney-general, who first prosecuted him, and of the king, who ratify'd the sentence.

How happy is he, who can satisfy his hunger with any food, quench his thirst with any drink, please his ear with any musick, delight his eye with any painting, any sculpture, any architecture, and divert his mind with any book or any company! How many mortifications must he suffer, that cannot bear any thing but beauty, order, elegance & perfection! *Your man of* taste, *is nothing but a man of* distaste.

❧ NOVEMBER

Nor be the Husband idle, tho' his Land
Yields plenteous Crops without his lab'ring Hand:
Tho' his collected Rent his Bags supply,
Or honest, careful Slaves scarce need his Eye.
Let him whom Choice allures, or Fortune yields,
To live amidst his own extended Fields,
Diffuse those Blessings which from Heav'n he found,
In copious Streams to bless the World around.

Pardoning the Bad, is injuring the Good.

He is not well-bred, that cannot bear Ill-Breeding in others.

On the 2d of this month, *Anno* 1641, the Long Parliament met, who began the *great rebellion*, as some call it, or the *glorious opposition* to arbitrary power, as others term it; for to this day *party* divides us on this head, and we are not (perhaps never shall be) agreed about it. ————
Party, says one, *is the madness of many, for the gain of a few*: To which may be added, *There are* honest *men in* all *parties*, wise men *in* none: Unless those may be call'd *wise*, for whose profit the rest are *mad*.

To thy lov'd haunt return, my happy muse,
For now behold the joyous winter-days
Frosty, succeed; and thro' the blue serene
For sight too fine, th' etherial nitre flies,
Killing infectious damps, and the spent air
Storing afresh with elemental life.
Close crouds the shining atmosphere; and binds
Our strengthen'd bodies in its cold embrace,
Constringent; feeds and animates our blood;
Refines our spirits, thro' the new-strung nerves
In swifter sallies darting to the brain;
Where sits the soul, intense, collected, cool,
Bright as the skies, and as the season keen.
All nature feels the renovating force
Of WINTER, only to the thoughtless eye
In Ruin seen – – – –.[10]

Muse, Shoes; Days, Stays; Serene, between; Air, Fair; Life, Wife, Strife, &c. &c. Rhimes, you see, are plenty enow; he that does not like blank verse, may add them at his leisure, as the poets do at *Manhatan*.

DECEMBER

Open to all his hospitable Door,
His Tennent's Patron, Parent to the Poor:
In Friendships dear, discording Neighbours bind,
Aid the distress'd, and humanise Mankind:
Wipe off the sorrowing Tear from *Virtue*'s Eyes,
Bid *Honesty* oppress'd, again arise:
Protect the Widow, give the Aged Rest,
And blessing live, and die for ever blest.

In Christmas feasting pray take care;
Let not your table be a Snare;
But with the Poor God's Bounty share.
Adieu my Friends! till the next Year.

On the 13th of this month, 1545, the famous council of *Trent* began.
On the 23d, 1688, K. *James* abdicated his kingdoms, and embarked for *France*.

The fall of *Niagara*, which *Popple*'s map lays down in the N-West corner of this province, is, according to *Henepin*, compounded of two great cross streams of water, and two falls, with an isle sloping along between. The waters fall from a horrible precipice above 600 foot, and foam and boil in an hideous manner, making an outrageous noise, more terrible than thunder; for when the wind blows out of the South, their dismal roaring may be heard more than 15 Leagues off.

Conrad, the 3d emperor of *Germany*, besieged *Guelph*, duke of *Bavaria*, in the city of *Warsburg*. The women perceiving the town could not hold out, petitioned the emperor that they might depart only with so much as they could carry on their backs; which the emperor condescended to, expecting they would have laden themselves with silver and gold; but they all came forth with every one her husband on her back; whereat the emperor was so moved that he wept, received the duke into his favour, gave all the men their lives, and extolled the women with deserved praises. – – – – *Quere*, Is this story more to the honour of the wives or of the husbands? My dame BRIDGET *says* the first, I *think* the latter: But we submit our dispute to the decision of the candid reader.

A wit's a feather, *and a chief a* rod;
An honest man's *the noblest work of God.*

POPE.

*A Spoonful of Honey will catch more Flies
than a Gallon of Vinegar.*

1749

Poor Richard's *Almanack, &c.*

Kind READER,

BY way of preface (for *custom* says there must be a preface to every almanack) I present thee with an *essay* wrote by a celebrated *naturalist* of our country, which if duly attended to, may be of more service to the publick, than 375 prefaces of my own writing[11]: Take it as follows, *viz.* An Essay *for the improvement of estates, by raising a durable timber for fencing, and other uses.*

Vale, & fruere.

JANUARY

Advice to Youth.

First, Let the Fear of HIM who form'd thy Frame,
Whose Hand sustain'd thee e'er thou hadst a Name,
Who brought thee into Birth, with Pow'r of Thought
Receptive of immortal Good, be wrought
Deep in thy Soul. His, not thy own, thou art;
To him resign the Empire of thy Heart.
His Will, thy Law; His Service, thy Employ;
His Frown, thy Dread, his Smile be all thy Joy.

[*Cont'd Febr.*

Wealth and Content are not always Bed-fellows.

Wise Men learn by others harms; Fools by their own.

On the 7th of this month 1692 died *Robert Boyle*, Esq; one of the greatest philosophers the last age produced. He first brought the machine called an *Airpump*, into use; by which many of the surprizing properties of that wonderful element were discovered and demonstrated. His knowledge of natural history, and skill in chymistry, were very great and extensive; and his piety inferior to neither.

> – – – – BOYLE, *whose pious search*
> *Amid the dark recesses of his works*
> *The great* CREATOR *sought* – – – –
>   THOMSON.

is therefore an instance, that tho' *Ignorance* may in some be the *Mother of Devotion*, yet true learning and exalted piety are by no means inconsistent.

When we read in antient history of the speeches made by generals to very numerous armies, we sometimes wonder how they could be well heard; but supposing the men got together so close, that each took up no more ground than two foot in breadth, and one in depth, 45000 might stand in a space that was but 100 yards square, and 21780 on a single acre of ground. There are many voices that may be heard at 100 yards distance.

⨯ FEBRUARY

> Wak'd by the Call of Morn, on early Knee,
> Ere the World thrust between thy God and thee,
> Let thy pure Oraisons, ascending, gain
> His Ear, and Succour of his Grace obtain,
> In Wants, in Toils, in Perils of the Day,
> And strong Temptations that beset thy Way.
> Thy best Resolves then in his Strength renew
> To walk in Virtue's Paths, and Vice eschew.
>   [*Cont'd Mar.*

The end of Passion is the beginning of Repentance.

Words may shew a man's Wit, but *Actions* his Meaning.

On the 18th of this month, *anno* 1546 died that famous reformer, LUTHER: who struck the great blow to papal tyranny in *Europe*. He was remarkably *temperate* in meat and drink, sometimes fasting four days together; and at other times, for many days, eating only a little bread and a herring. *Cicero* says, *There was never any* great *man who was not an* industrious *man*; to which may, perhaps, be added, *There was never any* industrious *man who was not a* temperate *man*: For intemperance in diet, abates the vigour, and dulls the action both of mind and body.

MARCH

To HIM intrust thy Slumbers, and prepare
The fragrant Incense of thy Ev'ning Prayer.
But first tread back the Day, with Search severe,
And *Conscience*, chiding or applauding, hear.
Review each Step; *Where, acting, did I err?*
Omitting, where? Guilt either Way infer.
Labour this Point, and while thy Frailties last,
Still let each following Day correct the last.

[*Cont'd Apr.*

'Tis a well spent penny that saves a groat.

Many Foxes grow grey, but few grow good.

Presumption first blinds a Man, then sets him a running.

The earth according to Mr. *Whiston*, is 7970 miles in diameter, which will make nigh 24000 miles in circumference. It revolves about its axis in 23 hours and 56 minutes: It moves in the space of one hour 56,000 miles; and is 365 days 6 hours and 9 minutes revolving about the sun.

The nose of a lady here, is not delighted with perfumes that she understands are in *Arabia*. Fine musick in *China* gives no pleasure to the nicest ear in *Pennsilvania*. Nor does the most exquisite dish serv'd up in *Japan*, regale a luxurious palate in any other country. But the benevolent mind of a virtuous man, is pleas'd, when it is inform'd of good and generous actions, in what part of the world soever they are done.

🐖 APRIL

Life is a shelvy Sea, the Passage fear,
And not without a skilful Pilot steer.
Distrust thy Youth, experienc'd Age implore,
And borrow all the Wisdom of Threescore.
But chief a Father's, Mother's Voice revere;
'Tis Love that chides, 'tis Love that counsels here.
Thrice happy is the Youth, whose pliant Mind
To all a Parent's Culture is resign'd.

[Cont'd May

A cold April, The Barn will fill.

Content makes poor men rich; Discontent
makes rich Men poor.

Too much plenty makes Mouth dainty.

On the 7th of this month, 1626, died that *great little* man, Sir
FRANCIS BACON; *great* in his prodigious genius, parts and learning; and
little, in his servile compliances with a *little* court, and submissive
flattery of a *little* prince. *Pope* characterises him thus, in one strong line;

> *If Ports allure thee, think how* BACON *shin'd,*
> *The wisest, brightest, meanest of mankind.*

He is justly esteem'd the father of the modern experimental philosophy.
And another poet treats him more favourably, ascribing his blemishes
to a wrong unfortunate choice of his way of Life;

> – – – – BACON, *hapless in his choice,*
> *Unfit to stand the civil storm of state,*
> *And thro' the smooth barbarity of courts,*
> *With firm, but pliant virtue, forward still*
> *To urge his course. Him for the studious shade*
> *Kind nature form'd, deep, comprehensive, clear,*
> *Exact, and elegant; in one rich soul,*
> PLATO, *the* STAGYRITE, *and* TULLY *join'd.*
> *The great deliverer he! who from the gloom*
> *Of cloister'd monks, and jargon-teaching schools,*

Led forth the true Philosophy, there long
Held in the magic chain of words and forms,
And definitions void: He led her forth,
Daughter of HEAV'N *! that slow ascending still,*
Investigating sure the chain of things,
With radiant finger points to HEAV'N *again.*[12]

✿ MAY

O, well begun, Virtue's great Work pursue,
Passions at first we may with Ease subdue;
But if neglected, unrestrain'd too long,
Prevailing in their Growth, by Habit strong,
They've warp'd the Mind, have fix'd the stubborn Bent,
And Force of Custom to wild Nature lent;
Who then would set the crooked Tree aright,
As soon may wash the tawny Indian white.

[*Cont'd June*

If *Passion* drives, let *Reason* hold the Reins.

Neither trust, nor contend, nor lay wagers, nor lend;
And you'll have peace to your Lives end.

Drink does not drown *Care*, but waters it,
    and makes it grow faster.

Who dainties love, shall Beggars prove.

On the 18th of this Month, 1684, the superbe city of GENOA, was barbarously bombarded by the *French*, and a great part of its beautiful buildings reduced to rubbish; in chastisement of a small affront taken by the *Gallic* King. The *English*, tho' lately in open war with that republic, have generously & humanely abstain'd from so cruel a proceeding.

On the 27th, anno 1564, died at *Geneva* that famous reformer, Mr. *John Calvin*, A man of equal *temperance* and *sobriety* with *Luther*, and perhaps yet greater *industry*. His lectures were yearly 186, his sermons yearly 286; he published besides every year some great volume in folio; to which add his constant employments, in governing the church, answering letters from all parts of the reformed world, from pastors, concerning doubts, or asking counsel, &c. &c. He ate little meat, and slept but very little; and as his whole time was filled up with useful action, he may be said to have *lived* long, tho' he died at 55 years of age; since *sleep* and *sloth* can hardly be called *living*.

🦞 JUNE

> *Industry*'s bounteous Hand may *Plenty* bring,
> But wanting *frugal Care*, 'twill soon take wing.
> Small thy Supplies, and scanty in their Source,
> 'Twixt *Av'rice* and *Profusion* steer thy Course.
> *Av'rice* is deaf to *Want*'s Heart-bursting Groan,
> *Profusion* makes the Beggar's Rags thy own:
> Close Fraud and Wrong from griping *Av'rice* grow,
> From rash *Profusion* desp'rate Acts and Woe.
> [*Cont'd July*

A Man has no more *Goods* than he gets Good by.

Welcome, Mischief, if thou comest alone.

Different Sects like different clocks,
   may be all near the matter, 'tho they don't quite agree.

On the 15th of this month, anno 1215, was *Magna Charta* sign'd by King *John*, for declaring and establishing *English Liberty*.

It was wise counsel given to a young man, *Pitch upon that course of life which is most excellent, and* CUSTOM *will make it the most delightful.* But many pitch on no course of life at all, nor form any scheme of living, by which to attain any valuable end; but wander perpetually from one thing to another.

> *Hast thou not yet propos'd some certain end,*
> *To which thy life, thy every act may tend?*
> *Hast thou no mark at which to bend thy bow?*
> *Or like a boy pursu'st the carrion crow*
> *With pellets and with stones, from tree to tree,*
> *A fruitless toil, and liv'st extempore?*
> *Watch the disease in time: For when, within*
> *The dropsy rages, and extends the skin,*

In vain for helebore the patient cries,
And sees the doctor, but too late is wise:
Too late for cure, he proffers half his wealth;
Ten thousand doctors cannot give him health.
    Learn, wretches, learn the motions of the mind,
Why you were made, for what you were design'd,
And the great moral end *of human kind.*
Study thy self; what rank or what degree,
The wise creator has ordain'd for thee:
And all the offices of that estate,
Perform, and with thy prudence guide thy fate.

JULY

Honour the softer Sex; with courteous Style,
And Gentleness of Manners, win their Smile;
Nor shun their virtuous Converse; but when Age
And Circumstance consent, thy Faith engage
To some discreet, well-natur'd, chearful Fair,
One not too stately for the Houshold Care,
One form'd in Person and in Mind to please,
To season Life, and all its Labours ease.

[*Cont'd Aug.*

If your head is wax, don't walk in the Sun.

Pretty & *Witty*, will wound if they hit ye.

Having been poor is no shame, but being ashamed of it, is.

On the 12th of this month, *anno* 1712, died *Richard* the son of *Oliver Cromwell*, aged 90 years. And on the 13th, *anno* 1713, was the treaty of *Utrecht* signed, ending a glorious war by an inglorious peace. *The Preliminaries of the new Peace, are copied from those of the old one;* *'tis to be hoped the Peace itself will be better.*

'Tis raging NOON, *and, vertical, the Sun*
Darts on the Head direct his forceful rays.
All-conqu'ring HEAT, *oh intermit thy wrath!*
And on my throbbing temples potent thus

Beam not so fierce! Incessant still you flow,
And still another fervent flood succeeds,
Pour'd on the head profuse. In vain I sigh,
And restless turn, and look around for night;
Night is far off; and hotter hours approach.
Thrice happy he! that on the sunless side
Of a romantic mountain, forest-crown'd,
Beneath the whole collected shade reclines:
Or in the gelid caverns, woodbine-wrought
And fresh bedew'd with ever-spouting streams,
Sits coolly calm; while all the world without
Unsatisfy'd and sick, tosses in noon.
Emblem instructive of the virtuous man,
Who keeps his temper'd mind serene and pure,
And every Passion aptly harmoniz'd,
Amid a jarring world, with vice enflam'd.[13]

AUGUST

Gaming, the Vice of Knaves and Fools, detest,
Miner of Time, of Substance and of Rest;
Which, in the Winning or the Losing Part,
Undoing or undone, will wring the Heart:
Undone, self-curs'd, thy Madness thou wilt rue;
Undoing, Curse of others will pursue
Thy heated Head. A Parent's, Houshold's Tear,
A Neighbour's Groan, and *Heav'n*'s Displeasure fear.

[Cont'd Sept.

'Tis a laudable Ambition, that aims at being better
     than his Neighbours.

The wise Man draws more Advantage from his Enemies,
     than the Fool from his Friends.

On the 17th of this month, *anno* 1657, died the famous Admiral *Blake*, who was a soldier as well as seaman, and by several examples taught *Great Britain*, that her *wooden castles*, properly managed, were an over-match for the stone-walls of her enemies.

PRIDE is said to be the *last* vice the good man gets clear of. 'Tis a meer *Proteus*, and disguises itself under all manner of appearances, putting on sometimes even the mask of *humility*. If some are proud of neatness and propriety of dress; others are equally so of despising it, and acting the perpetual sloven.

> Morose *is sunk with shame, whene'er surpriz'd*
> *In linnen clean, or peruke undisguis'd.*
> *No sublunary chance his vestments fear,*
> *Valu'd, like leopards, as their spots appear.*
> *A fam'd surtout he wears, which once was blue,*
> *And his foot swims in a capacious shoe.*
> *One day his wife (for who can wives reclaim)*
> *Level'd her barbarous needle at his fame;*
> *But open force was vain; by night she went,*
> *And while he slept, surpriz'd the darling rent;*
> *Where yawn'd the frize, is now become a doubt,*
> *And glory at one entrance quite shut out.*[14]

Numbers that are equal to the sum of all their aliquot parts, are called *perfect numbers*; such are 6, 28, 120, &c. Of these numbers Mr. *Stone*, in his *Mathematical Dictionary*, says, there are but ten, between one and 1,000000,000000. I shall leave my curious reader to find the rest.

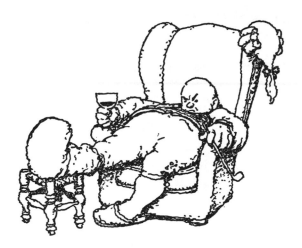

Pride and Gout are seldom cur'd throughout.

Poor Richard: 1749

✤ SEPTEMBER

Wouldst thou extract the purest Sweet of Life,
Be nor Ally nor Principal in Strife.
A Mediator there, thy Balsam bring,
And lenify the Wound, and draw the Sting;
On *Hate* let *Kindness* her warm Embers throw,
And mould into a Friend the melting Foe.
The weakest Foe boasts some revenging Pow'r;
The weakest Friend some serviceable Hour.

[*Cont'd Oct.*

All would live long, but none would be old.

Declaiming against Pride, is not always a Sign of Humility.

On the 12th of this month, *anno* 1604, the town of *Ostend* was surrender'd to the *Spaniards*, after a siege of three years, in which they lost 70,000 men. In the two last sieges, it was taken in fewer weeks.

It is the opinion of all the modern philosophers and mathematicians, that the planets are habitable worlds. If so, what sort of constitutions must those people have who live in the planet *Mercury*? where, says Sir *Isaac Newton*, the heat of the sun is seven times as great as it is with us; and would make our Water boil away. For the same person found by experiments, that an heat seven times as great as the heat of the sun in summer, is sufficient to set water a boiling.

✤ OCTOBER

In Converse be reserv'd, yet not morose,
In Season grave, in Season, too, jocose.
Shun Party-Wranglings, mix not in Debate
With Bigots in Religion or the State.
No Arms to Scandal or Detraction lend,
Abhor to wound, be fervent to defend.
Aspiring still to know, a Babbler scorn,
But watch where Wisdom opes her golden Horn.

[*Cont'd Nov.*

Neglect kills Injuries, Revenge increases them.

9 Men in 10 are suicides.

Doing an Injury puts you below your Enemy; *Revenging* one makes you but *even* with him; *Forgiving* it sets you *above* him.

On the 14th of this month, 1722, was the present King of *France* crowned.

That famous specific for the cure of intermitting fevers, agues, *&c.* called the Jesuits Bark, after it had been introduced into *Europe* with great applause, fell into a general disrepute (from some accidents attending the injudicious use of it) and was a long time neglected. At length one *Talbot*, an illiterate *Englishman*, grew remarkable for curing those disorders speedily and effectually, by a medicine which no one knew; and his fame reaching *France*, *Lewis* XIV. sent for him to the Dauphin, who had long labour'd under an obstinate ague, that resisted all the medicines then used by the best physicians. When he arriv'd at *Paris* and had seen the Dauphin, he boldly undertook his cure; but being first, for form-sake, examined by the King's physicians, they asked among other things, *What he judg'd the Dauphin's distemper to be? 'Tis an ague,* says he. *What is an ague?* said they, *give us a definition of it. Pray,* says he, *what is a definition? A definition,* says one, *is a clear, short, and proper description of a thing in words. Why then, gentlemen,* says he, *I will give you a definition of an ague; 'Tis a distemper – – – – that I can cure, and you can't. – – – –* They were affronted, told the King that *Talbot* was an ignorant quack, and not fit to be trusted with the Dauphin's health. The King however was resolv'd to try him and the Dauphin was cured. That munificent prince, besides rewarding *Talbot*, bought his secret at a great price for the publick good, and it prov'd no other thing than the Bark disguis'd, and some rules for giving it, now well known to physicians – – – – Thenceforward the bark grew into repute again, and is now in high esteem, daily gaining ground, and overcoming by the success attending it the prejudices that were once so universal against the use of it. 'Tis not unlikely, that some other valuable old medicines have been disused, from like causes, and may in time be advantageously revived again, to the benefit of mankind.

NOVEMBER

In quest of Gain be just: A Conscience clear
Is Lucre, more than Thousands in a Year;
Treasure no Moth can touch, no Rust consume;
Safe from the Knave, the Robber, and the Tomb.
Unrighteous Gain is the curs'd Seed of Woe,
Predestin'd to be reap'd by them who sow;
A dreadful Harvest! when th' avenging Day
Shall like a Tempest, sweep the Unjust away.

[Cont'd Dec.

Most of the Learning in use, is of no great Use.

Great Good-nature, without Prudence, is a great Misfortune.

Keep Conscience clear,
Then never fear.

DECEMBER

But not from Wrong alone thy Hand restrain,
The *Appetite* of Gold demands the Rein.
What Nature asks, what Decency requires,
Be this the Bound that limits thy Desires:
This, and the gen'rous godlike Pow'r to feed
The Hungry, and to warm the Loins of *Need*:
To dry *Misfortune*'s Tear, and scatter wide
Thy Blessings, like the *Nile*'s o'erflowing Tide.

[Finis

A Man in a Passion rides a mad Horse.

Reader farewel, all Happiness attend thee;
May each New-Year, better and richer find thee.

On the 25th of this month, *anno* 1642, was born the great Sir ISAAC
NEWTON, prince of the modern astronomers and philosophers. But what
is all our little boasted knowledge, compar'd with that of the angels? If
they see our actions, and are acquainted with our affairs, our whole body
of science must appear to them as little better than ignorance; and the

common herd of our learned men, scarce worth their notice. Now and then one of our very great philosophers, an *Aristotle*, or a *Newton*, may, perhaps, by his most refined speculations, afford them a little entertainment, as it seems a mimicking of their own sublime amusements. Hence *Pope* says of the latter,

> *Superior beings, when of late they saw*
> *A mortal man unfold all nature's law,*
> *Admir'd such wisdom in a human shape,*
> *And shew'd a Newton, as we shew an ape.*[15]

On WINTER.

> *'Tis done! dread Winter spreads his latest glooms,*
> *And reigns tremendous o'er the conquer'd year!*
> *How dead the vegetable kindgom lies!*
> *How dumb the tuneful! Horror wide extends*
> *His melancholy empire. Here fond man!*
> *Behold thy pictur'd life! pass some few years,*
> *Thy flowering Spring, thy Summer's ardent strength,*
> *Thy sober Autumn fading into age,*
> *And pale concluding Winter comes at last,*
> *And shuts the scene. Ah! whither now are fled*
> *Those dreams of greatness? Those unsolid hopes*
> *Of happiness? Those longings after fame?*
> *Those restless cares? those busy bustling days?*
> *Those gay-spent festive nights? those veering thoughts,*
> *Lost between good and ill, that shar'd thy life?*
> *All now are vanish'd!* VIRTUE *sole survives,*
> *Immortal, never-failing friend of man,*
> *His guide to happiness on high. – – – –*

THOMSON.[16]

How to get RICHES.

The Art of getting Riches consists very much in THRIFT. All Men are not equally qualified for getting Money, but it is in the Power of every one alike to practise this Virtue.

He that would be beforehand in the World, must be

beforehand with his Business: It is not only ill Management, but discovers a slothful Disposition, to do that in the Afternoon, which should have been done in the Morning.

Useful Attainments in your Minority will procure Riches in Maturity, of which Writing and Accounts are not the meanest.

Learning, whether Speculative or Practical is, in Popular or Mixt Governments, the Natural Source of Wealth and Honour.

PRECEPT I.

In Things of moment, on thy self depend,
Nor trust too far thy Servant or thy Friend:
With private Views, thy Friend may promise fair,
And Servants very seldom prove sincere.

PRECEPT II.

What can be done, with Care perform to Day,
Dangers unthought-of will attend Delay;
Your distant Prospects all precarious are,
And Fortune is as fickle as she's fair.

PRECEPT III.

Nor trivial Loss, nor trivial Gain despise;
Molehills, if often heap'd, to Mountains rise:
Weigh every small Expence, and nothing waste,
Farthings long sav'd, amount to Pounds at last.

The Cat in Gloves catches no Mice!

1750

Poor Richard's *Almanack*, &c.

To the READER.

THE Hope of acquiring lasting Fame, is, with many Authors, a most powerful Motive to Writing. Some, tho' few, have succeeded; and others, tho' perhaps fewer, may succeed hereafter, and be as well known to Posterity by their Works, as the Antients are to us. We *Philomaths*, as ambitious of Fame as any other Writers whatever, after all our painful Watchings and laborious Calculations, have the constant Mortification to see our Works thrown by at the End of the Year, and treated as mere waste Paper. Our only Consolation is, that short-lived as they are, they out-live those of most of our Cotemporaries.

Yet, condemned to renew the *Sisyphean* Toil, we every Year heave another heavy Mass up the Muses Hill, which never can the Summit reach, and soon comes tumbling down again.

This, kind Reader, is my seventeenth Labour of the Kind. Thro' thy continued Good-will, they have procur'd me, if no *Bays*, at least *Pence*; and the latter is perhaps the better of the two; since 'tis not improbable that a Man may receive more solid Satisfaction from *Pudding*, while he is *living*, than from *Praise*, after he is *dead*.

173

In my last, a few Faults escap'd; some belong to the Author, but most to the Printer: Let each take his Share of the Blame, confess, and amend for the future. In the second Page of *August*, I mention'd 120 as the next perfect Number to 28; it was wrong, 120 being no perfect Number; the next to 28 I find to be 496. The first is 6; let the curious Reader, fond of mathematical Questions, find the fourth. In the 2d Page of *March*, in some Copies, the Earth's Circumference was said to be nigh 4000, instead of 24000 Miles, the Figure 2 being omitted at the Beginning. This was Mr. Printer's Fault; who being also somewhat niggardly of his Vowels, as well as profuse of his Consonants, put in one Place, among the Poetry, *mad*, instead of made, and in another *wrapp'd*, instead of *warp'd*; to the utter demolishing of all Sense in those Lines, leaving nothing standing but the Rhime.[17] These, and some others, of the like kind, let the Readers forgive, or rebuke him for, as to their Wisdom and Goodness shall seem meet: For in such Cases the Loss and Damage is chiefly to the Reader, who, if he does not take my Sense at first Reading, 'tis odds he never gets it; for ten to one he does not read my Works a second Time.

Printers indeed should be very careful how they omit a Figure or a Letter: For by such Means sometimes a terrible Alteration is made in the Sense. I have heard, that once, in a new Edition of the *Common Prayer*, the following Sentence, *We shall all be changed in a Moment, in the Twinkling of an Eye*; by the Omission of a single Letter, became, *We shall all be hanged in a Moment*, &c. to the no small Surprize of the first Congregation it was read to.

May this Year prove a happy One to Thee and Thine, is the hearty Wish of, Kind Reader,

Thy obliged Friend,

R. SAUNDERS.

JANUARY

So weak are human Kind by Nature made,
Or to such Weakness by their Vice betray'd,
Almighty *Vanity*! to thee they owe
Their Zest of Pleasure, and their Balm of Woe.
Thou, like the Sun, all Colours dost contain,

Varying like Rays of Light on Drops of Rain;
For every Soul finds Reason to be proud,
Tho' hiss'd and hooted by the pointing Croud.

There are three Things extreamly hard, Steel,
   a Diamond and to know one's self.

Hunger is the best Pickle.

He is a Governor that governs his Passions,
   and he a Servant that serves them.

On the 9th of this Month, 1744-5, died CHARLES ALBERT, Elector of *Bavaria*, and Emperor of *Germany*. 'Tis thought his Death was hastened by Grief and Vexation at the Success of the Queen of *Hungary*, and the Disappointments of his own Ambition. O *Content*! What art thou! And where to be found! Art thou not an inseparable Companion of Honour, Wealth and Power? No. This Man was rich, great, a Sovereign Prince: But he wanted to be *richer*, *greater*, and *more a Sovereign*. At first his Arms had vast Success; but a Campaign or two left him not a Foot of Land he could call his own, and reduc'd him to live with his Empress in a *hired house* at *Frankfort*!

The bold Bavarian, *in a luckless Hour,*
Tries the dread summits of Cesarean *Power,*
With unexpected Legions bursts away,
And sees defenceless Realms receive his Sway;
Short Sway! Fair Austria *spreads her mournful Charms,*
The Queen, the Beauty, sets the World in Arms;
From Hill to Hill the Beacon's rousing Blaze
Spreads wide the Hope of Plunder and of Praise;
The fierce Croatian, *and the wild* Hussar,
And all the Sons of Ravage, crowd the War;
The baffled Prince, in Honour's flatt'ring Bloom,
Of hasty Greatness, finds the fatal Doom;
His Foes Derision, and his Subjects Blame,
And steals to Death from Anguish, and from Shame.[18]

175

≋ FEBRUARY

We smile at Florists, we despise their Joy,
And think their Hearts enamour'd of a Toy;
But are those wiser, whom we most admire,
Survey with Envy, and pursue with Fire?
What's he, who fights for Wealth, or Fame, or Power?
Another *Florio*, doating on a Flower,
A short-liv'd Flower, and which has often sprung,
From sordid Arts, as *Florio's* out of Dung.

A Cypher and Humility make the other Figures & Virtues
of ten-fold Value.

If it were not for the Belly, the Back might wear Gold.

Let thy Servant be faithful, strong, and homely.

For LIBERALITY.

Tho' safe thou think'st thy Treasure lies,
Hidden in Chests from Human Eyes,
Thieves, Fire, may come, and it may be
Convey'd, my Friend, as far from thee.
Thy Vessel that yon Ocean sails,
Tho' favour'd now with prosp'rous Gales,
Her Cargo which has Thousands cost,
All in a Tempest may be lost.
Cheats, Whores and Quacks, a thankless Crew,
Priests, Pickpockets, and Lawyers too,
All help by several Ways to drain,
Thanking themselves for what they gain;
The Liberal *are secure alone,*
For what they frankly give, for ever is their own.

MARCH

What's the bent Brow, or Neck in Thought reclin'd?
The Body's Wisdom, to conceal the Mind.
A Man of Sense can Artifice disdain,
As Men of Wealth may venture to go plain;
And be this Truth eternal ne'er forgot,
Solemnity's a Cover for a Sot;
I find the Fool, when I behold the Screen:
For 'tis the Wise Man's Interest to be seen.

Wouldst thou confound thine Enemy, be good thy self.

Pride is as loud a Beggar as *Want*,
  and a great deal more saucy.

Pay what you owe, and what you're worth you'll know.

The Reason, says *Swift*, why so few Marriages are happy, is, because young Ladies spend their Time in making *Nets*, not in making *Cages*.

177

Why, Celia, is your spreading Waist
So loose, so negligently lac'd?
How ill that Dress adorns your Head;
Distain'd and rumpled from the Bed?
Those Clouds that shade your blooming Face,
A little Water might displace,
As Nature ev'ry Morn bestows
The chrystal Dew to cleanse the Rose.
Those Tresses as the Raven black,
That wav'd in Ringlets down your Back,
Uncomb'd, and injur'd by Neglect,
Destroy the Face that once they deck'd,
Whence this Forgetfulness of Dress?
Pray, Madam, are you marry'd? Yes.
Nay then indeed the Wonder ceases,
No matter now how loose your Dress is;
The End is won, your Fortune's made,
Your Sister now may take the Trade.
*   Alas, what Pity 'tis to find*
This Fault in Half the Female kind!
From hence proceed Aversion, Strife,
And all that sours the wedded Life.
Beauty *can only point the Dart,*
'Tis Neatness *guides it to the Heart;*
Let Neatness then, and Beauty strive
To keep a wav'ring Flame alive.

APRIL

When e'er by seeming Chance, *Fop* throws his Eye
On Mirrors flushing with his Finery,
With how sublime a Transport leaps his Heart;
Pity such Friends sincere should ever part.
    So have I seen on some bright Summer's Day,
A spotted *Calf*, sleek, frolicksome and gay;
Gaze from the Bank, and much delighted seem,
Fond of the pretty Fellow in the Stream.

Sorrow is good for nothing but Sin.

Many a Man thinks he is buying Pleasure,
  when he is really selling himself a Slave to it.

Graft good Fruit all,
Or graft not at all.

❊ MAY

Content let all your Virtues lie unknown,
If there's no Tongue to praise them, but your own,
Of Boasting more than of a Bomb afraid,
Merit should be as modest as a Maid.
Fame is a Bubble the Reserv'd enjoy,
Who strive to grasp it, as they touch, destroy;
'Tis the World's Debt to Deeds of high Degree;
But if you pay yourself, the World is free.

Tis hard (but glorious) to be poor and honest: An empty
  Sack can hardly stand upright; but if it does, 'tis a
  stout one!

He that can bear a Reproof, and mend by it,
  if he is not wise, is in a fair way of being so.

Beatus esse sine Virtute, nemo potest.

On the 22d of this Month, 1453, was the famous City of *Constantinople*, the Capital of the *Greek* Empire, taken from the Christians by the *Turks*, who have ever since held it in Possession. When it was besieg'd, the Emperor made most earnest Application to his People, that they would contribute Money to enable him to pay his Troops, and defray the Expence of defending it; but they thro' Covetousness refused, pretending Poverty, *&c.* Yet the *Turks* in pillaging it, found so much Wealth among them, that even their common Soldiers were enriched: And it became a Saying, which continues to this Day, when they observe a Man grown suddenly rich, *He has been at the Sack of Constantinople.*

O *Avarice*! How blind are thy Votaries! How often by grasping at too much, do they lose all, and themselves with it! The Thirst of *More*, encreases with the *Heap*; and to the *restless* Desire of Getting, is added the *cruel Fear* of Losing, a Torment from which the Poor are free. And Death often scatters all we have with so much Care and Toil been gathering;

High built Abundance, *Heap on Heap for what?*
To breed new Wants, and beggar us the more;
Then make a richer Scramble for the Throng?
   Soon as this feeble Pulse, which leaps so long
Almost by Miracle, is tir'd with Play,
Like Rubbish from disploding Engines thrown,
Our Magazines of hoarded Trifles fly;
Fly adverse; fly to Foreigners, to Foes:
New Masters court, and call the former Fool,
(How justly!) for Dependance on their Stay,
Wide scatter, first, our Playthings, then our Dust.[19]

JUNE

Daphnis, says *Clio*, has a charming Eye;
What Pity 'tis her Shoulder is awry?
Aspasia's Shape indeed – – – – *but* then her Air,
'Twould ask a Conj'rer to find Beauty there.
Without a *But*, *Hortensia* she commends,
The first of Women, and the best of Friends;
Owns her in Person, Wit, Fame, Virtue, bright;
But how comes this to pass? – – – – She dy'd last Night.

Sound, & sound Doctrine, may pass through a Ram's Horn, and a Preacher, without straitening the one, or amending the other.

Clean your Finger, before you point at my Spots.

JULY

On TIME.

See TIME launch'd forth, in solemn Form proceed,
And Man on Man advance, and Deed on Deed!

No Pause, no Rest in all the World appears,
Ev'n live long Patriarchs waste their 1000 Years.
Some Periods void of Science and of Fame,
Scarce e'er exist, or leave behind a Name;
Meer sluggish Rounds, to let Succession climb,
Obscure, and idle Expletives of Time.

[*Cont'd Aug.*

He that spills the Rum, loses that only; He that drinks it,
    often loses both that and himself.

That Ignorance makes devout, if right the Notion,
'Troth, *Rufus*, thou'rt a Man of great Devotion.

A plain, clean, and decent Habit, proportioned to one's Circumstances, is one Mark of Wisdom. Gay Cloathing so generally betokens a light and empty Mind, that we are surpriz'd if we chance to find good Sense under that disguise.

Vain are the Studies of the Fop and Beau,
Who all their Care expend on outward Show.
Of late abroad was young Florello *seen;*
How blank his Look! How discompos'd his Mien!
So hard it proves in Grief sincere to feign,
Sunk were his Spirits, – – – – for his Coat was plain?
   Next Day his Breast regain'd its wonted Peace,
His Health was mended – – – – with a Silver Lace.[20]

What an admirable Invention is Writing, by which a Man may communicate his Mind without opening his Mouth, and at 1000 Leagues Distance, and even to future Ages, only by the Help of 22 Letters, which may be joined 5852616738497664000 Ways, and will express all Things in a very narrow Compass. 'Tis a Pity this excellent Art has not preserved the Name and Memory of its Inventor.

⚜ AUGUST

Others behold each nobler Genius thrive,
And in their generous Labours long survive;
By Learning grac'd, extend a distant Light;

Thus circling Science has her Day and Night.
　Rise, rise, ye dear Cotemporaries, rise;
On whom devolve these Seasons and these Skies!
Assert the Portion destin'd to your Share,
And make the Honour of the Times your Care.

[Cont'd Sept.

Those that have much Business must have much Pardon.

Discontented Minds, and Fevers of the Body
　are not to be cured by changing Beds or Businesses.

Genius without Education is like Silver in the Mine.

Little Strokes,
Fell great Oaks.

From MARTIAL.

Vitam quæ faciunt beatiorem, &c.

I fancy, O my Friend, that this
In Life bids fair for Happiness;
Timely an Estate to gain,
Left, or purchased by your Pain:
Grounds that pay the Tiller's Hire,
Woods to furnish lasting Fire;
Safe from Law t' enjoy your own,
Seldom view the busy Town;
Health with moderate Vigour join'd;
True well-grounded Peace of Mind;
Friends, your Equals in Degree,
Prudent, plain Simplicity;
Easy Converse Mirth afford,
Artless Plenty fill the Board;
Temp'rate Joy your Ev'nings bless,
Free from Care as from Excess:
Short the Night by Sleep be made,
Chaste, not chearless, be the Bed:
Chuse to be but what you are;
And Dying neither wish nor fear.

✢ SEPTEMBER

Still be your darling Study Nature's Laws;
And to its Fountain trace up every Cause.
Explore, for such it is, this high Abode,
And tread the Paths which *Boyle* and *Newton* trod.
Lo, Earth smiles wide, and radiant Heav'n looks down,
All fair, all gay, and urgent to be known!
Attend, and here are sown Delights immense,
For every Intellect, and every Sense.

［*Cont'd Oct.*

You may be too cunning for One, but not for All.

Many would live by their Wits, but break for want of Stock.

Poor *Plain dealing*! dead with out Issue!

Tho' Modesty is a Virtue, Bashfulness is a Vice.

Tim was so learned, that he could name a Horse in nine Languages.
So ignorant, that he bought a Cow to ride on.

The 3d of this Month, 1658, died OLIVER CROMWELL, aged 60 Years. A great Storm happen'd the Night he died, from whence his Enemies took Occasion to say, The D——l fetch'd him away in a Whirlwind: But his Poet *Waller*, in some Verses[21] on his Death, gave that Circumstance quite a different Turn. He begins with these lofty Lines;

> *We must resign, Heav'n his great Soul does claim,*
> *In Storms as loud as his immortal Fame;*
> *His dying Groans, his last Breath shakes our Isle,*
> *And Trees uncut fall for his Fun'ral Pile,* &c.

When the King came in, *Waller* made his Peace by a congratulatory Poem to his Majesty. And one Day 'tis said the King asked him jocularly, *What is the Reason,* Mr. Waller, *that your Verses on* Oliver *are so much better than those you made on me? We Poets, my Liege,* reply'd he, *always succeed better in Fiction than in Truth.*

> *Much Learning shows how little Mortals* know;
> *Much Wealth, how little Worldlings can* enjoy.
> *At best it baby's us with endless Toys,*
> *And keeps us Children 'till we drop to Dust.*
> *As Monkies at a Mirror stand amaz'd,*
> *They fail to find what they so plainly see;*
> *Thus Men, in shining Riches, see the Face*
> *Of Happiness, nor know it is a Shade;*
> *But gaze, and touch, and peep, and peep again,*
> *And wish, and wonder it is absent still.*[22]

OCTOBER

> With Adoration think, with Rapture gaze,
> And hear all Nature chant her Maker's Praise;
> With Reason stor'd, by Love of Knowledge fir'd,
> By Dread awaken'd, and by Love inspir'd,
> Can We, the Product of another's Hand,
> Nor whence, nor how, nor why we are, demand?
> And, not at all, or not aright employ'd,
> Behold a Length of Years, and all a Void?

[*Cont'd Nov.*

You can bear your own Faults,
   and why not a Fault in your Wife.

Hide not your Talents, they for Use were made.
What's a Sun-Dial in the Shade!

On the first of this Month, 1680, the great Comet appeared in *England*, and continued blazing near 3 Months. Of these suprizing Bodies, Astronomers hitherto know very little; Time and Observation, may make us better acquainted with them, and if their Motions are really regular, as they are supposed to be, enable us hereafter to calculate with some Certainty the Periods of their Return. They have heretofore been thought Forerunners of National Calamities, and Threateners of Divine Vengeance on a guilty World. Dr. *Young*, intimates this Opinion, in his Paraphrase on that Chapter of *Job*, where the Deity challenges the Patriarch, and convinces him of the Weakness of Man;

> *Who drew the* Comet *out to such a Size,*
> *And pour'd his flaming Train o'er Half the Skies!*
> *Did thy Resentment hang him out? Does he*
> *Glare on the Nations, and denounce from Thee?*

> *The Summer Fruits now gathered in,*
> *Let thankful Hearts in chearful Looks be seen;*
> *Ope the hospitable Gate,*
> *Ope for Friendship, not for State;*
> *Neighbours and Strangers enter there*
> *Equal to all of honest Air;*
> *To Rich or Poor of Soul sincere.*
> *Cheap bought Plenty, artless Store,*
> *Feed the Rich, and fill the Poor;*
> *Converse chear the sprightly Guest,*
> *Cordial Welcome crown the Feast;*
> *Easy Wit with Candour fraught,*
> *Laughter genuine and unsought;*
> *Jest from double Meaning free,*
> *Blameless, harmless Jollity;*
> *Mirth, that no repenting Gloom*
> *Treasures for our Years to come.*

NOVEMBER

Happy, thrice happy he! whose conscious Heart,
Enquires his Purpose, and discerns his Part;
Who runs with Heed, th' involuntary Race,
Nor lets his Hours reproach him as they pass;
Weighs how they steal away, how sure, how fast,
And as he weighs them, apprehends the last.
Or vacant, or engag'd, our Minutes fly;
We may be negligent, but we must die.

[*Cont'd Dec.*

What signifies knowing the Names,
    if you know not the Natures of Things.

Tim was so learned, that he could name a Horse in
    nine Languages: So ignorant, that he bought a Cow
    to ride on.

On the 30th of this Month, 1718, *Charles* XII. of *Sweden*, the modern *Alexander*, was kill'd before *Fredericstadt*. He had all the Virtues of a *Soldier*, but, as is said of the Virtues of *Cesar*, *They undid his Country*: Nor did they upon the whole afford himself any real Advantage. For after all his Victories and Conquests, he found his Power less than at first, his Money spent, his Funds exhausted, and his Subjects thinn'd extreamly. Yet he still warr'd on, in spite of Reason and Prudence, till a small Bit of Lead, more powerful than they, *persuaded* him to be quiet.

On what Foundation stands the Warrior's Pride?
How just his Hopes, let Swedish Charles *decide;*
A Frame of Adamant, a Soul of Fire,
No Dangers fright him, and no Labours tire;
O'er Love, o'er Force, extends his wide Domain,
Unconquer'd Lord of Pleasure and of Pain;
No Joys to him pacific Scepters yield,
War sounds the Trump, he rushed to the Field;
Behold surrounding Kings their Pow'r combine,
And one capitulate, and one resign;
Peace courts his Hand, but spreads her Charms in vain,

"Think nothing gain'd, he cries, 'till nought remain;
  On Moscow's *Walls* till Gothic *Standards fly,*
  And all is mine beneath the Polar Sky."
    The March begins in military State,
  And Nations on his Eye suspended wait;
  Stern Famine guards the solitary Coast,
  And Winter barricades the Realms of Frost;
  He comes, nor Want nor Cold his Course delay;
  Hide, blushing Glory, hide Pultowa's *Day:*
  The vanquish'd Hero leaves his broken Bands,
  And shews his Miseries in distant Lands;
  Condemn'd a needy Supplicant to wait,
  While Ladies interpose, and Slaves debate.
    But did not Chance at length her Error mend?
  Did no subverted Empire mark his End?
  Did rival Monarchs give the fatal Wound?
  Or hostile Millions press him to the Ground?
  His Fall was destin'd to a barren Strand,
  A petty Fortress, and a dubious Hand;
  He left the Name at which the World grew pale,
  To point a Moral, or adorn a Tale.[23]

❧ DECEMBER

And thou *supreme of Beings* and of Things!
Who breath'st all Life, and giv'st Duration Wings;
Intense, O let me for thy Glory burn,
Nor fruitless view my Days and Nights return;
Give me with Wonder at thy Works to glow;
To grasp thy Vision, and thy Truths to know;
To reach at length thy everlasting Shore,
And live and sing 'till Time shall be no more.
                                        [*Finis*

'Tis a Shame that your Family is an Honour to you!
  You ought to be an Honour to your Family.

Glass, China, and Reputation, are easily crack'd,
  and never well mended.

The Golden Age never was the present Age.

Adieu, my Task's ended.

Of COURTS.

If any Rogue vexatious Suits advance
Against you for your known Inheritance:
Enter by Violence your fruitful Grounds,
Or take the sacred Land-mark from your Bounds,
Or if your Debtors do not keep their Day,
Deny their Hands, and then refuse to pay;
You must with Patience all the Terms attend,
Among the common Causes that depend,
Till yours is call'd: – – – And that long-look'd-for Day,
Is still encumber'd with some new Delay:
Your Proofs and Deeds all on the Table spread,
Some of the B – – – ch perhaps are sick a-bed;
That J – – – ge steps out to light his Pipe, while this
O'er night was boozy, and goes out to p – – ss.
Some Witness miss'd; some Lawyer not in Town, ⎫
So many Rubs appear, the Time is gone, ⎬
For Hearing, and the tedious Suit goes on. ⎭
  Then rather let two Neighbours end your Cause,
And split the Difference; tho' you lose one Half;
  Than spend the Whole, entangled in the Laws,
While merry Lawyers sly, at both Sides laugh.

The Wolf sheds his Coat once a Year, his Disposition never.

1751

Poor Richard's *Almanack, &c.*

Courteous READER,

ASTROLOGY is one of the most ancient Sciences, had in high Esteem of old, by the Wise and Great. Formerly, no Prince would make War or Peace, nor any General fight a Battle, in short, no important Affair was undertaken without first consulting an *Astrologer*, who examined the Aspects and Configurations of the heavenly Bodies, and mark'd the *lucky Hour*. Now the noble Art (more Shame to the Age we live in!) is dwindled into Contempt; the Great neglect us, Empires make Leagues, and Parliaments Laws, without advising with us; and scarce any other Use is made of our learned Labours, than to find the best Time of cutting Corns, or gelding Pigs. − − − − This Mischief we owe in a great Measure to ourselves: The Ignorant Herd of Mankind, had they not been encourag'd to it by some of us, would never have dared to depreciate our sacred Dictates; but *Urania* has been betray'd by her own Sons; those whom she had favour'd with the greatest Skill in her divine Art, the most eminent Astronomers among the Moderns, the *Newtons*, *Halleys*, and *Whistons*, have wantonly contemn'd and abus'd her, contrary to the Light of their own Consciences. Of these, only the last nam'd, *Whiston*, has liv'd to repent, and

189

speak his Mind honestly. In his former Works he had treated *Judiciary Astrology* as a Chimera, and asserted, That not only the fixed Stars, but the Planets (Sun and Moon excepted) were at so immense a Distance, as to be incapable of any Influence on this Earth, and consequently nothing could be foretold from their Positions: but now in the Memoirs of his Life, publish'd 1749, in the 82d Year of his Age, he foretels, Page 607, the sudden Destruction of the *Turkish* Empire, and of the House of *Austria*, *German* Emperors, *&c.* and *Popes* of *Rome*; the Restoration of the *Jews*, and Commencement of the *Millennium*; all by the Year 1766; and this not only from Scripture Prophecies; but (take his own Words) – – – – "From the remarkable *astronomical* Signals that are to alarm Mankind of what is coming, *viz.* The *Northern Lights* since 1715; the six Comets at the Protestant Reformation in four Years, 1530, 1531, 1533, 1534, compar'd with the seven Comets already seen in these last eleven Years 1737, 1739, 1742, 1743, 1744, 1746, and 1748. – – – – From the great Annular Eclipse of the Sun, *July* 14, 1748, whose Center pass'd through all the four Monarchies, from *Scotland* to the *East-Indies*.– – – – From the Occultation of the *Pleiades* by the Moon each periodical Month, after the Eclipse last *July*, for above three Years, visible to the whole *Roman* Empire; as there was a like Occultation of the *Hyades* from *A.* 590, to *A.* 595, for six Years foretold by *Isaiah*. – – – – From the Transit of *Mercury* over the *Sun*, *April* 25, 1753, which will be visible thro' that Empire. – – – – From the Comet of *A. D.* 1456, 1531, 1607, and 1682, which will appear again about 1757 ending, or 1758 beginning, and will also be visible thro' that Empire. – – – – From the Transit of *Venus* over the *Sun*, *May* 26, 1761, which will be visible over the same Empire: And lastly, from the annular Eclipse of the *Sun*, *March* 11, 1764, which will be visible over the same Empire." – – – – From these *Astronomical Signs*, he foretels those great Events, That within 16 Years from this Time, "the *Millennium* or 1000 Years Reign of Christ shall begin, there shall be a *new Heavens*, and a *new Earth*: there shall be no more an Infidel in *Christendom*, Page 398, nor a Gaming-Table at *Tunbridge*!" – – – – When these Predictions are accomplished, what glorious Proofs they will be of the Truth of our Art? – – – – And if they happen to fail, there is no doubt but so profound an Astronomer as Mr. *Whiston*, will be able to see *other* Signs in the Heavens, foreshowing that the Conversion of Infidels was to be postponed, and the *Millennium* adjourn'd. – – – – After these great Things can any Man doubt our being capable of predicting a little Rain or Sun-shine? – – – – Reader, Farewell, and make the best Use of your Years and your Almanacks, for you see, that according to *Whiston*, you may have at most, but sixteen more of them.

Patowmack, July 30, 1750.

R. SAUNDERS.

When the young Trader, aided by your Loan,
Thrives in his Trade, a worthy Merchant grown;
When, snatch'd from Ruin's Jaws by your kind Hand,
The Farmer pays his Debts and saves his Land;
When Good like this is done, your Money lent
Brings you, besides your Interest, *Cent. per Cent.*
In pleasing Satisfaction and Content.

JANUARY

Who rise to *Glory*, must by VIRTUE rise,
'Tis *in the Mind* all *genuine Greatness* lies:
On that eternal Base, on that alone,
The World's Esteem you build, and more — your own.
For what avails Birth, Beauty, Fortune's Store,
The Plume of Title, and the Pride of Pow'r,
If, deaf to *Virtue*, deaf to *Honour*'s Call,
To Tyrant *Vice* a wretched Slave you fall?

Pray don't burn my House to roast your Eggs.

Some *Worth* it argues, a Friend's *Worth* to know;
Virtue to own the Virtue of a Foe.

Prosperity discovers Vice, Adversity Virtue.

The *Romans* were 477 Years, without so much as a Sun-dial to show the Time of Day: The first they had was brought from *Sicily*, by *Valerius Messala*: One hundred and eighteen Years afterwards, *Scipio Nasica*, produced to them an Invention for measuring the Hours in cloudy Weather, it was by the Dropping of Water out of one Vessel into another, somewhat like our Sand-Glasses. Clocks and Watches, to shew the Hour, are very modern Inventions. The Sub-dividing Hours into

Minutes, and Minutes into Seconds, by those curious Machines, is not older than the Days of our Fathers, but now brought to a surprising Nicety.

Since our Time is reduced to a Standard, and the Bullion of the Day minted out into Hours, the Industrious know how to employ every Piece of Time to a real Advantage in their different Professions: And he that is prodigal of his Hours, is, in Effect, a Squanderer of Money. I remember a notable Woman, who was fully sensible of the intrinsic Value of *Time*. Her Husband was a Shoemaker, and an excellent Craftsman, but never minded how the Minutes passed. In vain did she inculcate to him, That *Time is Money*. He had too much Wit to apprehend her, and it prov'd his Ruin. When at the Alehouse among his idle Companions, if one remark'd that the Clock struck Eleven, *What is that*, says he, *among us all?* If she sent him Word by the Boy, that it had struck Twelve; *Tell her to be easy, it can never be more.* If, that it had struck One, *Bid her be comforted, for it can never be less.*

If we lose our Money, it gives us some Concern. If we are cheated or robb'd of it, we are angry: But Money lost may be found; what we are robb'd of may be restored: The Treasure of Time once lost, can never be recovered; yet we squander it as tho' 'twere nothing worth, or we had no Use for it.

> *The Bell strikes* One: *We take no Note of Time,*
> *But from its Loss. To give it then a Tongue*
> *Is wise in Man. If heard aright*
> *It is the Knell of our departed Hours;*
> *Where are they? With the Years beyond the Flood:*
> *It is the Signal that demands Dispatch;*
> *How much is to be done? – – –*
>   *Be wise To-day, 'tis Madness to defer;*
> *Next day the fatal Precedent will plead;*
> *Thus on, till Wisdom is push'd out of Life:*
> Procrastination *is the Thief of Time,*
> *Year after Year it steals till all are fled,*
> *And to the Mercies of a Moment leaves*
> *The vast Concerns of an eternal Scene.*
> *If not so frequent, would not this be strange?*
> *That 'tis so frequent, This is stranger still.*[24]

FEBRUARY

Affect not that vain Levity of Thought,
Which sets Religion, Virtue, all at nought.
For true Religion like the Sun's blest Beam,
Darts thro' the conscious Mind a heav'nly Gleam,
Irradiates all the Soul, no Care allows,
Calms the best Heart, and smooths the easy Brows.
 Yet think it not enough what's right to know,
But let your Practice that right Knowledge show.
To *Christians* bad rude *Indians* we prefer;
'Tis better not to know, than knowing err.

Many a Man would have been worse,
 if his Estate had been better.

We may give Advice, but we cannot give Conduct.

Many have quarrel'd about Religion,
that never practised it.

Poor Richard: 1751

MARCH

Some sweet Employ for leisure Minutes chuse,
And let your very Pleasures have their Use.
But if you read, your Books with Prudence chuse.
Or Time mis-spent is worse than what you lose.
Be fully e'er you speak your Subject known,
And let e'en then some Diffidence be shown.
Keep something silent, and we think you wise,
But when we see the Bottom, we despise.

He that is conscious of a Stink in his Breeches,
    is jealous of every Wrinkle in another's Nose.

Love and *Tooth-ach* have many Cures, but none infallible,
    except *Possession* and *Dispossession*.

On the 15th of this Month, *Anno Romæ* 709, JULIUS CÆSAR was
slain in the Senate-House: He *fought*! he *conquer'd*! he *triumph'd*! For
what? For FAME.

And with what rare Inventions *do we strive*
        Ourselves *then to survive.*
Some with vast costly Tombs *would purchase it,*
        And by the Proofs of Death *pretend to* live.
Here lies the Great – – – – *False Marble, where?*
        Nothing but small *and* sordid *Dust lies there.*
                Some build enormous Mountain Palaces
                The Fools *and* Architects *to please:*
A lasting Life *in well hewn* Stone *they rear.*
CÆSAR *an higher Place does claim,*
        In the Seraphic Entity *of* FAME:
                He, since that Toy *his* Death,
Does fill all Mouths, and breathes *in all Men's* Breath;
– – – *The two* immortal Syllables *remain;*
                But O ye learned Men explain,
        What Essence, *what* Existence *this*
                In six poor Letters *is?*
In those alone does the great CÆSAR *live;*

194

'Tis all the conquer'd World *could give,*
We Poets *madder yet than all,*
With a refin'd fantastick Vanity
Think we not only have *but* give Eternity.
Fain would I see that Prodigal
Who his To-morrow *would bestow,*
For all old HOMER'S *Life, e'er since he* dy'd *till now.*

COWLEY.[25]

APRIL

O barb'rous Waggoners, your Wrath asswage,
Why vent you on the generous Steed your Rage?
Does not his Service earn you daily Bread?
Your Wives, your Children by his Labour fed?
  If, as the *Samian* taught, the Soul revives,
And, shifting Seats, in other Bodies lives,
Severe shall be the brutal Carter's Change,
Doom'd in a Thill-horse o'er rough Roads to range;
And while transform'd the groaning Load he draws,
Some Horse turn'd Carter shall avenge the Cause.

There are lazy Minds as well as lazy Bodies.

Most People return small Favours, acknowledge middling
  ones, and repay great ones with Ingratitude.

MAY

With ceaseless Streams a well-plac'd Treasure flows,
When spent increases, and by lessening grows.
Sarepta's Widow, hoping no Supply,
Thought, on her little Store, to eat and die:
Soon as she welcom'd her prophetic Guest,
The Cruse flow'd liberal, and the Corn increas'd,
Th' Almighty Pow'r unfailing Plenty sent,
The Oil unwasted, and the Meal unspent.

Fond Pride of Dress is sure an empty Curse;
E're *Fancy* you consult, consult your Purse.

Youth is pert and positive, *Age* modest and doubting:
    So Ears of Corn when young and light, stand bold upright,
    but hang their Heads when weighty, full, and ripe.

⚜ JUNE

What will not *Lux'ry* taste? Earth, Sea, and Air,
Are daily ransack'd for the Bill of Fare.
Blood stuff'd in Guts is *British* Christian's Food,
And *France* robs Marshes of the croaking Brood;
But he had sure a Palate cover'd o'er
With Brass or Steel, that on the rocky Shore,
First broke the oozy Oister's pearly Coat,
And risk'd the living Morsel down his Throat.

'Tis easier to suppress the first Desire,
    than to satisfy all that follow it.

Don't judge of Mens Wealth or Piety,
    by their *Sunday* Appearances.

Friendship increases by visiting Friends,
    but by visiting seldom.

⚜ JULY

Vice luring, in the Way of *Virtue* lies,
God suffers This; but tempts not; tho' He tries.
Go wrong, go right, 'tis your own Action still;
He leaves you to your Choice, of Good, or Ill.
Then chuse the Good! the Ill submisly bear!
The Man of Virtue is above Despair.
Safe on this Maxim with the Writer rest,
That all that happens, happens for the best.

If your Riches are yours, why don't you take them
    with you to the t'other World?

What more valuable than Gold? Diamonds.
Than Diamonds? Virtue.

❧ AUGUST

Ye Party Zealots, thus it fares with you,
When Party Rage too warmly you pursue;
Both Sides club Nonsense and impetuous Pride,
And *Folly* joins whom *Sentiments* divide.
You vent your Spleen as Monkeys when they pass,
Scratch at the mimic Monkey in the Glass,
While both are *one*; and henceforth be it known,
Fools of both Sides shall stand as Fools alone.

If worldly Goods cannot save me from Death,
    they ought not to hinder me of eternal Life.

To-day is Yesterday's Pupil.

'Tis great Confidence in a Friend to tell him *your* Faults,
    greater to tell him *his*.

❧ SEPTEMBER

Ah! what is Life? With Ills encompass'd round,
Amidst our Hopes, Fate strikes the sudden Wound;
To-day the Statesman of new Honour dreams,
To-morrow Death destroys his airy Schemes.
Is mouldy Treasure in thy Chest confin'd;
Think, all that Treasure thou must leave behind;
Thy Heir with Smiles shall view thy blazon'd Hearse,
And all thy Hoards, with lavish Hand disperse.

[Cont'd Oct.

Talking against Religion is unchaining a Tyger;
    The Beast let loose may worry his Deliverer.

Ambition often spends foolishly what *Avarice*
    had wickedly collected.

❧ OCTOBER

Should certain Fate th'impending Blow delay,
Thy Mirth will sicken, and thy Bloom decay;

Then feeble Age will all thy Nerves disarm,
No more thy Blood its narrow Channels warm;
Who then would wish to stretch this narrow Span,
To suffer Life beyond the Date of Man?
    The virtuous Soul pursues a nobler Aim,
And Life regards but as a fleeting Dream.

[Cont'd Nov.

Pillgarlic was in the *Accusative* Case, and bespoke a
Lawyer in the *Vocative*, who could not understand him
till he made use of the *Dative*.

Great Estates may venture more;
Little Boats must keep near Shore.

Nice Eaters seldom meet with a good Dinner.

❧ November

She longs to wake, and wishes to get free,
To launch from Earth into Eternity.
For while the boundless Theme extends our Thought,
Ten thousand thousand rolling Years are nought.
O endless Thought! divine *Eternity*!
Th' immortal Soul shares but a Part of thee;
For thou wert present when our Life began,
When the warm Dust shot up in breathing Man.

[Cont'd Dec.

Not to oversee Workmen, is to leave them your Purse open.

The Wise and Brave dares own that he was wrong.

Cunning proceeds from Want of Capacity.

It is an amusing Speculation to look back, and compute what Numbers of Men and Women among the Ancients, clubb'd their Endeavours to the Production of a single Modern. As you reckon backwards the Number encreases in the same Proportion as the Price of the Coat which was sold for a Half-penny a Button, continually doubled.

Thus, a present Nobleman (for Instance) is				1
His Father and Mother were				2
His Grandfathers and Grandmothers				4
His Great Grandfathers and Great Grandmothers				8
And, supposing no Intermarriages among Relations, the next Predecessors will be				16

The next Ditto,	32	The next Ditto,	8192
The next Ditto,	64	The next Ditto,	16384
The next Ditto,	128	The next Ditto,	32768
The next Ditto,	256	The next Ditto,	65536
The next Ditto,	512	The next Ditto,	131072
The next Ditto,	1024	The next Ditto,	262144
The next Ditto,	2048	The next Ditto,	524288
The next Ditto,	4096	The next Ditto,	1048576

Here are only computed 21 Generations, which, allowing 3 Generations to 100 Years, carry us back no farther than the *Norman* Conquest, at which Time each present Nobleman, to exclude all ignoble Blood from his Veins, ought to have had One Million, Forty-eight Thousand, Five Hundred and Seventy six noble Ancestors. Carry the Reckoning back 300 Years farther, and the Number amounts to above 500 Millions; which are more than exist at any one Time upon Earth, and shews the Impossibility of preserving Blood free from such Mixtures, and that the Pretension of such Purity of Blood in ancient Families is a mere Joke. Hence we see how it happens that every Nation has a kind of general Cast of Feature, by which it may be distinguished; continual Intermarriages for a Course of Ages rendring all the People related by Blood, and, as it were, of one Family.

⫷ DECEMBER

Ere the Foundations of the World were laid,
Ere kindling Light th'Almighty Word obey'd,
Thou wert; and when the subterraneous Flame,
Shall burst its Prison, and devour this Frame,
From angry Heav'n when the keen Lightning flies,
When fervent Heat dissolves the melting Skies,

Thou still shalt be; still as thou wert before,
And know no Change when *Time* shall be no more.
⌈*Finis*

The Proud hate Pride—in others.

Who judges best of a Man, his Enemies or himself?

Drunkenness, that worst of Evils, makes some Men Fools,
some Beasts, some Devils.

'Tis not a Holiday that's not kept holy.

On the 6th of this Month, 1711. died in *England*, Mrs. *Jane Schrimshaw*, aged 127 Years: – – – – But *England* boasts some much longer Livers. *James Sands*, of *Horburn*, in the County of *Stafford*, near *Birmingham*, lived 140 Years, and his Wife 120, in a perfect State of Health till the Day of their Deaths. He out-liv'd 5 Leases of 21 Years each, all made after his Marriage. *Thomas Parr*, married his first Wife at 80 Years of Age, by whom he had two Children; his second Wife after he was 120 Years old, by whom he had one Child, and lived till he was something above 150. *Henry Jenkins* of the Parish of *Bolton*, in *York-shire*, died the 8th of this same Month, 1670, aged 169 Years. In these *American* Parts we have no such very old Men; not that the Climate is unhealthy, but because the present Inhabitants *were not born soon enough*.

Great Talkers, little Doers.

1752

Poor Richard's *Almanack, &c.*

Kind READER,

SINCE the King and Parliament have thought fit to alter our Year, by taking eleven Days out of *September*, 1752, and directing us to begin our Account for the future on the First of *January*, some Account of the Changes the Year hath heretofore undergone, and the Reasons of them, may a little gratify thy Curiosity.

The Vicissitude of *Seasons* seems to have given Occasion to the first Institution of the *Year*. Man naturally curious to know the Cause of that Diversity, soon found it was the Nearness and Distance of the Sun; and upon this, gave the Name *Year* to the Space of Time wherein that Luminary, performing his whole Course, returned to the same Point of his Orbit.

And hence, as it was on Account of the Seasons, in a great Measure, that the *Year* was instituted, their chief Regard and Attention was, that the same Parts of the *Year* should always correspond to the same Seasons; *i.e.* that the Beginning of the Year should always be when the Sun was in the same Point of his Orbit; and that they should keep Pace, come round, and end together.

This, different Nations aimed to attain by different Ways; making the *Year* to commence from different Points of the Zodiac; and even the

Time of his Progress different. So that some of their Years were much more perfect than others, but none of them quite just; *i.e.* none of them but whose Parts shifted with Regard to the Parts of the Sun's Course.

It was the *Egyptians*, if we may credit *Herodotus*, that first formed the *Year*, making it to contain 360 Days, which they subdivided into twelve Months, of thirty Days each.

Mercury Trismegistus added five Days more to the Account. - - - - And on this Footing *Thales* is said to have instituted the Year among the *Greeks*. Tho' that Form of the Year did not hold throughout all *Greece*. Add that the *Jewish*, *Syrian*, *Roman*, *Persian*, *Ethiopic*, *Arabic*, &c. Years, are all different.

In effect, considering the poor State of Astronomy in those Ages, it is no Wonder different People should disagree in the Calculus of the Sun's Course. We are even assured by *Diodorus Siculus*, *Plutarch*, and *Pliny*, that the *Egyptian Year* itself was at first very different from what it became afterwards.

According to our Account, the *Solar Year*, or the Interval of Time in which the Sun finishes his Course thro' the Zodiac, and returns to the same Point thereof from which he had departed, is 365 Days, 5 Hours, 49 Minutes; tho' some Astronomers make it a few Seconds, and some a whole Minute less; as *Kepler*, for Instance, who makes it 365 Days, 5 Hours, 48 Minutes, 57 Seconds, 39 Thirds. *Ricciolus*, 365 Days, 5 Hours, 48 Minutes. *Tycho Brahe*, 365 Days, 5 Hours, 48 Minutes.

The *Civil Year* is that Form of *Year* which each Nation has contrived to compute Time by; or the *Civil* is the *Tropical Year*, considered as only consisting of a certain Number of whole Days; the odd Hours and Minutes being set aside, to render the Computation of Time in the common Occasions of Life more easy.

Hence as the *Tropical Year* is 365 Days, 5 Hours, 49 Minutes; the *Civil Year* is 365 Days. And hence also, as it is necessary to keep Pace with the Heavens, it is required that every fourth Year consist of 366 Days, which would for ever keep the Year exactly right, if the odd Hours of each Year were precisely 6.

The ancient *Roman Year*, as first settled by *Romulus*, consisted of ten Months only; *viz.* I. *March*, containing 31 Days. II. *April*, 30. III. *May*, 31. IV. *June* 30. V. *Quintilis*, 31. VI. *Sextilis*, 30. VII. *September*, 30. VIII. *October*, 31. IX. *November*, 30. X. *December*, 30; in all 304 Days; which came short of the *Solar Year*, by 61 Days.

Hence the Beginning of *Romulus*'s Year was vague, and unfixed to any precise Season; which Inconvenience to remove, that Prince ordered so many Days to be added yearly, as would make the State of the Heavens correspond to the first Month, without incorporating these additional Days, or calling them by the Name of any Month.

Numa Pompilius corrected this irregular Constitution of the Year, and composed two new Months, *January* and *February*, of the Days that were used to be added to the former Year. Thus, *Numa*'s *Year* consisted of twelve Months; *viz.* I. *January*, containing 29 Days. II. *February*, 28. III. *March*, 31. IV. *April*, 29. V. *May*, 31. VI. *June*, 29. VII. *Quintilis*, 31. VIII. *Sextilis*, 29. IX. *September*, 29. X. *October*, 31. XI. *November*, 29. XII. *December*, 29; in all 355 Days, which came short of the common Solar Year by ten Days; so that its Beginning was vague and unfixed.

Numa, however, desiring to have it fixed to the Winter Solstice, ordered 22 Days to be intercalated in *February* every second Year, 23 every fourth, 22 every sixth, and 23 every eighth Year.

But this Rule failing to keep Matters even, Recourse was had to a new Way of Intercalating; and instead of 23 Days every eighth Year, only 15 were added; and the Care of the whole committed to the *Pontifex Maximus*, or High Priest; who, neglecting the Trust, let Things run to the utmost Confusion. And thus the *Roman* Year stood till *Julius Cæsar* made a Reformation.

The *Julian Year*, is a Solar Year, containing commonly 365 Days; tho' every fourth Year, called *Bissextile*, contains 366. – – – – The Names and Order of the Months of the *Julian Year*, and the Number of Days in each, are well known to us, having been long in Use.

The astronomical Quantity, therefore, of the *Julian Year*, is 365 Days, 6 Hours, which exceeds the true Solar Year by 11 Minutes; which Excess in 131 Years amounts to a Whole Day. – – – – And thus the *Roman Year* stood, till the Reformation made therein by Pope *Gregory*.

Julius Cæsar, in the Contrivance of his Form of the Year, was assisted by *Sosigenes*, a famous Mathematician, called over from *Egypt* for this very Purpose; who, to supply the Defect of 67 Days which had been lost thro' the Fault of the High Priests, and to fix the Beginning of the Year to the Winter Solstice, made that Year to consist of 15 Months, or 445 Days; which for that Reason is used to be called *Annus Confusionis*, the *Year of Confusion*.

This Form of the Year was used by all Christian Nations, till the

Middle of the 16th Century; and still continues to be so by several Nations; among the Rest, by the *Swedes, Danes,* &c. and by the *English* till the second of *September* next, when they are to assume the Use of the *Gregorian Year.*

The GREGORIAN YEAR is the *Julian Year* corrected by this Rule; that whereas on the common Footing, every Secular or Hundredth Year, is *Bissextile*; on the new Footing, three of them are common Years, and only the fourth *Bissextile*.

The Error of eleven Minutes in the *Julian Year*, little as it was, yet, by being repeated over and over, at length became considerable; and from the Time when *Cæsar* made his Correction, was grown into 13 Days, by which the Equinoxes were greatly disturbed. To remedy this Irregularity, which was still a growing, Pope *Gregory* the XIII. called together the chief Astronomers of his Time, and concerted this Correction; and to restore the Equinoxes to their Place threw out the ten Days that had been got from the Council of *Nice*, and which had shifted the fifth of *October* to the 15th.

In the Year 1700, the Error of ten Days was grown to eleven; upon which the Protestant States of *Germany*, to prevent further Confusion, accepted the *Gregorian* Correction. And now in 1752, the *English* follow their Example.

Yet is the *Gregorian Year* far from being perfect, for we have shewn, that, in four Centuries, the *Julian Year* gains three Days, one Hour, twenty Minutes: But it is only the three Days are kept out in the *Gregorian Year*; so that here is still an Excess of one Hour, twenty Minutes, in four Centuries; which in 72 Centuries will amount to a whole Day.

As to the Commencement of the Year, the *legal Year* in *England* used to begin on the Day of the *Annunciation*; *i.e.* on the 25th of *March*; tho' the historical Year began on the Day of the *Circumcision*; *i.e.* the first of *January*, on which Day the *Italian* and *German* Year also begins; and on which Day ours is to begin from this Time forward, the first Day of *January* being now by Act of Parliament declared the first Day of the Year 1752.

At the Yearly Meeting of the People called *Quakers*, held in *London*, since the Passing of this Act, it was agreed to recommend to their Friends a Conformity thereto, both in omitting the eleven Days of *September* thereby directed to be omitted, and beginning the Year hereafter on the first Day of the Month called *January*, which is henceforth to be by them called and written, *The First Month*, and the rest likewise in their Order, so that *September* will now be the *Ninth Month*, *December* the *Twelfth*.

This *Act of Parliament*, as it contains many Matters of Importance, and extends expressly to all the *British Colonies*, I shall for the Satisfaction of the Publick, give at full length:[26] Wishing withal, according to ancient Custom, that this *New Year* (which is indeed a New Year, such an one as we never saw before, and shall never see again) may be a happy Year to all my kind Readers.

I am, Your faithful Servant,

R. SAUNDERS.

JANUARY

On *PUBLICK SPIRIT*.[27]

Where never Science beam'd a friendly Ray,
Where one vast Blank neglected Nature lay;
From PUBLICK SPIRIT there, by Arts employ'd,
Creation, varying, glads the chearless Void.
By Arts, which Safety, Treasure and Delight,
On Land, on Wave, in wondrous Works unite!
Myriads made happy, *Publick Spirit* bless,
Parent of Trade, Wealth, Liberty and Peace.

[*Cont'd Febr.*

Observe old *Vellum*; he praises former Times,
    as if he'd a mind to sell 'em.

Kings have long Arms, but Misfortune longer:
    Let none think themselves out of her Reach.

FEBRUARY

Unlike where Tyranny, the Rod maintains
O'er turfless, leafless and uncultur'd Plains,
Here Herbs of Food and Physic, Plenty showers,
Gives Fruits to blush, and colours various Flowers.

Where Sands or stony Wilds once starv'd the Year,
Laughs the green Lawn, and nods the golden Ear.
White shine the fleecy Race, which Fate shall doom,
The Feast of Life, the Treasure of the Loom.

[Cont'd Mar.

For want of a Nail the Shoe is lost; for want of a Shoe,
    the Horse is lost; for want of a Horse the Rider is lost.

ꝏ MARCH

What tho' no *Arch of Triumph* is assign'd
To laurel'd Pride, whose Sword has thinn'd Mankind;
Tho' no vast Wall extends from Coast to Coast,
No Pyramid aspires sublimely lost.
Lo! stately Streets, lo! ample Squares invite
The salutary Gale that breathes Delight.
Lo! Structures mark the hospitable Strand,
Where *Charity* extends her tender Hand;

[Cont'd Apr.

The busy Man has few idle Visitors;
    to the boiling Pot the Flies come not.

Calamity and Prosperity are the Touchstones of Integrity.

ꝏ APRIL

Where the sick Stranger joys to find a Home,
Where casual Ill, maim'd Labour, freely come;
Those worn with Age, Infirmity or Care,
Find Rest, Relief, and Health returning fair.
There too the Walls of rising Schools ascend,
For PUBLICK SPIRIT still is *Learning*'s Friend,
Where Science, Virtue, sown with liberal Hand,
In future Patriots shall inspire the Land.

[Cont'd May

The Prodigal generally does more Injustice than the Covetous.

Generous Minds are all of kin.

✿ MAY

And when too populous at length confess'd,
From confluent Strangers refug'd and redress'd:
When War so long withdraws his barb'rous Train,
That Peace o'erstocks us with the Sons of Men:
So long Health breathes thro' the pure ambient Air,
That Want must prey on those Disease would spare;
Then will be all the *gen'rous Goddess* seen,
Then most diffus'd she shines, and most benign.

[*Cont'd June*

'Tis more noble to forgive, and more manly to despise,
  than to revenge an Injury.

A Brother may not be a Friend,
  but a Friend will always be a Brother.

Meanness is the Parent of Insolence.

A true Friend is the best Possession.

☙ JUNE

Her Eye far piercing, round extends its Beams,
To *Erie*'s Banks, or smooth *Ohio*'s Streams,
It fixes where kind Rays till then have smil'd,
(Vain Smile!) on some luxuriant houseless Wild;
How many Sons of Want might here enjoy
What Nature gives for Age but to destroy?
'Blush, blush, O *Sun* (she cries) here vainly found
To rise, to set, to roll the Seasons round!

[*Cont'd July*

Mankind are very odd Creatures: One Half censure
what they practise, the other half practise what they
censure; the rest always say and do as they ought.

Severity is often Clemency; Clemency Severity.

☙ JULY

'Shall Heav'n distil in Dews, descend in Rain,
From Earth gush Fountains, Rivers flow in vain?
There shall the *watry Lives* in Myriads stray,
And be, to be alone each other's Prey?
Unsought shall here the teeming Quarries own
The various Species of mechanic Stone?
From Structure This, from Sculpture That confine?
Shall Rocks forbid the latent Gem to shine?

[*Cont'd Aug.*

Bis dat qui cito dat: He gives twice that gives soon;
i.e. he will soon be called upon to give again.

A Temper to bear much, will have much to bear.

Pride dines upon Vanity, sups on Contempt.

☙ AUGUST

'Shall Mines obedient aid no Artist's Care,
Nor give the martial Sword and peaceful Share?

Ah! shall they never precious Ore unfold,
To smile in Silver, or to flame in Gold?
Shall here the vegetable World alone,
For Joys, for various Virtues rest unknown?
While Food and Physic, Plants and Herbs supply,
Here must they shoot alone to bloom and die?

[Cont'd Sept.

Great Merit is coy, as well as great Pride.

An undutiful Daughter, will prove an unmanageable Wife.

Old Boys have their Playthings as well as young Ones;
    the Difference is only in the Price.

September

'Shall Fruits, which none, but brutal Eyes survey,
Untouch'd grow ripe, untasted drop away?
Shall here th' irrational, the salvage Kind
Lord it o'er Stores by Heav'n for Man design'd,
And trample what mild Suns benignly raise,
While Man must lose the Use, and Heav'n the Praise?
Shall it then be?' (Indignant here she rose,
Indignant, yet humane, her Bosom glows)

[Cont'd Oct.

The too obliging Temper is evermore disobliging itself.

Hold your Council before Dinner;
    the full Belly hates Thinking as well as Acting.

October

'No! By each honour'd *Grecian Roman* Name,
By Men for Virtue Deified by Fame,
Who peopled Lands, who model'd infant State,
And then bad Empire be maturely great,
By *These* I swear (be witness Earth and Skies!)
Fair Order here shall from Confusion rise,

Rapt I a future Colony survey!
Come then, ye Sons of Mis'ry! come away!

[*Cont'd Nov.*

The Brave and the Wise can both pity and excuse;
   when Cowards and Fools shew no Mercy.

Ceremony is not Civility; nor Civility Ceremony.

If Man could have Half his Wishes,
   he would double his Troubles.

❧ NOVEMBER

'Let Those, whose Sorrows from Neglect are known,
(Here taught compell'd empower'd) Neglect attone!
Let Those enjoy (who never merit Woes)
In Youth th' industrious Wish, in Age Repose!
Allotted Acres (no reluctant Soil)
Shall prompt their Industry, and pay their Toil.
Let Families, long Strangers to Delight,
Whom wayward Fate dispers'd, by Me unite;

[*Cont'd Dec.*

It is ill Jesting with the Joiner's Tools,
   worse with the Doctor's.

Children and Princes will quarrel for Trifles.

Praise to the undeserving, is severe Satyr.

☃ DECEMBER

'Here live enjoying Life, see Plenty, Peace;
Their Lands encreasing as their Sons increase!
As Nature yet is found in leafy Glades
To intermix the Walks with Lights and Shades;
Or as with Good and Ill, in chequer'd Strife,
Various the Goddess colours human Life;
So in this fertile Clime if yet are seen
Moors, Marshes, Cliffs, by Turns to intervene:
Where Cliffs, Moors, Marshes desolate the View,

Where haunts the Bittern, and where screams the Mew,
Where prowls the Wolf, where roll'd the Serpent lies,
Shall solemn Fanes, and Halls of Justice rise.
And Towns shall open (all of Structure fair!)
To bright'ning Prospects, and to purest Air,
Frequented Ports and Vineyards green succeed,
And Flocks encreasing whiten all the Mead;
On Science Science, Arts on Arts refine;
On these from high all Heav'n shall smiling shine,
And *Publick Spirit* here a People show,
Free num'rous pleas'd and busy all below.
   'Learn future Natives of this promis'd Land,
What your Forefathers ow'd my saving Hand!
Learn when *Despair* such sudden Bliss shall see,
Such Bliss must shine from *Providence* thro' *ME*!
Do you the neighb'ring blameless *Indian* aid,
Culture what he neglects, not His invade;
Dare not, oh dare not, with ambitious View,
Force or demand Subjection never due;
Let by My specious Name no *Tyrants* rise,
And cry, while they enslave, they civilize!
Know, *LIBERTY* and *I* are still the *same*,
Congenial – – – – ever mingling Flame with Flame!
Nor let me *Afric*'s sable Children see,
Vended for Slaves tho' form'd by Nature free;
If Those you dare, albeit unjust Success
Empow'rs you now unpunish'd to oppress,
Revolving Empire you and yours may doom
(*Rome* all subdu'd, yet *Vandals* vanquish'd *Rome*)
Yes, Empire may revolve, give them the Day,
And Yoke may Yoke, and Blood may Blood repay.'
   Thus (Ah! how far unequall'd by *my* Lays,
Unskill'd the Heart to melt or Mind to raise)
Sublime benevolent deep sweetly clear,
Worthy a *Thomson*'s Muse, an – – – –'s Ear,
Thus spoke the *Goddess*. Thus I faintly tell
In what lov'd Works Heav'n gives her to excel.
But who her Sons, that to her Int'rest true,

Still plan with Wisdom, and with Zeal pursue?
These found most frequent in Life's *middle* State,
Rich without Gold, and without Titles great:
Knowledge of Books and Men exalts their Thought,
In Wit accomplish'd tho' in Wiles untaught,
Careless of Whispers meant to wound their Name,
Not sneer'd nor brib'd from Virtue into Shame;
In Letters elegant, in Honour bright,
Form'd to give Happiness, their sole Delight.

  When Gifts like these conferr'd by bounteous Heav'n,
Talents and Will to the same Person giv'n,
The Man ennobled doth an HERO rise,
Fame and his Virtues lift him to the Skies.
While we admire what we can't imitate,
Deny'd by Nature, and forbid by Fate.

  O! were I form'd to share this heav'nly Fire,
In Parts and Pow'rs strong as in Desire,
Moses, *Lycurgus*, *Numa* I revere,
Their Wisdom great, their Love to Man sincere,
By *Publick Spirit* rank'd the first of Men,
Yet I'd not envy them, nor even P———.

[Finis

Success has ruin'd many a Man.

Great Pride and Meanness sure are near ally'd;
Or thin Partitions do their Bounds divide.

Drink does not drown Care, but waters it,
and makes it grow fast.

Poor Richard's *Almanack, &c.*

Courteous READER,

THIS is the twentieth Time of my addressing thee in this Manner, and I have reason to flatter myself my Labours have not been unacceptable to the Publick. I am particularly pleas'd to understand that my *Predictions of the Weather* give such general Satisfaction; and indeed, such Care is taken in the Calculations, on which those Predictions are founded, that I could almost venture to say, there's not a single One of them, promising *Snow, Rain, Hail, Heat, Frost, Fogs, Wind,* or *Thunder,* but what comes to pass *punctually* and *precisely* on the very Day, in some Place or other on this little *diminutive* Globe of Ours; (and when you consider the vast Distance of the Stars from whence we take our Aim, you must allow it no small Degree of Exactness to hit any Part of it) I say on this Globe; for tho' in other Matters I confine the Usefulness of my *Ephemeris* to the *Northern Colonies,* yet in that important Matter of the Weather, which is of such *general Concern,* I would have it more extensively useful, and therefore take in both Hemispheres, and all Latitudes from *Hudson's Bay* to *Cape Horn.*

You will find this Almanack in my former Method, only conformable to the *New-Stile* established by the Act of Parliament, which I gave you in my last at length; the new Act since made for Amendment of that first Act, not affecting us in the least, being intended only to regulate some Corporation Matters in *England*, before unprovided for. I have only added a Column in the second Page of each Month, containing the Days of the *Old Stile* opposite to their corresponding Days in the *New*, which may, in many Cases, be of Use; and so conclude (believing you will excuse a short Preface, when it is to make Room for something better)

Thy Friend and Servant,

R. SAUNDERS.

HYMN *to the* CREATOR, *from Psalm* CIV.[28]

Awake, my Soul! with Joy thy God adore;
Declare his Greatness; celebrate his Pow'r;
Who, cloath'd with Honour, and with Glory crown'd,
Shines forth, and cheers his Universe around.
Who with a radiant Veil of heavenly Light
Himself conceals from all created Sight.
Who rais'd the spacious Firmament on high,
And spread the azure Curtain of the Sky.
Whose awful Throne Heav'n's starry Arch sustains,
Whose Presence not Heav'n's vast Expanse retains.
Whose Ways unsearchable no Eye can find,
The Clouds his Chariot, and his Wings the Wind.
Whom Hosts of mighty Angels own their Lord,
And flaming Seraphim fulfil his Word.
Whose Pow'r of old the solid Earth did found,
Self-pois'd, self-center'd, and with Strength girt round;
From her appointed Sphere forbid to fly,
Or rush unbalanc'd thro' the trackless Sky.
To reas'ning Man the sov'reign Rule assign'd,
His Delegate o'er each inferior Kind;
Too soon to fall from that distinguish'd Place,
His Honours stain'd with Guilt and foul Disgrace.
  He saw the Pride of Earth's aspiring Lord,
And in his Fury gave the dreadful Word:
Straight o'er her peopled Plains his Floods were pour'd,

And o'er her Mountains the proud Billows roar'd.
Athwart the Face of Earth the Deluge sweeps,
And whelms the impious Nations in the Deeps.
Again God spake – – – – and at his pow'rful Call
The raging Floods asswage, the Waters fall,
The Tempests hear his Voice, and straight obey,
And at his Thunder's Roar they haste away:
From off the lofty Mountains they subside,
And gently thro' the winding Vallies glide,
Till in the spacious Caverns of the Deep
They sink together, and in Silence sleep.
There he hath stretch'd abroad their liquid Plains,
And there Omnipotence their Rage restrains,
That Earth no more her Ruins may deplore,
And guilty Mortals dread their Wrath no more.

He bids the living Fountains burst the Ground,
And bounteous spread their Silver Streams around:
Down from the Hills they draw their shining Train,
Diffusing Health and Bounty o'er the Plain.
There the fair Flocks allay the Summer's Rage,
And panting Savages their Flame asswage,
On their sweet winding Banks th' aerial Race
In artless Numbers warble forth his Praise,
Or chant the harmless Raptures of their Loves,
And cheer the Plains, and wake the vocal Groves.
Forth from his Treasures in the Skies he pours
His precious Blessings in refreshing Show'rs,
Each dying Plant with Joy new Life receives,
And thankful Nature smiles, and Earth revives.
The fruitful Fields with Verdure he bespreads,
The Table of the Race that haunts the Meads,
And bids each Forest, and each flow'ry Plain
Send forth their native Physic for the Swain.
Thus doth the various Bounty of the Earth
Support each Species crowding into Birth.
In purple Streams she bids her Vintage flow,
And Olives on her Hills luxuriant grow,
One with its generous Juice to cheer the Heart,

And one illustrious Beauty to impart;
And Bread of all Heav'n's precious gifts the chief
From desolating Want the sure Relief.
Which with new Life the feeble Limbs inspires,
And all the Man with Health and Courage fires.
The Cloud-topt Hills with waving Woods are crown'd,
Which wide extend their sacred Shades around,
There *Lebanon's* proud Cedars nod their Heads;
There *Bashan's* lofty Oaks extend their Shades:
The pointed Firs rise tow'ring to the Clouds,
And Life and warbling Numbers fill the Woods.
   Nor gentle Shades alone, nor verdant Plains,
Nor fair enamell'd Meads, nor flow'ry Lawns,
But e'en rude Rocks and dreary Desarts yield
Retreats for the wild Wand'rers of the Field.
The Pow'r with Life and Sense all Nature fills,
Each Element with varied Being swells,
Race after Race arising view the Light,
Then silent pass away, and sink in Night.
The Gift of Life thus boundlesly bestow'd,
Proclaims th' exhaustless Hand, the Hand of God.
   Nor less thy Glory in th' etherial Spheres,
Nor less thy ruling Providence appears.
There from on high the gentle Moon by Night
In solemn Silence sheds her Silver Light,
And thence the glorious Sun pours forth his Beams,
Thence copious spreads around his quick'ning Streams.
Each various Orb enjoys the golden Day,
And Worlds of Life hang on his chearful Ray.
Thus Light and Darkness their fix'd Course maintain,
And still the kind Vicissitudes remain:
For when pale Night her sable Curtain spreads,
And wraps all Nature in her awful Shades,
Soft Slumbers gently seal each mortal Eye,
Stretch'd at their Ease the weary Lab'rers lie.
The restless Soul 'midst Life's vain Tumults tost,
Forgets her Woes, and ev'ry Care is lost.

[*Cont'd Jan.*

JANUARY

Then from their Dens the rav'nous Monsters creep,
Whilst in their Folds the harmless Bestial sleep.
The furious Lion roams in quest of Prey,
To gorge his Hunger till the Dawn of Day;
His hideous Roar with Terror shakes the Wood,
As from his Maker's Hand he asks his Food.
Again the Sun his Morning Beams displays,
And fires the eastern Mountain with his Rays.

[*Cont'd Febr.*

'Tis against some Mens Principle to pay Interest,
    and seems against others Interest to pay the Principal.

Philosophy as well as Foppery often changes Fashion.

Fond Pride of Dress is, sure, a very Curse;
Ere Fancy you consult, consult your Purse.

≋ FEBRUARY

Before him fly the Horrors of the Night;
He looks upon the World—and all is Light.
Then the lone Wand'rers of the dreary Waste
Affrighted to their Holds return in Haste,
To Man give up the World, his native Reign,
Who then resumes his Pow'r, and rules the Plain.
　　How various are thy Works, Creator wise!
How to the Sight Beauties on Beauties rise!

[Cont'd Mar.

Setting too good an Example is a Kind of Slander
　　seldom forgiven; 'tis *Scandalum Magnatum.*

A great Talker may be no Fool,
　　but he is one that relies on him.

☞ MARCH

Where Goodness worthy of a God bestows
His Gifts on all, and without Bounds o'erflows;
Where Wisdom bright appears, and Pow'r divine,
And where Infinitude itself doth shine;
Where Excellence invisible's exprest,
And in his glorious Works the God appears confest.
　　With Life thy Hand hath stock'd this earthly Plain,
Nor less the spacious Empire of the Main.

[Cont'd Apr.

When Reason preaches, if you won't hear her
　　she'll box your Ears.

It is not Leisure that is not used.

☞ APRIL

There the tall Ships the rolling Billows sweep,
And bound triumphant o'er th' unfathom'd Deep.
There great Leviathan in regal Pride,
The scaly Nations crouding by his Side,

Far in the dark Recesses of the Main
O'er Nature's Wastes extends his boundless Reign.
Round the dark Bottoms of the Mountains roves,
The hoary Deep swells dreadful as he moves.

[*Cont'd May*

The Good-will of the Governed will be starv'd,
   if not fed by the good Deeds of the Governors.

Paintings and Fightings are best seen at a distance.

❧ MAY

Now views the awful Throne of antient Night,
Then mounts exulting to the Realms of Light;
Now launches to the Deep, now stems the Shore,
An Ocean scarce contains the wild Uproar.
   Whate'er of Life replenishes the Flood,
Or walks the Earth, or warbles thro' the Wood,
In Nature's various Wants to thee complains,
The Hand, which gave the Life, the Life sustains.

[*Cont'd June*

If you would reap Praise you must sow the Seeds,
Gentle Words and useful Deeds.

Ignorance leads Men into a Party,
   and *Shame* keeps them from getting out again.

❧ JUNE

To each th' appointed Sustenance bestows,
To each the noxious and the healthful shows.
Thou spread'st thy Bounty—meagre Famine flies:
Thou hid'st thy Face—their vital Vigour dies.
Thy pow'rful Word again restores their Breath;
Renew'd Creation triumphs over Death.
Th' Almighty o'er his Works casts down his Eye,
And views their various Excellence with Joy;

[*Cont'd July*

Many have quarrel'd about Religion, that never practis'd it.

Sudden Power is apt to be insolent, *Sudden Liberty* saucy;
    that behaves best which has grown gradually.

He that best understands the World, least likes it.

Haste makes Waste.

❧ JULY

His Works with Rev'rence own his pow'rful Hand,
And humble Nature waits his dread Command,
He looks upon the Earth — her Pillars shake,
And from her Centre her Foundations quake.
The Hills he touches — Clouds of Smoke arise,
And sulph'rous Streams mount heavy to the Skies.
    Whilst Life informs this Frame, that Life shall be
(O First and Greatest!) sacred all to Thee.

[Cont'd Aug.

Anger is never without a Reason,
    but seldom with a good One.

He that is of Opinion Money will do every Thing,
    may well be suspected of doing every Thing for Money.

An ill Wound, but not an ill Name, may be healed.

♌ AUGUST

Thy Praise my Morning Song, my daily Theme,
My Ev'ning Subject, and my Midnight Dream;
When Grief oppresses, and when Pain assails;
When all the Man, and all the Stoic fails;
When fierce Tentation's stormy Billows roll;
When Guilt and Horror overwhelm my Soul;
With outward Ills contending Passions join'd,
To shake frail Virtue, and unhinge the Mind;

[Cont'd Sept.

A lean Award is better than a fat Judgment.

When out of Favour, none know thee;
    when in, thou dost not know thyself.

God, *Parents*, and *Instructors*, can never be requited.

⚘ SEPTEMBER

When Nature sinks, when Death's dark Shades arise,
And this World's Glories vanish from these Eyes;
Then may the Thought of Thee be ever near,
To calm the Tumult, and compose the Fear.
In all my Woes thy Favour my Defence;
Safe in thy Mercy, not my Innocence,
And through what future Scenes thy Hand may guide
My wond'ring Soul, and thro' what States untry'd,

                                 [*Cont'd Oct.*

He that builds before he counts the Cost, acts foolishly; and
    he that counts before he builds, finds he did not count
    wisely.

Patience in Market, is worth Pounds in a Year.

Danger is Sauce for Prayers.

⚘ OCTOBER

What distant Seats soe'er I may explore,
When frail Mortality shall be no more;
If aught of meek or contrite in thy Sight
Shall fit me for the Realms of Bliss and Light,
Be this the Bliss of all my future Days,
To view thy Glories, and to sing thy Praise.
When the dread Hour, ordain'd of old, shall come,
Which brings on stubborn Guilt its righteous Doom,

                                 [*Cont'd Nov.*

If you have no Honey in your Pot, have some in your Mouth.

A Pair of good Ears will drain dry an hundred Tongues.

❧ NOVEMBER

When Storms of Fire on Sinners shall be pour'd,
And all th' Obdurate in thy Wrath devour'd;
May I then hope to find a lowly Place
To stand the meanest of th' etherial Race;
Swift at thy Word to wing the liquid Sky,
And on thy humblest Messages to fly.
Howe'er thy blissful Sight may raise my Soul,
While vast Eternity's long Ages roll,

[*Cont'd Dec.*

Serving God is Doing Good to Man, but Praying is thought
an easier Service, and therefore more generally chosen.

Nothing humbler than *Ambition*, when it is about to climb.

❧ DECEMBER

Perfection on Perfection tow'ring high,
Glory on Glory rais'd, and Joy on Joy,
Each Pow'r improving in the bright'ning Mind,
To humble Virtues, lofty Knowledge join'd;
Be this my highest Aim, howe'er I soar,
Before thy Footstool prostrate to adore,
My brightest Crown before thy Feet to lay,
My Pride to serve, my Glory to obey.

[*Cont'd Jan. 1754*

The discontented Man finds no easy Chair.

Virtue and a Trade, are a Child's best Portion.

Gifts much expected, are *paid*, not *given*.

– – – – It is astonishing, and even frightful to think, that this vast and cumbrous Globe of Earth and Sea, which is almost twenty-five thousand Miles in Circumference, had received such an Impulse from the Almighty Arm, as has carried it constantly for above these five thousand Years, that we know of, round the Sun at the Rate of at least fifty thousand Miles every Hour, which it must absolutely do, to go round the Sun in a Year at the Distance of eighty Millions of Miles from him. So that, if an Angel were to come from some other World, and to place himself near the Earth's Way, he would see it pass by him with a Swiftness, to which that of a Cannon Ball is but as one to one hundred, and would be left behind by it no less than the above Number of Miles in the Space of one Hour. There is no more Reason to doubt, that the Earth goes in this Manner round the Sun, than there would be for a Passenger in a Ship on smooth Water, who saw the Objects upon Land continually passing by, to doubt whether the Vessel he was in, or the Shore, was in Motion. We see the Sun continually changes his Place with respect to the fixed Stars, and must own it to be highly improbable that this Change of Place is owing to any Change in the whole Heavens, which, considering the Distance of the starry Heavens, would require a Motion infinitely more rapid than that above ascribed to the Earth. As for the common Objection against the Earth's Motion, that we are not sensible of it, and that a Stone thrown up from the Earth ought not to fall down upon the same Place again; it is answered at once by the above Comparison of a Ship, from which (as has been often found by Experiment) a Ball fired directly up in the Air, does not fall behind the Ship, let her Motion be ever so swift, but, partaking of the Ship's Motion, is carried forward in the Air, and falls down again upon the Deck. And as to the Objections taken from some Scripture Expressions, which seem to contradict the Theory of the Earth's Motion, it is plain, from innumerable Instances, that Revelation was not given to Mankind to make them Philosophers or deep Reasoners, but to improve them in Virtue and Piety; and that it was therefore proper it should be expressed in a Manner accommodated to common Capacities and popular Opinions in all Points merely speculative, and which were not to have any direct Influence upon the Hearts and Lives of Men – – – – [28a]

How to secure Houses, &c. from LIGHTNING.

It has pleased God in his Goodness to Mankind, at length to discover to them the Means of securing their Habitations and other Buildings from Mischief by Thunder and Lightning. The Method is this: Provide a small Iron Rod (it may be made of the Rod-iron used by the Nailers) but of such a Length, that one End being three or four Feet in the moist Ground, the other may be six or eight Feet above the highest

Part of the Building. To the upper End of the Rod fasten about a Foot of Brass Wire, the Size of a common Knitting-needle, sharpened to a fine Point; the Rod may be secured to the House by a few small Staples. If the House or Barn be long, there may be a Rod and Point at each End, and a middling Wire along the Ridge from one to the other. A House thus furnished will not be damaged by Lightning, it being attracted by the Points, and passing thro the Metal into the Ground without hurting any Thing. Vessels also, having a sharp pointed Rod fix'd on the Top of their Masts, with a Wire from the Foot of the Rod reaching down, round one of the Shrouds, to the Water, will not be hurt by Lightning.

He that whines for Glass without G,
Take away L and that's he.

1754

Poor Richard's *Almanack, &c.*

Kind READER,

I HAVE now serv'd you three Apprenticeships, yet, old as I am, I have no Inclination to quit your Service, but should be glad to be able to continue in it three times three Apprenticeships longer.

The first *Astrologers* I think, were honest Husbandmen; and so it seems are the last; for my Brethren *Jerman*, and *Moore*, and myself, the only remaining Almanack-makers of this Country, are all of that Class: Tho' in intermediate Times our Art has been cultivated in great Cities, and even in the Courts of Princes; witness History, from the Days of King NEBUCHADNEZZAR I. of *Babylon*, to those of Queen JAMES I. of *England*. – – – – But you will ask, perhaps, how I prove that the first Astrologers were Countrymen? – – – – I own this is a Matter beyond the Memory of History, for Astrology was before Letters; but I prove it from the Book of the Heavens, from the Names of the twelve Signs, which were mostly given to remark some Circumstance relative to rural Affairs, in the several successive Months of the Year, and by that Means to supply the Want of Almanacks. – – – – Thus, as the Year of the Ancients began most naturally with the Spring, *Aries* and *Taurus*, that is, the Ram and the Bull, represented the successive Addition to their

Flocks of Sheep and Kine, by their Produce in that Season, Lambs and Calves. – – – – *Gemini* were originally the Kids, but called the Twins, as Goats more commonly bring forth two than one: These follow'd the Calves. – – – – *Cancer*, the Crab, came next, when that Kind of Fish were in Season. – – – – Then follow'd *Leo*, the Lion, and *Virgo*, the Wench, to mark the Summer Months, and Dog-days, when those Creatures were most mischievous. In Autumn comes first *Libra*, the Ballance, to point out the Time for weighing and selling the Summer's Produce; or rather, a Time of Leisure for holding Courts of Justice in which they might plague themselves and Neighbours; I know some suppose this Sign to signify the equal Poise, at that Time, of Day and Night; but the other Signification is the truer, as plainly appears by the following Sign *Scorpio*, or the Scorpion, with the Sting in his Tail, which certainly denotes the Paying of Costs. – – – – Then follows *Sagittary*, the Archer, to show the Season of Hunting; for now the Leaves being off the Trees and Bushes, the Game might be more easily seen and struck with their Arrows. – – – – The *Goat* accompanies the short Days and long Nights of Winter, to shew the Season of Mirth, Feasting and Jollity; for what can *Capricorn* mean, but Dancing or Cutting of *Capers*? – – – – At length comes *Aquarius*, or the Water-bearer, to show the Season of Snows, Rains and Floods; and lastly *Pisces*, or the two Shads, to denote the approaching Return of those Fish up the Rivers: Make your Wears, hawl your Seins; Catch 'em and pickle 'em, my Friends; they are excellent Relishers of old Cyder. – – – – But if you can't get Shad, Mackrell may do better.

I know, gentle Readers, that many of you always expect a Preface, and think yourselves slighted if that's omitted. So here you have it, and much good may't do ye. As little as it is to the Purpose, there are many less so, now-a-days. – – – – I have left out, you see, all the usual Stuff about the *Importunity of Friends*, and the like, or I might have made it much bigger. You think, however, that 'tis big enough o' Conscience, for any Matter of Good that's in it; – – – – I think so too, if it fills the Page, which is the Needful at present, from

Your loving Friend to serve,

R. SAUNDERS.

JANUARY

[*Cont'd from Dec. 1753*

Hail, *infinite* CREATOR! with thy Praise
The Muse began, with thee shall end my Lays,
These are thy Works, blest *Architect* divine!
This *Earth*, and all this beauteous Offspring thine.
Thy Breath first bid *inactive Matter* move,
And strait with Life the genial Atoms strove
Producing *Animal*, and *Plant*, and *Flow'r*,
Concurrent proof of *Wisdom*, and of *Pow'r*.

[*Cont'd Febr.*

The first Degree of Folly, is to conceit one's self wise;
   the second to profess it; the third to despise Counsel.

Take heed of the Vinegar of sweet Wine,
   and the Anger of Good-nature.

FEBRUARY

Thy potent Word infus'd the *solar* Light,
And spread the Curtain of refreshing *Night*;
With splendid *Orbs* enrich'd the *Void* profound,
Rang'd the bright *Worlds*, and roll'd their Courses round.
  O sing his Praises then! How justly due,
Created Kinds, the Strains of Praise from You?
How grateful the deserv'd Returns of Love!
Praise him thou *Earth*, ye *Worlds* that roll above,
Each Pow'r, whole Nature, all his Works, conspire
In Songs of Praise, an universal Choir.

[*Cont'd Mar.*

The Bell calls others to Church,
   but itself never minds the Sermon.

Cut the Wings of your Hens and Hopes,
   lest they lead you a weary Dance after them.

The Cat in Gloves catches no Mice.

Poor Richard: 1754

MARCH

Thou SUN, Creation's pure resplendent Eye;
And all ye *solar Orbs* that deck the Sky,
Round whose vast *Systems*, peopled Planets move.
Ye central Suns of numerous *Earths* above.
Praise the *dread Pow'r*, whose *Goodness* ye proclaim,
And let your warbling Spheres attune his Name.
Thou MOON, who with thy Rays of silver Light,
Dost gild the shapeless Gloom of awful Night;

[*Cont'd Apr.*

In Rivers & bad Governments, the lightest Things
    swim at top.

APRIL

And you *satellitary Orbs* on high,
Who kindly Beams to distant Worlds supply,
Hymn your *Creator*'s Praise, whose Skill divine
Impow'r'd your Mass to roll, your Globes to shine.
Ye *Comets*! that in long Ellipses stray,
Whole Ages finishing your annual Way;
Thou *Darkness*! Nature's *emblematic* Tomb,
Yield him your Reverence of impressive Gloom,
In silent Praise – – – And thou dread *Space* profound,
Thro' all thy waste interminable Bound.

[*Cont'd May*

If you'd know the Value of Money, go and borrow some.

The Horse thinks one thing, and he that saddles him another.

Love thy Neighbour; yet don't pull down your Hedge.

MAY

Winds! who in troubled Air your Voices raise,
Sweet with loud Accents in your *Maker*'s Praise;
And you, soft *Breezes*, that perfume the Spring,
Bear him a Tribute on your gentler Wing.

Spread it, ye pealing *Thunders*, round the Sky,
Wide as your Vollies roll, or *Lightnings* fly.
Ye *Meteors*! your *Creator*'s Praises show;
The spangled *Dew*, the Cloud-reflected *Bow*,

[*Cont'd June*

When *Prosperity* was well mounted, she let go the Bridle,
and soon came tumbling out of the Saddle.

Some make Conscience of wearing a Hat in the Church,
who make none of robbing the Altar.

JUNE

And moist'ning *Show'r*,—ye *Frosts*! his Praise proclaim;
The pendant *Icicle*'s clear native Gem;
Hoar Mists congeal'd, that dress the Meadow pale:
Blue *Vapour*, whitening *Snows*, and pearly *Hail*.
Praise him, ye *Seasons*! *Spring* with youthful Face,
And *Summer* blooming with maturer Grace;
Ripe *Autumn* clad in Vines, with *Harvests* crown'd,
And *Winter* old—his solemn Praise resound.

[*Cont'd July*

In the Affairs of this World Men are saved, not by Faith,
but by the Want of it.

Friendship cannot live with *Ceremony*, nor without *Civility*.

Praise little, dispraise less.

JULY

The *Flow'ry Tribes*, in all their bright Array,
Their lovely Forms and dazzling Hues display.
Ye fruitful Branches! white with vernal Bloom,
In rich Oblations breathe your fresh Perfume.
Praise him, ye *Plants*! with all your sweet Supplies;
Ye od'rous *Herbs*, in grateful Incense rise.
Insects! that creep on Earth, or spread the Wing,
In Troops your tributary Homage bring.

[*Cont'd Aug.*

The learned Fool writes his Nonsense in better Language
than the unlearned; but still 'tis Nonsense.

A Child thinks 20 *Shillings* and 20 Years
can scarce ever be spent.

✠ AUGUST

Fowls of the upper Air! and Brutes supine!
And Fish! that swim the Floods or Ocean Brine.
  Ye *Seraphims*, bright Flames! ye Angel Choirs!
To the lov'd Theme tune all your sounding Lyres.
Saints! thron'd in Bliss, who once convers'd below,
In noblest Strains your loftier Praise bestow.
Man! *Image of thy Maker's moral Pow'r*,
Last, labour'd Work of Heav'n's creating Hour;

[*Cont'd Sept.*

Don't think so much of your own Cunning, as to forget
other Mens: A cunning Man is overmatch'd by a
cunning Man and a Half.

Willows are weak, but they bind the Faggot.

You may give a Man an Office,
but you cannot give him Discretion.

☯ SEPTEMBER

O shall his Goodness, his Indulgence move
No warm Returns, nor swell the Breath of Love?
Priest of the mute Creation, *He* demands
Their Off'rings from thy consecrated Hands,
Deputed *Lord*; – – – from thy dead Slumber part;
Let *Nature* wake, awake the Pow'rs of *Art*,
And with exerted Force attune his Praise,
In Notes may emulate cælestial Lays.
Let *Music* her divinest Succours bring,
The breathing *Flute*, the *Viol's* warbling String,

[*Cont'd Oct.*

He that doth what he should not,
   shall feel what he would not.

To be intimate with a foolish Friend,
   is like going to bed to a Razor.

Little Rogues easily become great Ones.

❧ OCTOBER

And dulcid *Voice* – – – Ye *Concerts* louder grow!
Let the shrill *Trump*, the deep'ning *Organ* blow,
While with the Notes, the tremulating Ground,
And ecchoing Roofs, strike awful Rapture round.
Praise him each Creature, *Plenitude* and *Space*;
Inanimate, and Things of *living Race*.
From the terrestrial to the starry Pole,
Praise him his *Works*, and thou my prostrate Soul!
[*Cont'd Nov.*

You may sometimes be much in the wrong,
   in owning your being in the right.

Friends are the true Sceptres of Princes.

Where Sense is wanting, every thing is wanting.

❧ NOVEMBER

  Thus while in vain the wretched human Brood,
Pursue on Earth a false, imagin'd Good;
That Good, which Creatures never can bestow,
With him still only found from whom they flow;
While *Gold* or *Lust*, with a deceitful Bribe,
Tempt to sure Woes the easy list'ning Tribe;
While *Faction* leads th' unsteady Herd aside,
And *Vanity* perverts the Sons of Pride;
[*Cont'd Dec.*

For Age and Want save while you may;
No Morning Sun lasts a whole Day.

Many Princes sin with *David*, but few repent with him.

He that hath no *ill* Fortune will be troubled with *good*.

ꙮ December

Would I from Vice, from Luxury remove,
Conversing with the Themes of heav'nly Love.
These shall my Hours of virtuous Life amuse,
Cheer its dull Glooms, and brighter Hopes infuse;
Pleas'd the lov'd Visit frequent to renew,
While certain Bliss my rais'd Desires pursue,
To meditate my *Maker*, and my Lays
Tune to his Pow'r, who gave me Breath to praise.
[*Finis*

Learning to the Studious; Riches to the Careful;
  Power to the Bold; Heaven to the Virtuous.

Now glad the Poor with *Christmas* Cheer;
Thank God you're able so to end the Year.

Do not squander Time, for that's what Life is made of.

Of the GREAT *Works* of NATURE

The sixth and outermost of the primary Planets is *Saturn*; he revolves round the Sun in the Space of almost thirty Years, at the Distance of about 800 Millions of Miles. His great Distance from us has hitherto prevented Astronomers from observing his Revolution on his own Axis. To make the Appearance he does to us, at the Distance of above 700 Millions of Miles, he must be several Hundreds of Times larger than the Earth, though his Magnitude is supposed to be much inferior to that of *Jupiter*. There is belonging to this Planet the most extraordinary and unaccountable Phænomenon in Nature, *viz.* A huge bright Circle, or Ring, surrounding his Body, supposed, by the Appearance it makes to us, to be no less than 20,000 Miles broad, and about as many from the Body of the Planet. Whether this amazing Appearance has been occasioned by any Disruption of the Body of the Planet, as our Earth has been by some supposed to have been reduced to her present shattered Condition by the Deluge; or whether this Ring has been designed by the Author of Nature as an original Appendage of the Planet, to encrease their Light, which, according to our Notions, must be very necessary at the Distance of *Saturn*; which of these, I say, or whether either of them is the Case, is not yet known. To the Inhabitants of *Saturn*, if there are any, this Ring must appear to be in the Heavens, and not to belong to the Planet itself. *Saturn* has no less than five Moons, very distinctly visible through a good Telescope, revolving round him. – – – –

To suppose that the Author of Nature had any View to us, when he created these secondary Planets or Moons, and gave them their Revolutions round *Jupiter* and *Saturn*; to imagine that he intended those vast Bodies (for some of those Moons cannot be supposed to be less than the Earth we inhabit) for any Benefit or Advantage to us, which he knew should never be seen by any but a few Astronomers peeping through Telescopes; to imagine, I say, that the divine Wisdom should contrive Things so ill, is as much to his Honour, as if we should suppose he had placed a Sun and planetary System within the Globe of the Earth, and intended it for our Use. But, to return, if there are Inhabitants in *Saturn*, which I know no Reason we have to doubt, their five Moons must not only be of vast Use in increasing their Light, which at that Distance can never, at mid Day, be so bright as our Twilight, but must likewise afford them great Entertainment in observing them as they rise, sometimes altogether, sometimes separately, and as they eclipse one another in their Revolutions. – – – –

Besides the six primary Planets, which revolve round the Sun, – – – – and the ten Secondaries or Moons, – – – – modern Astronomy shews, that there are a great many other stupendous Bodies, called Comets, to be considered as Part of the Solar System – – – – The Comets differ very much in Appearance one from another, and all from the Planets, in that they all look dusky and gloomy, as if surrounded with a very gross Atmosphere, and project behind them, that is, toward the Part of the Heavens that is opposite to the Sun, a Stream of Mist or Vapour, commonly called their Tails. It is most likely that the Tail of a Comet is only its Atmosphere rarified to a great Degree by the extreme Heat of the Sun, on its Approach to him: For it is always observed, that the Tail becomes longer as the Comet approaches nearer to the Sun, and contrariwise. The Tail of the Comet, which appeared in 1680, extended itself over no less than sixty Degrees, or a third Part of our whole Heavens from East to West. To make such an Appearance at the Distance that Comet was supposed to be at, the Tail must have been many Millions of Miles in Length.

Whether these tremendous Bodies, which the Almighty has set a traversing in this fearful Manner through the vast Expanse, be Worlds formerly inhabited, and now reduced to a Chaos, with their wicked Inhabitants left in them in a State of Punishment; or whether they are future Worlds, not yet reduced to an habitable State; or whether they are vast Masses of combustible Matter, made to pass periodically round the Sun, and after a Number of Revolutions, approaching every Time nearer and nearer, as it is supposed some of them do, are at last to drop into the Sun, as an Addition of Fewel to make up for his immense and continual Waste of Light and Heat; or whether they are intended to impregnate from Time to Time the Regions of the Planets with a Quantity of salutary Particles to make up for the Decay or Waste of those necessary Principles; or whether they are form'd to bring about Deluges or Conflagrations, and so prove the Instruments of the Divine Vengeance upon his offending Creatures; whether any of these, I say, be the Design for which infinite Wisdom formed these amazing Bodies, and let them loose to wander through the Sky, is above human Understanding to determine. It is plain, that the Shock of a Body, of the Size of a

Comet, against the Earth, or any of the Planets, moving with the Rapidity they have in their Approach to, or Recess from the Sun, especially if the Motion of both the Comet and Planet should happen to be contrary, must be attended with Consequences frightful beyond all Imagination. But it is highly probable, that even the near Approach of a Comet to the Earth would cause terrible Effects. Our Comfort is, that the whole Machine of Nature is in the Hands of one who knows how to conduct and manage all its vast and unwieldy Parts, and that the Motions of those dreadful Bodies, though to such puny Creatures as we are, they seem the more terrible the more we consider them, are entirely under his Rule and Guidance, and that no one Part of Nature can break loose upon, or bear down another, without his Permission. – – – –

If we consider the immense Distance of the fixed Stars, and consequently, the Magnitude they must be of, to be visible by us at this Distance, we can hardly suppose the Divine Wisdom, which does nothing in vain, has created such Numbers of luminous Bodies, of Magnitudes inconceivable, and at Distances almost infinite, for no other Purpose but to afford us a little glimmering Light in the Night, which could have been done more effectually, and with infinitely less Exertion of creating Power, by one single additional Moon. For what Purpose then shall we suppose such a Profusion of stupendous Luminaries created? In all Probability, or rather without all Doubt, to enlighten innumerable Systems of Worlds, which revolve round them, in the same Manner as our Earth and the other Planets of our System revolve round the Sun. – – – –

If each of those innumerable Millions and Myriads of Luminaries be in fact, as is highly probable, a glorious Sun, a stupendous World of Light and Heat, with its System of Planets, Moons and Comets going round it; and if all those Planets and Moons be Worlds inhabited by various Orders of Beings, enjoying or preparing themselves for such Degrees of Happiness as the divine Wisdom and Goodness has appointed for them; if this, I say, be a just Idea of the Universe (and surely no Idea we can frame is too grand for Omnipotence to produce) we have here a View of that Expanse to which the Epithet VAST, is not improperly given, in our Poem of last Year, and must own, that the Universe, considered in this Manner, is a Theatre truly fit for a God to display his infinite Power, Wisdom and Goodness. But after we have, by Computation, extended the created Universe to a Space containing the greatest Number of Miles human Arithmetic can express, what is that Space to Infinitude? It is even a Point that bears no Proportion to the unbounded and unlimited Presence of the divine Nature. Were an angelic Being to take his Flight from this Part of the Universe, and to proceed in a direct Course with the Swiftness of Light, it is certain, that, should he continue his Flight to all Eternity, he must still find himself in the Centre of the divine Presence. So strictly just, as well as inimitably sublime, are those Expressions of Scripture, "In him we live, and move, and have our Being. There is no flying from his Presence. The Heavens, even the Heaven of Heavens cannot contain him," &c.[28a]

A good Wife lost, is God's Gift lost.

Poor Richard's *Almanack, &c.*

Courteous READER,

IT is a common Saying, that *One Half of the World does not know how the other Half lives*. To add somewhat to your Knowledge in that Particular, I gave you in a former Almanack, an Account of the Manner of living at *Hudson's-Bay*, and the Effects produced by the excessive Cold of that Climate, which seem'd so strange to some of you, that it was taken for a Romance, tho' really authentick. – – – – In this, I shall give you some Idea of a Country under the Torrid Zone, which for the Variety of its Weather (where one would naturally expect the greatest Uniformity) is extreamly remarkable. The Account is extracted from the Journal of Monsieur *Bouguer*, one of the *French* Academicians, sent by their King to measure a Degree of Latitude under the Equinoctial, in order to settle a Dispute between the *English* and *French* Philosophers concerning the Shape of the Earth, others being at the same Time sent for the same Purpose to *Lapland*, under the Polar Circle. – – – – The Mountains in that Country are so lofty, that the highest we have, being compared to them, are mere Mole-hills. This Extract relates chiefly to the Country among those Mountains.

 The Method of this Almanack is the same I have observed for some Years past; only in the third Column the Names of some of the principal fixed Stars are put down against those Days on which they come to the Meridian at nine a Clock in the Evening, whereby those unacquainted, may learn to know them. I am,

Your obliged Friend and Servant,

R. SAUNDERS.

The HAPPY MAN.[29]

Sure Peace is his: A solid Life, estrang'd
To Disappointment and fallacious Hope,
Rich in Content.

THOMSON.

Happy the Man, who free from noisy Sports,
And all the Pomp and Pageantry of Courts:
Far from the venal World can live secure,
Be moral, honest, virtuous – – – – tho' but poor,
Who walking still by Equity's just Rules,
Detesting sordid Knaves, and flatt'ring Fools:
Regarding neither Fortune, Pow'r, nor State,
Nor ever wishing to be vainly great,
Without Malevolence and Spleen can live,
And what his Neighbour wants, with Joy would give;—
A Foe to Pride, no Passion's guilty Friend,
Obeying Nature, faithful to her End;
Severe in Manners, as in Truth severe,
Just to himself, and to his Friends sincere;
His Temper even, and his steady Mind
Refin'd by Friendship, and by Books refin'd.
Some low roof'd Cottage holds the happy Swain,
Unknown to Lux'ry, or her servile Train;
He studying Nature grows serenely wise,
Like *Socrates* he lives, or like him dies.
He asks no Glory gain'd by hostile Arms,
Nor sighs for Grandeur with her painted Charms.
With calm Indiff'rence views the shifting Scene,
Thro' all magnanimous resign'd, serene.
On Hope sustain'd he treads Life's devious Road,

And knows no Fear, except the Fear of GOD.
Would Heav'n indulgent grant my fond Desire,
Thus would I live, and thus should Life expire.

EPITAPH on a worthy Clergyman.

Still like his Master, known by breaking Bread,
The Good he entertain'd, the Needy fed;
Of Humour easy, and of Life unblam'd,
The Friend delighted, while the Priest reclaim'd.
The Friend, the Father, and the Husband gone,
The Priest still lives in this recording Stone;
Where pious Eyes may read his Praises o'er,
And learn each Grace his Pulpit taught before.

EPITAPH on another Clergyman.

Here lies, who need not here be nam'd,
For Theologic Knowledge fam'd;
Who all the Bible had by rote,
With all the Comments Calvin wrote;
Parsons and Jesuits could confute,
Talk Infidels and Quakers mute,
To every Heretick a Foe;
Was he an honest Man? – – So so.

🐝 JANUARY

The FARMER.

O happy he! happiest of mortal Men!
Who far remov'd from Slavery, as from Pride,
Fears no Man's Frown, nor cringing waits to catch
The gracious Nothing of a great Man's Nod;
Where the lac'd Beggar bustles for a Bribe,
The Purchase of his Honour; where Deceit,
And Fraud, and Circumvention, drest in Smiles,

[*Cont'd Febr.*

239

A Man with out a Wife, is but half a Man.

Speak little, do much.

He that would travel much, should eat little.

⊗ February

Hold shameful Commerce, and beneath the Mask
Of Friendship and Sincerity, betray.
Him, nor the stately Mansion's gilded Pride,
Rich with whate'er the imitative Arts,
Painting or Sculpture, yield to charm the Eye;
Nor shining Heaps of massy Plate, enwrought
With curious, costly Workmanship, allure.
Tempted nor with the Pride nor Pomp of Power,

[*Cont'd Mar.*

When the Wine enters, out goes the Truth.

If you would be loved, love and be loveable.

⊗ March

Nor Pageants of Ambition, nor the Mines
Of grasping Av'rice, nor the poison'd Sweets
Of pamper'd Luxury, he plants his Foot
With Firmness on his old paternal Fields,
And stands unshaken. There sweet Prospects rise
Of Meadows smiling in their flow'ry Pride,
Green Hills and Dales, and Cottages embower'd,
The Scenes of Innocence, and calm Delight.

[*Cont'd Apr.*

Ask and have, is sometimes dear buying.

The hasty Bitch brings forth blind Puppies.

⊗ April

There the wild Melody of warbling Birds,
And cool refreshing Groves, and murmuring Springs,

Invite to sacred Thought, and lift the Mind
From low Pursuits, to meditate the God!

RURAL LIFE *in an higher Class.*

But sing, O Muse! the Swain, the happy Swain,
Whom Taste and Nature leading o'er his Fields,

[*Cont'd May*

Where there is Hunger, Law is not regarded; and
  where Law is not regarded, there will be Hunger.

Two dry Sticks will burn a green One.

🐟 MAY

Conduct to every rural Beauty. See!
Before his Footsteps winds the waving Walk,
Here gently rising, there descending slow
Thro' the tall Grove, or near the Water's Brink,
Where Flow'rs besprinkled paint the shelving Bank,
And weeping Willows bend to kiss the Stream.
Now wand'ring o'er the Lawn he roves, and now
Beneath the Hawthorn's secret Shade reclines;

[*Cont'd June*

The honest Man takes Pains, and then enjoys Pleasures;
  the Knave takes Pleasure, and then suffers Pains.

Think of three Things, whence you came, where you are
  going, and to whom you must account.

🐛 JUNE

Where purple Violets hang their bashful Heads,
Where yellow Cowslips, and the blushing Pink,
Their mingled Sweets, and lovely Hues combine.
  Here, shelter'd from the North, his ripening Fruits
Display their sweet Temptations from the Wall,
Or from the gay Espalier; while below,

His various Esculents, from glowing Beds,
Give the fair Promise of delicious Feasts.

[*Cont'd July*

Necessity has no Law; Why? Because
  'tis not to be had without Money.

There was never a good Knife made of bad Steel.

The Wolf sheds his Coat once a Year, his Disposition never.

♜ JULY

There from his forming Hand new Scenes arise,
The fair Creation of his Fancy's Eye.
Lo! bosom'd in the solemn shady Grove,
Whose rev'rend Branches wave on yonder Hill,
He views the Moss-grown Temple's ruin'd Tower,
Cover'd with creeping Ivy's cluster'd Leaves,
The Mansion seeming of some rural God,
Whom Nature's Choristers, in untaught Hymns

[*Cont'd Aug.*

Who is wise? He that learns from every One.
Who is powerful? He that governs his Passions.
Who is rich? He that is content.
Who is that? Nobody.

♞ AUGUST

Of wild yet sweetest Harmony, adore.
From the bold Brow of that aspiring Steep,
Where hang the nibbling Flocks, and view below
Their downward Shadows in the glassy Wave,
What pleasing Landscapes spread before his Eye!
Of scatter'd Villages, and winding Streams,
And Meadows green, and Woods, and distant Spires,
Seeming, above the blue Horizon's Bound,

[*Cont'd Sept.*

A full Belly brings forth every Evil.

The Day is short, the Work great, the Workmen lazy, the
    Wages high, the Master urgeth; Up, then, and be doing.

The Doors of Wisdom are never shut.

⚖ SEPTEMBER

To prop the Canopy of Heaven. Now lost
Amidst a blooming Wilderness of Shrubs,
The golden Orange, Arbute ever green,
The early blooming Almond, feathery Pine,
Fair *Opulus, to Spring, to Autumn dear,
And the sweet Shades of varying Verdure, caught
                                       [*Cont'd Oct.*

Much Virtue in Herbs, little in Men.

The Master's Eye will do more Work than both his Hands.

When you taste Honey, remember Gall.

♋ OCTOBER

From soft *Acacia*'s gently waving Branch,
Heedless he wanders; while the grateful Scents
Of Sweet-briar, Roses, Honeysuckles wild,
Regale the Smell; and to th' enchanted Eye
Mezareon's purple *Laurustinus*' white,
And pale *Laburnum*'s pendent Flow'rs display
Their diff'rent Beauties. O'er the smooth shorn Grass
His lingering Footsteps leisurely proceed,
                                    [*Cont'd Nov.*

Being ignorant is not so much a Shame,
    as being unwilling to learn.

God gives all Things to Industry.

An hundred Thieves cannot strip one naked Man,
    especially if his Skin's off.

**The Gelder Rose.*

✄ NOVEMBER

In Meditation deep:—When, hark! the Sound
Of distant Water steals upon his Ear;
And sudden opens to his pausing Eye
The rapid rough Cascade, from the rude Rock
Down dashing in a Stream of lucid Foam:
Then glides away, meand'ring o'er the Lawn,
A liquid Surface; shining seen afar,
At Intervals, beneath the shadowy Trees;

[*Cont'd Dec.*

Diligence overcomes Difficulties, Sloth makes them.

Neglect mending a small Fault,
    and 'twill soon be a great One.

Bad Gains are truly Losses.

✄ DECEMBER

Till lost and bury'd in the distant Grove.
Wrapt into sacred Musing, he reclines
Beneath the Covert of embow'ring Shades;
And painting to his Mind the bustling Scenes
Of Pride and bold Ambition, pities Kings.

[*Finis*

A long Life may not be good enough,
    but a good Life is long enough.

Be at War with your Vices, at Peace with your Neighbours,
    and let every New-Year find you a better Man.

Virtue may not always make a Face handsome,
but Vice will certainly make it ugly.

1756

Poor Richard's *Almanack, &c.*

PREFACE

Courteous READER,

I SUPPOSE my Almanack may be worth the Money thou hadst paid for it, hadst thou no other Advantage from it, than to find the *Day of the Month*, the *remarkable Days*, the *Changes of the Moon*, the *Sun and Moon's Rising and Setting*, and to foreknow the *Tides* and the *Weather*; these, with other Astronomical Curiosities, I have yearly and constantly prepared for thy Use and Entertainment, during now near two Revolutions of the Planet *Jupiter*. But I hope this is not all the Advantage thou hast reaped; for with a View to the Improvement of thy *Mind* and thy *Estate*, I have constantly interspers'd in every little Vacancy, *Moral Hints, Wise Sayings,* and *Maxims of Thrift*, tending to impress the Benefits arising from *Honesty, Sobriety, Industry* and *Frugality*; which if thou hast duly observed, it is highly probable thou art *wiser* and *richer* many fold more than the Pence my Labours have cost thee. Howbeit, I shall not therefore raise my Price because thou art better able to pay; but being thankful for past Favours, shall endeavor to make my little Book more worthy thy Regard, by adding to those *Recipes* which were intended for the *Cure* of the *Mind*, some valuable Ones regarding the *Health* of the *Body*. They are recommended by the Skilful, and by successful Practice. I wish a Blessing may attend the Use of them, and to thee all Happiness, being

Thy obliged Friend,

R. SAUNDERS.

JANUARY

ASTRONOMY, hail, Science heavenly born!
Thy Schemes the Life assist, the Mind adorn.
To changing Seasons give determin'd Space,
And fix to Hours and Years their measur'd Race
The pointing *Dial*, on whose figur'd Plane,
Of Time's still Flight we Notices obtain;
The *Pendulum*, dividing lesser Parts,
Their Rise acquire from thy inventive Arts.[30]

[*Cont'd Febr.*

A Change of *Fortune* hurts a wise Man no more than
a Change of the *Moon*.

There is no Virtue, the Honour whereof gets a Man more Envy, than that of *Justice*, because it procures great Authority among the common People; they only revere the Valiant, and admire the Wise, while they truly love Just Men; for in these they have intire Trust and Confidence, but of the former, they always fear one, and mistrust the other. They look on Valour as a certain natural Ferment of the Mind, and Wisdom as the Effect of a fine Constitution, or a happy Education; but a Man has it in his own Power to be just; and that is the Reason it is so dishonourable to be otherwise; as *Waller* handsomely expresses it,

Of all the Virtues, Justice *is the best,*
Valour, without it, is a common Pest;
Pirates and Thieves, too oft with Courage *grac'd,*
Shew us how ill that Virtue may be plac'd;
'Tis Constitution makes us chaste *and* brave,
Justice *from Reason and from Heav'n we have;*
Our other Virtues dwell but in the Blood,
That in the Soul, and gives the Name of Good.[31]

Receipt against the HEART-BURN.

The Heart-burn is an uneasy Sensation of Heat in the Stomach, occasioned by Indigestion, which is the Mother of Gout, Rheumatism, Gravel and Stone. – – – – *To prevent it*, Eat no Fat, especially what is burnt or oily; and neither eat or drink any thing sour or acid. – – – – *To cure it*, Dissolve a Thimble-full of Salt or Wormwood in a Glass of Water, and drink it.

⁂ FEBRUARY

Th' acute *Geographer*, th' *Historian* sage,
By thy Discov'ries clear the doubtful Page.
From mark'd Eclipses, *Longitude* perceive,
Can settle *Distances*, and Æra's give.
From his known Shore the Seaman distant far,
Steers, safely guided, by thy *Polar Star*;
Nor errs, when Clouds and Storms obscure its Ray,
His Compass marks him as exact a Way.

[*Cont'd Mar.*

Does Mischief, Misconduct, & Warrings displease ye;
Think there's a Providence, 'twill make ye easy.

Mine is better than *Ours*.

Religion is so far from barring Men any innocent Pleasure, or Comfort of human Life, that it *purifies* the Pleasures of it, and renders them more *grateful* and generous; and besides this, it brings mighty Pleasures of its own, those of a *glorious Hope*, a *serene Mind*, a *calm* and *undisturbed Conscience*, which far out-relish the most studied artificial Luxuries. – – – – But here after,

How will the sensual Mind *its Loss sustain,*
When its gross Objects *shall be sought in vain?*
Incapable to act its darling Lust,
Yet spurr'd and prompted by a sharper Gust;
Pain'd for its Choice, would still its Choice resume,
Which (by sure Want) but more augments the Doom,
Made by wise Heav'n at one conjunctive Time,

247

Its Wish *and* Grief, *its* Punishment *and* Crime.
Nought there the destin'd *Wretched e'er shall find*
To please the Senses, or relieve the Mind;
No luscious Banquet, or delicious Bowl,
To drown, in lewd Excess, th' intemperate Soul;
Nor gay Amusement more, nor jovial Throng,
That to their thoughtless Hours did once belong![32]

An excellent Application for a FRESH BURN.

Beat or scrape *Irish* Potatoes to a soft pulpy Mass; mix some common Salt finely powder'd; and apply it cool to the Part. When it grows warm or dry, apply a fresh Quantity.

MARCH

When frequent Travels had th' instructive Chart
Supply'd, the Prize of Philosophic Art!
Two curious mimic Globes, to Crown the Plan,
Were form'd; by his CREATOR's Image, Man.
The first, with Heav'n's bright Constellations vast,
Rang'd on the Surface, with th' Earth's Climes *the last*.
Copy of this by human Race possest,
Which Lands indent, and spacious Seas invest.

[*Cont'd Apr.*

Love your Enemies, for they tell you your Faults.

He that has a Trade, has an Office of Profit and Honour.

The Wit of Conversation consists more in finding it in others, than shewing a great deal yourself. He who goes out of your Company pleased with his own Facetiouness and Ingenuity, will the sooner come into it again. Most Men had rather *please* than *admire* you and seek less to be *instructed* and *diverted*, than *approved* and *applauded*; and it is certainly the most delicate Sort of Pleasure, to *please another*.

But that Sort of *Wit*, which employs itself insolently in Criticising and Censuring the Words and Sentiments of others in Conversation, is absolute *Folly*; for it answers none of the Ends of Conversation. He who uses it, neither *improves others*, is *improved* himself, or *pleases* any one. How amiably contrary is POPE's Character of a Critic.

– – – – *the Man who Counsel can bestow,*
Still pleas'd to teach, and yet not proud to know?
Unbias'd, or by Favour, or by Spite;
Not dully prepossess'd, or blindly right;
Tho' learn'd, well-bred; and tho' well bred, sincere;
Modestly bold, and humanly severe:
Who to a Friend his Faults can freely show,
And gladly praise the Merit of a Foe;
Blest with a Taste exact, yet unconfin'd,
A Knowledge both of Books and human Kind;
Gen'rous Converse, a Soul exempt from Pride,
And Love to praise, and Reason on its Side.
Such once were Critics, *such the happy Few,*
Athens *and* Rome *in better Ages knew.*[33]

There are three faithful Friends—an old Wife,
an old Dog and ready Money.

🐂 APRIL

Fram'd on imaginary Poles to move,
With Lines, and different Circles mark'd above.
The pleasur'd Sense, by this Machine can tell,
In what Position various Nations dwell:
Round the wide Orb's exterior Surface spread;
How side-ways some the solid Convex tread:
While a more sever'd Race of busy Pow'rs
Project, with strange Reverse, their Feet to ours.

[*Cont'd May*

Be civil to *all*; serviceable to *many*; familiar with few;
   Friend to *one*; Enemy to *none*.

Vain-Glory flowereth, but beareth no Fruit.

As I spent some Weeks last Winter, in visiting my old Acquaintance in the *Jerseys*, great Complaints I heard for Want of Money, and that Leave to make more Paper Bills could not be obtained. *Friends and Countrymen*, my Advice on this Head shall cost you nothing, and if you will not be angry with me for giving it, I promise you not to be offended if you do not take it.

You spend yearly at least *Two Hundred Thousand Pounds*, 'tis said, in *European*, *East-Indian*, and *West-Indian* Commodities. Supposing one Half of this Expence to be in *Things absolutely necessary*, the other Half may be call'd *Superfluities*, or at best, Conveniences, which however you might live without for one little Year, and not suffer exceedingly. Now to save this Half, observe these few Directions.

1. When you incline to have new Cloaths, look first well over the old Ones, and see if you cannot shift with them another Year, either by Scouring, Mending, or even Patching if necessary. Remember a Patch on your Coat, and Money in your Pocket, is better and more creditable than a Writ on your Back, and no Money to take it off.

2. When you incline to buy China Ware, Chinces, *India* Silks, or any other of their flimsey slight Manufactures; I would not be so hard with you, as to insist on your absolutely *resolving against it*; all I advise, is, to *put it off* (as you do your Repentance) *till another Year*; and this, in some Respects, may prevent an Occasion of Repentance.

3. If you are now a Drinker of Punch, Wine or Tea, twice a Day; for the ensuing Year drink them but *once* a Day. If you now drink then but once a Day, do it but every other Day. If you do it now but once a Week, reduce the Practice to once a Fortnight. And if you do not exceed in Quantity as you lessen the Times, half your Expence in these Articles will be saved.

4thly and lastly, When you incline to drink Rum, fill the Glass *half* with Water.

Thus at the Year's End, there will be *An Hundred Thousand Pounds* more Money in your Country.

If Paper Money in ever so great a Quantity could be made, no Man could get any of it without giving something for it. But all he saves in this Way, will be *his own for nothing*; and his Country actually so much richer. Then the Merchants old and doubtful Debts may be honestly paid off, and Trading become surer thereafter, if not so extensive.

♊ May

So on the Apple's smooth suspended Ball,
(If greater we may represent by small)
The swarming Flies their reptile Tribes divide,
And cling Antipodal on every side.
Hence pleasant Problems may the Mind discern
Of ev'ry Soil their Length of Days to learn;
Can tell when round, to each fix'd Place, shall come,
Faint Dawn, Meridian Light, or Midnight Gloom.

[*Cont'd June*

Laws *too gentle* are seldom *obeyed*;
too severe, seldom *executed*.

Trouble springs from *Idleness*; *Toil* from *Ease*.

Love, and be *loved*.

♋ June

These Gifts to astronomic Art we owe,
Its Use extensive, yet its Growth but slow.
If back we look on ancient Sages Schemes,

They seem ridiculous as Childrens Dreams;
How shall the Church, that boasts unerring Truth,
Blush at the Raillery of each modern Youth,
When told her *Pope**, of Heresy arraign'd
The Sage†, who Earth's Rotation once maintain'd?

[*Cont'd July*

A wise Man will desire no more, than what he may get justly, use soberly, distribute chearfully, and leave contentedly.

The diligent Spinner has a large Shift.

LEWIS CORNARO, a *Venetian* of Quality and Learning, wrote a Book of the *Benefits* of a *sober Life*, and produced himself as a Testimony. He says, to the fortieth Year of his Age, he was continually perplex'd with Variety of *Infirmities*; at last he grew so careful of his Diet, that in one Year, he was almost freed from all his Diseases, and never after used Physick: He continued thus temperate all the rest of his Life, sound, chearful and vegete, and was so entire and perfect in his Strength at fourscore Years, as to be able to walk, ride, hunt, and perform every Office of Life as well as in his Youth. At length he died in his Chair, with very little Pain or Sickness, all his Senses being entire to the last, tho' in the 120th Year of his Age.

– – – – Mark, what Blessings flow
From frugal temperate Meals; 'tis they bestow
That prime of Blessings, HEALTH. *All will confess*
That various Meats the Stomach much oppress.
All may reflect how light, *how* well *they were,*
When plain and simple was their chearful Fare.
Who down to Sleep from a short Supper lies,
Can to the next Day's Business chearful rise,
Or jovially indulge, when the round Year
Brings back the festal Day to better Chear,
Or when his wasted Strength he would restore
When Years approach, and Age's feeble Hour
A softer Treatment claim. But if in Prime

---

* *Urban* VIII.   † *Galileo.*

Of Youth and Health, you take, before your Time,
The Luxuries of Life, where is their Aid
When Age and Sickness shall your Strength invade.

❧ JULY

Vain *Epicurus*, and his frantic Class,
Misdeem'd our Globe a plane quadrangle Mass;
A fine romantic Terras, spread in State,
On central Pillars that support its Weight;
Like *Indian Sophs*, who this terrestrial Mould,
Affirm, four sturdy Elephants uphold.
The Sun, new ev'ry Morn, flat, small of Size,
Just what it measures to the naked Eyes.

[Cont'd Aug.

A false Friend and a Shadow,
   attend only while the Sun shines.

To-morrow, every Fault is to be amended;
   but that *To-morrow* never comes.

It is observable that God has often called Men to Places of Dignity and Honour, when they have been busy in the honest Employment of their Vocation. *Saul* was seeking his Father's Asses, and *David* keeping his Father's Sheep when called to the Kingdom. The Shepherds were feeding their Flocks, when they had their glorious Revelation. God called the four Apostles from their Fishery, and *Matthew* from the Receipt of Custom; *Amos* from among the Herdsmen of *Tekoah*, *Moses* from keeping *Jethro*'s Sheep, *Gideon* from the Threshing Floor, *&c.* God never encourages Idleness, and despises not Persons in the meanest Employments.[34]

Learn of the Bees, see to their Toils they run
In clust'ring Swarms, and labour in the Sun:
See 'em instruct in Work their buzzing Race,
The Sweets to gather, and to form the Mass.
The busy Nation flies from Flow'r to Flow'r,
And hoards, in curious Cells, the golden Store.

The little Ant (Example too, to Man
Of Care and Labour) gathers all she can,
And brings it to enlarge her Heap at Home,
Against the Winter, which she knows will come.
 Man's Understanding, dull'd by Idleness,
Contracts a Rust, that makes it daily less.
Unless you often plow the fruitful Field,
No Grain, but mix'd with Thistles, will it yield.
Ill runs the Horse, and hindmost in the Race,
Who long has been unpractic'd in the Chace.

AUGUST

As pos'd the *Stagyrite*'s dark School appears,
Perplex'd with Tales devis'd of *Chrystal Spheres*,
Strange *solid Orbs*, and *Circles* oddly fram'd;
Who with Philosophy their Reveries nam'd.
How long did *Ptolomy*'s dark Riddle spread,
With Doubts deep puzzling each scholastic Head,
Till, like the *Theban* wise in Story fam'd,
COPERNICUS that *Sphynxian* Monster sham'd;

[*Cont'd Sept.*

Plough deep, while Sluggards sleep;
And you shall have Corn, to sell and to keep.

He that sows Thorns, should never go barefoot.

Cornaro, among other Advantages arising from *Temperance*, mentions this as a material one, that a Man by out living his Competitors, arrives at higher Dignities, and more profitable Employments, and by keeping his Mind clear, and his Body in Health, improves his Knowledge and Abilities, and can execute those Employments with greater Reputation. He might have added, That by living long, a Man long enjoys the Reputation and Fame he may have acquired. - - - - *Aristotle* was much more famous after his Death than during his Life; but *Newton*, who lived to the Age of 85, had been 60 Years a distinguish'd Philosopher, and many Years before he dy'd was universally esteem'd and admir'd. If Praise be, as *Plato* said, the sweetest Kind of Music,

Newton long enjoy'd a *Concert* of that Music; and the following Lines were by many thought not too extravagant for his *Epitaph.*

Approach, ye wise of Soul, with Awe divine,
'Tis Newton's *Name that consecrates this Shrine!*
That Sun *of Knowledge, whose meridian Ray*
Kindled the Gloom of Nature into Day!
That Soul of Science! That unbounded Mind!
That Genius, which exalted human Kind!
Confest supreme of Men! his Country's Pride!
And half esteem'd an Angel, till he dy'd;
Who in the Eye of Heav'n like Enoch *stood,*
And thro' the Paths of Knowledge walk'd with GOD;
Who made his Fame, a Sea without a Shore,
And but forsook one World to know the Laws of more.

Serving God is Doing Good to Man, but Praying is thought
an easier Service, and therefore more generally chosen.

❧ SEPTEMBER

He the true Planetary System taught,
Which the learn'd *Samian* first from *Egypt* brought;
Long from the World conceal'd, in Error lost,
Whose rich Recovery latest Times shall boast.
Then TYCHO rose, who with incessant Pains,
In their due Ranks replac'd the starry Trains,
His Labours by a fresh Industry mov'd,
HEVELIUS, FLAMSTEAD, HALLEY, since improv'd.

[*Cont'd Oct.*

Laziness travels so slowly, that *Poverty* soon overtakes him.

Sampson with his *strong Body*, had a *weak Head*,
or he would not have laid it in a Harlot's Lap.

Simplicity, Innocence, Industry, Temperance, are Arts that lead to Tranquility, as much as Learning, Knowledge, Wisdom and Contemplation. A *noble Simplicity* in Discourse is a Talent rare, and above the Reach of ordinary Men. Genius, Fancy, Learning, Memory, *&c.* are so far from helping, that they often hinder the Attaining of it.

By the Word *Simplicity*, is not always meant *Folly* or *Ignorance*; but often, pure and upright Nature, free from Artifice, Craft or deceitful Ornament. In this Sense *Pope* uses it, in the Epitaph he made for his Friend *Gay*, too beautiful and instructive to be here omitted.[35]

Of Manners gentle, of Affections mild,
In Wit a Man, Simplicity *a Child.*
Words ever pleasing, yet sincerely true,
Satire still just, and Humour ever new.
Above Temptation, in a low Estate,
And uncorrupted, ev'n *among the Great.*
A safe *Companion, and an easy Friend,*
Belov'd thro' Life, lamented in thy End:
These are thy Honours; – – – – *Not that here thy Bust*
Is mix'd with Heroes, or with Kings thy Dust;
But that the Worthy, and the Good shall say,
Striking their pensive Bosoms, Here lies GAY.

❧ OCTOBER

The *Lyncean* GALILEO then aspires
Thro' the rais'd Tube to mark the Stellar fires!
The *Galaxy* with clust'ring Lights o'erspread,
The new-nam'd Stars in bright *Orion*'s Head,
The varying *Phases* circling Planets show,
The *Solar Spots*, his Fame was first to know.
Of *Jove's Attendants*, Orbs till then unknown,
Himself the big Discovery claims alone.

[*Cont'd Nov.*

When a Friend deals with a Friend
Let the Bargain be clear and well penn'd,
That they may continue Friends to the End.

He that never eats too much, will never be lazy.

When an Army is to march thro' a Wilderness, where the Conveniences of Life are scarce to be obtained even for Money, many *Hardships*, *Wants* and *Difficulties* must necessarily be borne by the Soldiers; which nothing tends more to make tolerable, than the *Example* of their Officers. If *these* riot in Plenty, while *those* suffer Hunger and Thirst, Respect and Obedience are in Danger of being lost, and Mutiny or Desertion taking their Places. *Charles* the XIIth of *Sweden*, thus still'd a growing Clamour about *bad Bread* in his March thro' the Wilds of *Tartary*: The Soldiers complained of it, and presented him a Sample of what was daily distributed to them, mouldy as it was, and half rotten. He received it coolly, examined it, and said, *'Tis bad indeed, but it may be eaten.* And to prove his Words, he immediately ate it himself. *Lucan* gives us a glorious Picture of *Cato*, leading his Army thro' the parched Desarts of *Lybia*,

> *Foremost, on Foot, he treads the burning Sand,*
> *Bearing his Arms in his own patient Hand:*
> *Scorning another's weary Neck to press,*
> *Or in a lazy Chariot loll at Ease.*
> *The panting Soldier to his Toil succeeds,*
> *Where no Command but great Example leads.*
> *Sparing of Sleep, still for the rest he wakes,*

And at the Fountain last his Thirst he slakes:
Whene'er by Chance, some living Stream is found,
He stands, and sees the cooling Draughts go round,
Stays till the last and meanest Drudge be past,
And, till his Slaves have drank, disdains to taste.[36]

❧ NOVEMBER

CASSINI next, and HUYGENS, like renown'd,
The *Moons* and wondrous *Ring of Saturn* found.
Sagacious KEPLER, still advancing saw
Th' *elliptic Motion*, Nature's plainest Law,
That universal acts thro' every Part.
This laid the Basis of *Newtonian* Art.
NEWTON! vast Mind! whose piercing Pow'rs apply'd
The secret Cause of Motion first descry'd;
Found Gravitation was the primal Spring,
That wheel'd the Planets round their central King.

[*Cont'd Dec.*

To be *proud* of *Knowledge*, is to be *blind* with *Light*; to be
proud of *Virtue*, is to *poison* yourself with the *Antidote*.

Get what you can, and what you get, hold;
'Tis the *Stone* that will turn all your Lead into Gold.

There is really a great Difference in *Things* sometimes where there seems to be but little Distinction in *Names*. The *Man* of Honour is an internal, the *Person* of Honour an external, the one a real, the other a fictitious, Character. A *Person* of Honour may be a profane Libertine, penurious, proud, may insult his Inferiors, and defraud his Creditors; but it is impossible for a *Man* of Honour to be guilty of any of these. The *Person* of Honour may flatter for Court Favours, or cringe for Popularity; he may be *for* or *against* his Country's Good, as it suits his private Views. But the *Man* of Honour can do none of these. – – – – He

Upright and firm, and steady to his Trust,
Inflexible to Ill, and obstinately just;
The Fury of the Populace defies,

And dares the Tyrant's threatning Frown despise.
Always himself, nought can his Virtue move,
Unsway'd by Party, Hatred, Gain, or Love.
So the tall Summit of Olympus *knows,*
Nor raging Hurricanes, nor hoary Snows;
But high, in the superior Skies, is seen,
Above the Clouds, eternally serene;
While at its steady Foot, the rushing Rain
And rattling Thunder spend their Force in vain.[37]

DECEMBER

Mysterious Impulse! that more clear to know,
Exceeds the finite Reach of Art below.
Forbear, bold Mortal! 'tis an impious Aim;
Own GOD immediate acting thro' the Frame.
'Tis HE, unsearchable, in all resides;
HE the FIRST CAUSE their Operations guides,
Fear on his awful Privacy to press,
But, honouring HIM, thy Ignorance confess.

[*Finis*

An honest Man will receive neither *Money* nor *Praise*,
that is not his Due.

Saying and *Doing*, have quarrel'd and parted.

Tell me my Faults, and mend your own.

Well, my Friend, thou art now just entering the last Month of
another Year. If thou art a Man of Business, and of prudent Care, belike thou wilt now settle thy Accounts, to satisfy thyself whether thou
has gain'd or lost in the Year past, and how much of either, the better to
regulate thy future Industry or thy common Expences. This is com-
mendable.—But it is not all.—Wilt thou not examine also thy *moral*
Accompts, and see what Improvements thou hast made in the Conduct
of Life, what Vice subdued, what Virtue acquired; how much *better*,
and how much *wiser*, as well as how much *richer* thou art grown? What
shall it *profit* a Man, if he *gain* the whole World, and *lose* his own Soul?

Without some Care in this Matter, tho' thou may'st come to count thy Thousands, thou wilt possibly still appear poor in the Eyes of the Discerning, even *here*, and be really so for ever *hereafter*.

> *Of Man's miraculous Mistakes, this bears*
> *The Palm, "That all Men are about to live,"*
> *For ever on the Brink of being born.*
> *How excellent that Life they mean to lead!*
> *All Promise is poor dilatory Man,*
> *And that thro' every Stage. When young, indeed,*
> *In full Content, we, sometimes, nobly rest,*
> *Unanxious for ourselves; and only wish*
> *As duteous Sons, our Fathers were more wise.*
> *At Thirty Man suspects himself a Fool;*
> *Knows it at Forty, and reforms his Plan;*
> *At Fifty chides his infamous Delay,*
> *Pushes his prudent Purpose to Resolve;*
> *In all the Magnanimity of Thought*
> *Resolves; and re-resolves; then dies the same.*[38]

Experience keeps a dear School, but Fools will learn
in no other, and scarce in that.

Poor Richard's Almanack, &c.

Courteous READER,

AS no temporal Concern is of more Importance to us than *Health*, and that depends so much on the Air we every Moment breathe, the Choice of a good wholesome Situation to fix a Dwelling in, is a very serious Affair to every Countryman about to begin the World, and well worth his Consideration, especially as not only the *Comfort* of Living, but even the *Necessaries of Life*, depend in a great Measure upon it; since a Family frequently sick can rarely if ever thrive. – – – –

'Tis a Pleasure to me to be any way serviceable in communicating useful Hints to the Publick; and I shall be obliged to others for affording me the Opportunity of enjoying that Pleasure more frequently, by sending me from time to time such of their own Observations, as may be advantageous if published in the Almanack.

I am thy obliged Friend,

RICHARD SAUNDERS.

How to make a STRIKING SUNDIAL, *by which not only a Man's own Family, but all his Neighbours for ten Miles round, may know what a Clock it is, when the Sun shines, without seeing the Dial.*

Chuse an open Place in your Yard or Garden, on which the Sun may shine all Day without any Impediment from Trees or Buildings.

On the Ground mark out your Hour Lines, as for a horizontal Dial, according to Art, taking Room enough for the Guns. On the Line for One o'Clock, place one Gun; on the Two o'Clock Line two Guns, and so of the rest. The Guns must all be charged with Powder, but Ball is unnecessary. Your Gnomon or Style must have twelve burning Glasses annex'd to it, and be so placed as that the Sun shining through the Glasses, one after the other, shall cause the Focus or burning Spot to fall on the Hour Line of One, for Example, at one a Clock, and there kindle a Train of Gunpowder that shall fire one Gun. At Two a Clock, a Focus shall fall on the Hour Line of Two, and kindle another Train that shall discharge two Guns successively; and so of the rest.

Note, There must be 78 Guns in all. Thirty-two Pounders will be best for this Use; but 18 Pounders may do, and will cost less, as well as use less Powder, for nine Pounds of Powder will do for one Charge of each eighteen Pounder, whereas the Thirty-two Pounders would require for each Gun 16 Pounds.

Note also, That the chief Expence will be the Powder, for the Cannon once bought, will, with Care, last 100 Years.

Note moreover, That there will be a great Saving of Powder in cloudy Days.

Kind Reader, Methinks I hear thee say, *That is indeed a good Thing to know how the Time passes, but this Kind of Dial, notwithstanding the mentioned Savings, would be very expensive; and the Cost greater than the Advantage.* Thou art wise, my Friend, to be so considerate beforehand; some Fools would not have found out so much, till they had made the Dial and try'd it. – – – – Let all such learn that many a private and many a publick Project, are like this *Striking Dial*, great Cost for little Profit.

🐂 JANUARY

CONVERSATION *HINTS.*[39]

Good Sense and Learning may Esteem obtain,
Humour and Wit a Laugh, if rightly ta'en;
Fair Virtue Admiration may impart;
But 'tis GOOD-NATURE only wins the Heart:
It molds the Body to an easy Grace,
And brightens every Feature of the Face;

It smooths th' unpolish'd Tongue with Eloquence,
And adds Persuasion to the finest Sense.

[*Cont'd Febr.*

He that would rise at Court, must begin by Creeping.

Many a Man's own Tongue gives Evidence
  against his Understanding.

Nothing dries sooner than a Tear.

When a Man looks back upon his Day, Week or Year spent, and finds his Business has been worthy the Dignity of human Nature, it exhilarates and revives him, enables him to pass his own Approbation on himself, and, as it were, to anticipate the *Euge*, the *Well done, good and faithful Servant*, he shall one Day receive from his great Master. But he that gives himself only the idle Devertisements of a Child, cannot reflect on Time past without Confusion; and is forced to take Sanctuary in a total Inconsideration, or run from one Amusement to another, to avoid Thinking, or answering to himself the Question, *What have I done?* Idleness, and its Amusements are in the End more tiresome than Labour itself.[40]

Uneasy both in Country and in Town,
They search a Place to lay their Burthen down:
One, restless in his Parlour, walks abroad,
And vainly thinks to leave behind his Load;
But strait returns; for he's as restless there,
And finds there's no Relief in open Air.
To's Country Seat another would retire,
And spurs as hard as if it were on Fire,
There soon begins to yawn, and stretch and snore,
And seeks the City which he left before.

⚏ FEBRUARY

Would you both please, and be instructed too,
The Pride of shewing forth yourself subdue.
Hear ev'ry Man upon his fav'rite Theme,
And ever be more knowing than you seem.

The lowest Genius will afford some Light,
Or give a Hint that had escap'd your Sight.
Doubt, till he thinks you on Conviction yield,
And with fit Questions let each Pause be fill'd.
And the most knowing will with Pleasure grant,
You're rather much reserv'd than ignorant.

[*Cont'd Mar.*

'Tis easier to build two Chimneys, than maintain one in Fuel.

Anger warms the Invention, but overheats the Oven.

Is there any Duty in Religion more generally agreed on, or more justly required by God, than a perfect Submission to his Will in all Things? Can any Disposition of Mind, either please him more, or become us better, than that of being satisfied with all he gives, and content with all he takes away? None, certainly, can be of more Honour to God, nor of more Ease to ourselves; for if we consider him as our Maker, we dare not contend with him; if as our Father, we ought not to mistrust him; so that we may be confident whatever he does is for our Good, and whatever happens that we interpret otherwise, yet we can get nothing by Repining, nor save any thing by Resisting.[41]

'Tis done, O Lord, the Idol I resign,
Unfit to share a Heart so justly thine;
Nor can the heav'nly Call unwelcome be,
That still invites my Soul more near to thee:
Ye Shades, ye Phantoms, and ye Dreams adieu!
With Smiles, I now your parting Glories view.
I see the Hand; I worship, I adore,
And justify the great disposing Power.

RULES of LAW fit to be Observed in purchasing.

From an old Book.

First, see the Land which thou intend'st to buy,
Within the Seller's Title clear doth lie.
And that no Woman to it doth lay Claim,
By Dowry, Jointure, or some other Name,
That it may cumber. Know if bound or free

The Tenure stand, and that from each Feoffee
It be releas'd: That the Seller be so old
That he may lawful sell, thou lawful hold.
Have special Care that it not mortgag'd lie,
Nor be entailed on Posterity.
Then if it stand in Statute bound or no:
Be well advis'd what Quit-Rent out must go;
What Custom, Service hath been done of old,
By those who formerly the same did hold.
And if a wedded Woman put to Sale,
Deal not with her, unless she bring her Male.
For she doth under Covert-Baron go,
Altho' sometimes some also traffick so.
Thy Bargain being made, and all this done,
Have special Care to make thy Charter run
To thee, thine Heirs, Executors, Assigns,
For that beyond thy Life securely binds.
These Things foreknown and done, you may prevent
Those Things rash Buyers many times repent.
And yet, when as you have done all you can,
If you'd be sure, deal with an honest Man.

Very good Rules, these, and sweetly sung. If they are learnt by heart, and repeated often to keep them in Memory, they may happen to save the Purchaser more Pence than the price of my Almanack. In Imitation of this old Writer, I have Thoughts of turning *Coke's Institutes*, and all our Province Laws into Metre, hoping thereby to engage some of our young Lawyers and old Justices to *read a little*.

MARCH

The Rays of Wit gild wheresoe'er they strike,
But are not therefore fit for all alike;
They charm the lively, but the Grave offend,
And raise a Foe as often as a Friend;
Like the resistless Beams of blazing Light,
That chear the strong, and pain the weakly Sight.

If a bright Fancy therefore be your Share,
Let Judgment watch it with a Guardian's Care.

[*Cont'd Apr.*

It is Ill-Manners to silence a Fool, and Cruelty
   to let him go on.

Scarlet, Silk and Velvet, have put out the Kitchen Fire.

APRIL

'Tis like a Torrent, apt to overflow,
Unless by constant Government kept low;
And ne'er inefficacious passes by,
But overturns or gladdens all that's nigh.
Or else, like Trees, when suffer'd wild to shoot,
That put forth much, but all unripen'd Fruit;
It turns to Affectation and Grimace,
As like to Wit as Gravity to Grace.

[*Cont'd May*

He that would catch Fish, must venture his Bait.

Men take more pains to mask than mend.

One *To-day* is worth two *To-morrows*.

Since Man is but of a very limited Power in his own Person, and consequently can effect no great Matter merely by his own personal Strength, but as he acts in Society and Conjunction with others; and since no Man can engage the active Assistance of others, without first engaging their Trust; And moreover, since Men will trust no further than they judge one, for his *Sincerity*, fit to be trusted; it follows, that a discovered Dissembler can atchieve nothing great or considerable. For not being able to gain Mens Trust, he cannot gain their Concurrence; and so is left alone to act singly and upon his own Bottom; and while that is the Sphere of his Activity, all that he can do must needs be contemptible.

Sincerity *has such resistless Charms,*
She oft the fiercest of our Foes disarms:
No Art she knows, in native Whiteness dress'd.

Her Thoughts all pure, and therefore all express'd:
She takes from Error its Deformity;
And without her all other Virtues die.
Bright Source of Goodness! to my Aid descend,
Watch o'er my Heart, and all my Words attend.[42]

✿ MAY

How hard soe'er it be to bridle *Wit*,
Yet *Mem'ry* oft no less requires the Bit:
How many, hurried by its Force away,
For ever in the Land of Gossips stray!
Usurp the Province of the Nurse, to lull,
Without her Privilege for being dull!
Tales upon Tales they raise, ten Stories high,
Without Regard to Use or Symmetry.

[*Cont'd June*

The way to be safe, is never to be secure.

Dally not with other Folks Women or Money.

Work as if you were to live 100 years,
Pray as if you were to die To-morrow.

It is generally agreed to be Folly, *to hazard the Loss of a Friend,* *rather than lose a Jest.* But few consider how easily a Friend may be thus lost. Depending on the known Regard their Friends have for them, Jesters take more Freedom with Friends than they would dare to do with others, little thinking how much deeper we are wounded by an Affront from one we love. But the strictest Intimacy can never warrant Freedoms of this Sort; and it is indeed preposterous to think they should; unless we can suppose Injuries are less Evils when they are done us by Friends, than when they come from other Hands.

Excess of Wit may oftentimes beguile:
Jests are not always pardon'd – – – by a Smile.
Men may disguise their Malice at the Heart,
And seem at Ease – – – tho' pain'd with inward Smart.
Mistaken, we – – think all such Wounds of course

Reflection cures; – – alas! it makes them worse.
Like Scratches they with double Anguish seize,
Rankle with time, and fester by Degrees.

But sarcastical Jests on a Man's Person or his Manners, tho' hard to bear, are perhaps more easily borne than those that touch his Religion. Men are generally warm in what regards their religious Tenets, either from Tenderness of Conscience, or a high Sense of their own Judgments. People of plain Parts and honest Dispositions, look on Salvation as too serious a Thing to be jested with; and Men of speculative Religion, who profess from the Conviction rather of their Heads than Hearts, are not a bit less vehement than the real Devotees. He who says a slight or a severe Thing of their Faith, seems to them to have thereby undervalued their Understandings, and will consequently incur their Aversion, which no Man of common Sense would hazard for a lively Expression; much less a person of good Breeding, who should make it his chief Aim to be well with all.

Like some grave Matron of a noble Line,
With awful Beauty does Religion shine.
Just Sense should teach us to revere the Dame,
Nor, by imprudent Jests, to spot her Fame.
In common Life you'll own this Reas'ning right,
That none but Fools in gross Abuse delight:
Then use it here – – – nor think the Caution vain,
To be polite, *Men need not be profane.*

JUNE

A Story should, to please, at least seem true,
Be apropos, well told, concise, and new;
And whensoe'er it deviates from these Rules,
The Wise will sleep, and leave Applause to Fools.
But others, more intolerable yet,
The Waggeries that they've said, or heard, repeat;
Heavy by Mem'ry made, and what's the worst,
At second-hand as often as at first.

[*Cont'd July*

Pride breakfasted with *Plenty*, dined with *Poverty*,
  supped with *Infamy*.

Retirement does not always secure Virtue;
  Lot was upright in the City, wicked in the Mountain.

🐾 JULY

But above all Things, *Raillery* decline,
Nature but few does for that Task design;
'Tis in the ablest Hand a dangerous Tool,
But never fails to wound the meddling Fool:
For all must grant it needs no common Art
To keep Men patient while we make them smart.
Not *wit* alone, nor *Humour*'s self, will do,
Without *Good nature*, and *much Prudence* too.
                                    [*Cont'd Aug.*

Idleness is the Dead Sea, that swallows all Virtues: Be active
  in Business, that *Temptation* may miss her Aim: The Bird
  that sits, is easily shot.

Shame and the *Dry-belly-ach* were Diseases of the last Age;
  this seems to be cured of them.

In studying Law or Physick, or any other Art or Science, by which
you propose to get your Livelihood, though you find it at first hard, difficult and unpleasing, use *Diligence*, *Patience* and *Perseverance*; the Irk-
somness of your Task will thus diminish daily, and your Labour shall
finally be crowned with Success. You shall go beyond all your Competitors who are careless, idle or superficial in their Acquisitions, and be
at the Head of your Profession. – – – – *Ability* will command *Business*,
Business Wealth; and *Wealth* an easy and honourable *Retirement* when
Age shall require it.

Near to the wide extended Coasts of Spain,
Some Islands triumph o'er the raging Main;
Where dwelt of old, as tuneful Poets say,
Slingers, *who bore from all the Prize away.*
While Infants yet, their feeble Nerves they try'd;

269

Nor needful Food, till won by Art, supply'd.
Fix'd was the Mark, the Youngster oft in vain,
Whirl'd the misguided Stone with fruitless Pain:
'Till, by long Practice, to Perfection brought,
With easy Sleight their former Task they wrought.
Swift from their Arm th' unerring Pebble flew,
And high in Air, the flutt'ring Victim slew.
So in each Art Men rise but by Degrees,
And Months of Labour lead to Years of Ease.

⚜ AUGUST

Of all the Qualities that help to raise
In Men the universal Voice of Praise,
Whether in Pleasure or in Use they end,
There's none that can with MODESTY contend.
Yet 'tis but little that its *Form* be caught,
Unless its *Origin* be first in Thought;
Else rebel Nature will reveal the Cheat,
And the whole Work of Art at once defeat.

[*Cont'd Sept.*

Tho' the Mastiff be gentle, yet bite him not by the Lip.

Great-Almsgiving, lessens no Man's Living.

The royal Crown cures not the Head-ach.

On the *Freedom* of the PRESS.

While free from Force the Press remains,
Virtue and Freedom *chear our Plains,*
And Learning *Largesses bestows,*
And keeps unlicens'd open House.
We to the Nation's publick Mart
Our Works of Wit, and Schemes of Art,
And philosophic Goods, this Way,
Like Water carriage, cheap convey.
This Tree *which* Knowledge *so affords,*

Inquisitors with flaming Swords
From Lay-Approach with Zeal defend,
Lest their own Paradise should end.

The Press *from her fecundous Womb*
Brought forth the Arts of Greece *and* Rome;
Her Offspring, skill'd in Logic War,
Truth's *Banner wav'd in open Air;*
The Monster Superstition *fled,*
And hid in Shades her Gorgon Head;
And awless Pow'r, *the long kept Field,*
By Reason *quell'd, was forc'd to yield.*

This Nurse of Arts and Freedom's Fence,
To chain, is Treason against Sense:
And Liberty, *thy thousand Tongues*
None silence who design no Wrongs;
For those that use the Gag's Restraint,
First rob, before they stop Complaint.[43]

❦ SEPTEMBER

Hold forth upon yourself on no Pretence,
Unless invited, or in Self-Defence;
The Praise you take, altho' it be your Due,
Will be suspected, if it come from you.
If to seem modest, you some Faults confess,
The World suspect yet more, and never less:
For each Man, by Experience taught, can tell
How strong a Flatterer does within him dwell.

[*Cont'd Oct.*

Act uprightly, and despise Calumny; Dirt may stick to
a Mud Wall, but not to polish'd Marble.

PARADOXES.

I. The *Christians* observe the *first* Day of the Week for their *Sunday*, the *Jews* the *Seventh* for their Sabbath, the *Turks* the *sixth* Day of the Week for the Time of their Worship; but there is a particular Place of the Globe, to which if a *Christian*, *Jew*, and *Turk* sail in one and the same Ship, they shall keep the Time for their Worship on different Days, as above, all the Time they are sailing to that particular Place; but when they arrive at that Place, and during the Time they remain at it, they shall all keep their Sabbath on one and the same Day; but when they depart from that Place, they shall all differ as before.

II. There is a certain Port, from which if three Ships depart at one and the same time, and sail on three particular different Courses, till they return to the Port they departed from; and if in one of these Ships be *Christians*, in the second *Jews*, and in the third *Turks*, when they return to the Port they departed from, they shall differ so with respect to real and apparent Time, that they all shall keep their Sabbath on one and the same Day of the Week, and yet each of them separately shall believe that he keeps his Sabbath on the Day of the Week his Religion requires.

❧ OCTOBER

No part of Conduct asks for Skill more nice,
Tho' none more common, than to give *Advice*:
Misers themselves, in this will not be saving,
Unless their Knowledge makes it worth the having.
And where's the Wonder, when we will intrude,
An useless Gift, it meets Ingratitude?
Shun then, unask'd, this arduous Task to try;
But, if consulted, use Sincerity.

[Cont'd Nov.

The *Borrower* is a Slave to the *Lender*; the *Security* to *both*.

Singularity in the right, hath ruined many: Happy those
who are convinced of the general Opinion.

Ambition to be greater and richer, merely that a Man may have it in his Power to do more Service to his Friends and the Publick, is of a quiet orderly Kind, pleased if it succeeds, resigned if it fails. But the *Ambition* that has *itself* only in View, is restless, turbulent, regardless of publick Peace, or general Interest, and the secret Maker of most Mischiefs, between Nations, Parties, Friends and Neighbours.

Let Satyr blast, with every Mark of Hate,
The vain Aspirer, or dishonest Great.
Whom Love of Wealth, or wild Ambition's Sway
Push forward, still regardless of the Way;
High and more high who aim with restless Pride,
Where neither Reason nor fair Virtue guide;
And Him, the Wretch, who labours on with Pain,
For the low Lucre of an useless Gain,
(Wise but to get, and active but to save)
May Scorn deserv'd still follow to the Grave.
*   But he who fond to raise a splendid Name,*
On Life's ambitious Heights would fix his Fame,
In active Arts or ventrous Arms would shine,
Yet shuns the Paths which Virtue bids decline;
Who dignifies his Wealth by gen'rous Use,
To raise th' Oppress'd, or Merit to produce,
Reason's impartial Voice shall ne'er condemn,
The glorious Purpose of so wise an Aim.[44]

❧ NOVEMBER

Be rarely warm in Censure or in Praise;
Few Men deserve our Passion either ways:
For half the World but floats 'twixt Good and Ill,
As Chance disposes Objects, these the Will;
'Tis but a see-saw Game, where Virtue now
Mounts above Vice, and then sinks down as low.
Besides, the Wise still hold it for a Rule,
To trust that Judgment most, that seems most cool.

[*Cont'd Dec.*

Proportion your Charity to the Strength of your Estate,
    or God will proportion your Estate to the Weakness
    of your Charity.

The Tongue offends, and the Ears get the Cuffing.

Some antient Philosophers have said, that Happiness depends more
on the inward Disposition of Mind than on outward Circumstances;

and that he who cannot be happy in any State, can be so in no State. To be happy, they tell us we must be content. Right. But they do not teach how we may become content. *Poor Richard* shall give you a short good Rule for that. *To be content, look backward on those who possess less than yourself, not forward on those who possess more.* If this does not make you *content*, you don't deserve to be *happy*.

CONTENTMENT! *Parent of Delight,*
So much a Stranger to our Sight,
Say, Goddess, in what happy Place
Mortals behold thy blooming Face;
Thy gracious Auspices impart,
And for thy Temple chuse my Heart.
They whom thou deignest to inspire,
Thy Science learn, to bound Desire;
By happy Alchymy of Mind
They turn to Pleasure all they find.
Unmov'd when the rude Tempest blows,
Without an Opiate they repose;
And, cover'd by your Shield, defy
The whizzing Shafts that round them fly;
Nor, meddling with the Gods Affairs,
Concern themselves with distant Cares;
But place their Bliss in mental Rest,
And feast upon the Good possest.[45]

☙ DECEMBER

Would you be well receiv'd where'er you go,
Remember each Man vanquish'd is a Foe:
Resist not therefore to your utmost Might,
But let the Weakest think he's sometimes right;
He, for each Triumph you shall thus decline,
Shall give ten Opportunities to shine;
He sees, since once you own'd him to excel,
That 'tis his Interest you should reason well.
[*Finis*

Sleep without Supping, and you'll rise without owing for it.

When other Sins grow old by Time,
Then Avarice is in its prime,
Yet feed the Poor at *Christmas* time.

Learning is a valuable Thing in the Affairs of this Life, but of infinitely more Importance is *Godliness,* as it tends not only to make us happy here but hereafter. At the Day of Judgment, we shall not be asked, what Proficiency we have made in Languages or Philosophy; but whether we have liv'd virtuously and piously, as Men endued with Reason, guided by the Dictates of Religion. In that Hour it will more avail us, that we have thrown a Handful of Flour or Chaff in Charity to a Nest of contemptible Pismires, than that we could muster all the Hosts of Heaven, and call every Star by its proper Name. For then the Constellations themselves shall disappear, the Sun and Moon shall give no more Light, and all the Frame of Nature shall vanish. But our good or bad Works shall remain for ever, recorded in the Archives of Eternity.

Unmov'd alone the Virtuous *now appear,*
And in their Looks a calm Assurance wear.
From East, from West, from North and South they come,
To take from the most righteous Judge their Doom;
Who thus, to them, with a serene Regard;
(The Books of Life before him laid,
And all the secret Records wide display'd)
"According to your Works be your Reward:
Possess immortal Kingdoms as your Due,
Prepar'd from an eternal Date for you."

Of the expected COMET.

The great Blazing-star or Comet, which appeared in 1531, 1607, and 1682, is expected by Astronomers to return and appear again in this Year, or the next, for its Periods are somewhat unequal, and so cannot be exactly ascertained like those of the Planets which are more regular and better known. According to its last Period, its next Perihelion should be in *July* 1757; but the Length of that before would make it *October* 25, 1758.

As these huge tremendous Bodies travel thro' our System, they seem fitted to produce great Changes in it. Mr. *Whiston* has gone a good Way towards proving that the Comet of 1668, was, in one of its Revolutions, the Cause of the Deluge, by coming so near this Earth as to raise a vast Tide in the Abyss, by which the Shell was broke, and the whole overflowed; the Comet too was then in its Approach towards the Sun, and he supposes its Atmosphere crouded with the watery Vapours it had gathered in those inconceivably cold Regions, into which it had fled off in its Aphelion, and so produced the mentioned Rains. The same Comet Sir *Isaac Newton* has calculated, when in its Perihelion *December* the 8th, was heated by its Nearness to the Sun to a Degree 2000 times more hot than red hot Iron, and would require 50,000 Years to cool again. This same Comet, Dr. *Halley* observed *Nov.* 11, was not above a Semidiameter of the Earth from the Earth's Way; so that had the Earth at that time been in that Part of its Orbit, something very extraordinary might have happened either by Water or Fire.

Should a Comet in its Course strike the Earth, it might instantly beat it to Pieces, or carry it off out of the Planetary System. The great Conflagration may also, by Means of a Comet, be easily brought about; for as some of them are supposed to be much bigger than this Globe we live on, if one should meet with us in its Return from the Sun, all the Disputes between the Powers of Europe would be settled in a Moment; the World, to such a Fire, being no more than a Wasp's Nest thrown into an Oven.

But our Comfort is, the same great Power that made the Universe, governs it by his Providence. And such terrible Catastrophes will not happen till 'tis best they should. – – – – In the mean time, we must not presume too much on our own Importance. There are an infinite Number of Worlds under the divine Government, and if this was annihilated it would scarce be miss'd in the Universe.

> GOD *sees with equal Eye, as Lord of all,*
> *A Hero perish, or a Sparrow fall.*
> *Atoms, or Systems, into Ruin hurl'd,*
> *And now a Bubble burst, – – and now a World!*

1758

Poor Richard's *Almanack, &c.*

Courteous READER,

I HAVE heard that nothing gives an Author so great Pleasure, as to find his Works respectfully quoted by other learned Authors. This Pleasure I have seldom enjoyed; for tho' I have been, if I may say it without Vanity, an *eminent Author* of Almanacks annually now a full Quarter of a Century, my Brother Authors in the same Way, for what Reason I know not, have ever been very sparing in their Applauses; and no other Author has taken the least Notice of me, so that did not my Writings produce me some solid *Pudding*, the great Deficiency of *Praise* would have quite discouraged me.

I concluded at length, that the People were the best Judges of my Merit; for they buy my Works; and besides, in my Rambles, where I am not personally known, I have frequently heard one or other of my Adages repeated, with, *as Poor Richard says*, at the End on't; this gave me some Satisfaction, as it showed not only that my Instructions were regarded, but discovered likewise some Respect for my Authority; and I own, that to encourage the Practice of remembering and repeating those wise Sentences, I have sometimes *quoted myself* with great Gravity.

Judge then how much I must have been gratified by an Incident I am going to relate to you. I stopt my Horse lately where a great Number of People were collected at a Vendue of Merchant Goods. The Hour of Sale not being come, they were conversing on the Badness of the Times, and one of the Company call'd to a plain clean old Man, with white Locks, *Pray, Father* Abraham, *what think you of the Times? Won't these heavy Taxes quite ruin the Country? How shall we be ever able to pay them? What would you advise us to?* – – – – Father *Abraham* stood up, and reply'd, If you'd have my Advice, I'll give it you in short, for a *Word to the Wise is enough*, and *many Words won't fill a Bushel*, as *Poor Richard* says. They join'd in desiring him to speak his Mind, and gathering round him, he proceeded as follows;[46]

"Friends, says he, and Neighbours, the Taxes are indeed very heavy, and if those laid on by the Government were the only Ones we had to pay, we might more easily discharge them; but we have many others, and much more grievous to some of us. We are taxed twice as much by our *Idleness*, three times as much by our *Pride*, and four times as much by our *Folly*, and from these Taxes the Commissioners cannot ease or deliver us by allowing an Abatement. However let us hearken to good Advice, and something may be done for us; *God helps them that help themselves*, as *Poor Richard* says, in his Almanack of 1733.

It would be thought a hard Government that should tax its People one tenth Part of their *Time*, to be employed in its Service. But *Idleness* taxes many of us much more, if we reckon all that is spent in absolute *Sloth*, or doing of nothing, with that which is spent in idle Employments or Amusements, that amount to nothing. *Sloth*, by bringing on Diseases, absolutely shortens Life. *Sloth, like Rust, consumes faster than Labour wears, while the used Key is always bright*, as *Poor Richard* says. But *dost thou love Life, then do not squander Time, for that's the Stuff Life is made of*, as *Poor Richard* says. – – – – How much more than is necessary do we spend in Sleep! forgetting that *The sleeping Fox catches no Poultry*, and that *there will be sleeping enough in the Grave*, as *Poor Richard* says. If Time be of all Things the most precious, *wasting Time* must be, as *Poor Richard* says, *the greatest Prodigality*, since, as he elsewhere tells us, *Lost Time is never found again*; and what we call *Time-enough, always proves little enough.* Let us then up and be doing, and doing to the Purpose; so by Diligence shall we do more with less Perplexity. *Sloth makes all Things difficult, but Industry all easy*, as *Poor Richard* says; and *He that riseth late, must trot all Day, and shall scarce overtake his Business at Night.* While *Laziness travels so slowly, that*

Poverty soon overtakes him, as we read in *Poor Richard*, who adds, *Drive thy Business, let not that drive thee*; and *Early to Bed, and early to rise, makes a Man healthy, wealthy, and wise.*

So what signifies *wishing* and *hoping* for better Times. We may make these Times better if we bestir ourselves. *Industry need not wish*, as *Poor Richard* says, and *He that lives upon Hope will die fasting. There are no Gains, without Pains*; then *Help Hands, for I have no Lands*, or if I have, they are smartly taxed. And, as *Poor Richard* likewise observes, *He that hath a Trade hath an Estate*, and *He that hath a Calling hath an Office of Profit and Honour*; but then the *Trade* must be worked at, and the *Calling* well followed, or neither the *Estate*, nor the *Office*, will enable us to pay our Taxes. – – – – If we are industrious we shall never starve; for, as *Poor Richard* says, *At the working Man's House* Hunger *looks in, but dares not enter.* Nor will the Bailiff or the Constable enter, for *Industry pays Debts, while Despair encreaseth them*, says *Poor Richard.* – – – – What though you have found no Treasure, nor has any rich Relation left you a Legacy, *Diligence is the Mother of Good-luck*, as *Poor Richard* says, *and God gives all Things to Industry.* Then *plough deep, while Sluggards sleep, and you shall have Corn to sell and to keep*, says *Poor Dick.* Work while it is called To-day, for you know not how much you may be hindered To-morrow, which makes *Poor Richard* say, *One To-day is worth two To-morrows*; and farther, *Have you somewhat to do To-morrow, do it To-day.* If you were a Servant, would you not be ashamed that a good Master should catch you idle? Are you then your own Master, *be ashamed to catch yourself idle*, as *Poor Dick* says. When there is so much to be done for yourself, your Family, your Country, and your gracious King, be up by Peep of Day; *Let not the Sun look down and say, Inglorious here he lies.* Handle your Tools without Mittens; remember that *the Cat in Gloves catches no Mice*, as *Poor Richard* says. 'Tis true there is much to be done, and perhaps you are weak handed, but stick to it steadily, and you will see great Effects, for *constant Dropping wears away Stones*, and by *Diligence and Patience the Mouse ate in two the Cable*; and *little Strokes fell great Oaks*, as *Poor Richard* says in his Almanack, the Year I cannot just now remember.

Methinks I hear some of you say, *Must a Man afford himself no Leisure?* – – – – I will tell thee, my Friend, what *Poor Richard* says, *Employ thy Time well if thou meanest to gain Leisure*; and, *since thou art not sure of a Minute, throw not away an Hour.* Leisure, is Time for doing something useful; this Leisure the diligent Man will obtain, but the lazy Man never; so that, as *Poor Richard* says, a *Life of Leisure and a Life of Laziness are two Things.* Do you imagine that Sloth will afford you more Comfort than Labour? No, for as *Poor Richard* says, *Trouble springs from Idleness, and grievous Toil from needless Ease. Many without Labour, would live by their* WITS *only, but they break for want of Stock.* Whereas Industry gives Comfort, and Plenty, and Respect: *Fly Pleasures, and they'll follow you. The diligent Spinner has a large Shift;* and *now I have a Sheep and a Cow, every Body bids me Good morrow;* all which is well said by *Poor Richard.*

But with our Industry, we must likewise be *steady, settled* and *careful,* and oversee our own Affairs *with our own Eyes,* and not trust too much to others; for, as *Poor Richard* says,

> *I never saw an oft removed Tree,*
> *Nor yet an oft removed Family,*
> *That throve so well as those that settled be.*

And again, *Three Removes is as bad as a Fire;* and again, *Keep thy Shop, and thy Shop will keep thee;* and again, *If you would have your Business done, go; If not, send.* And again,

> *He that by the Plough would thrive,*
> *Himself must either hold or drive.*

And again, *The Eye of a Master will do more Work than both his Hands;* and again, *Want of Care does us more Damage than Want of Knowledge;* and again, *Not to oversee Workmen, is to leave them your Purse open.* Trusting too much to others Care is the Ruin of many; for, as the *Almanack* says, *In the Affairs of this World, Men are saved, not by Faith, but by the Want of it;* but a Man's own Care is profitable; for, saith *Poor Dick, Learning is to the Studious,* and *Riches to the Careful,* as well as *Power to the Bold,* and *Heaven to the Virtuous.* And farther, *If you would have a faithful Servant, and one that you like, serve yourself.* And again, he adviseth to Circumspection and Care, even in the smallest Matters, because sometimes *a little Neglect may breed great Mischief;* adding, *For want of a Nail the Shoe was lost; for want of a Shoe the Horse was lost; and for want of a Horse the Rider was lost,* being overtaken and slain by the Enemy, all for want of Care about a Horse-shoe Nail.

So much for Industry, my Friends, and Attention to one's own Business; but to these we must add *Frugality*, if we would make our *Industry* more certainly successful. A Man may, if he knows not how to save as he gets, *keep his Nose all his Life to the Grindstone*, and die not worth a *Groat* at last. *A fat Kitchen makes a lean Will*, as *Poor Richard* says; and,

> *Many Estates are spent in the Getting,*
> *Since Women for Tea forsook Spinning and Knitting,*
> *And Men for Punch forsook Hewing and Splitting.*

If you would be wealthy, says he, in another Almanack, *think of Saving as well as of Getting: The* Indies *have not made* Spain *rich, because her* Outgoes *are greater than her* Incomes. Away then with your expensive Follies, and you will not have so much Cause to complain of hard Times, heavy Taxes, and chargeable Families; for, as *Poor Dick* says,

> *Women and Wine, Game and Deceit,*
> *Make the Wealth small, and the Wants great.*

And farther, *What maintains one Vice, would bring up two Children.* You may think perhaps, That a *little* Tea, or a *little* Punch now and then, Diet a *little* more costly, Clothes a *little* finer, and a *little* Entertainment now and then, can be no *great* Matter; but remember what *Poor Richard* says, *Many a* Little *makes a Mickle*; and farther, *Beware of* little *Expences; a small Leak will sink a great Ship*; and again, *Who Dainties love, shall Beggars prove*; and moreover, *Fools make Feasts, and wise Men eat them.*

A small Leak will sink a great Ship.

Here you are all got together at this Vendue of *Fineries* and *Knick-nacks*. You call them *Goods*, but if you do not take Care, they will prove

Evils to some of you. You expect they will be sold *cheap*, and perhaps they may for less than they cost; but if you have no Occasion for them, they must be *dear* to you. Remember what *Poor Richard* says, *Buy what thou hast no Need of, and ere long thou shalt sell thy Necessaries.* And again, *At a great Pennyworth pause a while*: He means, that perhaps the Cheapness is *apparent* only, and not *real*; or the Bargain, by straitning thee in thy Business, may do thee more Harm than Good. For in another Place he says, *Many have been ruined by buying good Pennyworths.* Again, *Poor Richard* says, *'Tis foolish to lay out Money in a Purchase of Repentance*; and yet this Folly is practised every Day at Vendues, for want of minding the Almanack. *Wise Men*, as *Poor Dick* says, *learn by others Harms, Fools scarcely by their own; but, Felix quem faciunt aliena Pericula cautum.* Many a one, for the Sake of Finery on the Back, have gone with a hungry Belly, and half starved their Families; *Silks and Sattins, Scarlet and Velvets*, as *Poor Richard* says, *put out the Kitchen Fire.* These are not the *Necessaries* of Life; they can scarcely be called the *Conveniencies*, and yet only because they look pretty, how many *want* to *have* them. The *artificial* Wants of Mankind thus become more numerous than the *natural*; and, as *Poor Dick* says, *For one poor Person, there are an hundred* indigent. By these, and other Extravagancies, the Genteel are reduced to Poverty, and forced to borrow of those whom they formerly despised, but who through *Industry* and *Frugality* have maintained their Standing; in which Case it appears plainly, that a *Ploughman on his Legs is higher than a Gentleman on his Knees*, as *Poor Richard* says. Perhaps they have had a small Estate left them, which they knew not the Getting of; they think *'tis Day, and will never be Night*; that a little to be spent out of *so much*, is not worth minding; (*a Child and a Fool*, as *Poor Richard* says, *imagine* Twenty Shillings *and* Twenty Years can never be spent) but, *always taking out of the Meal-tub, and never putting in, soon comes to the Bottom*; then, as *Poor Dick* says, *When the Well's dry, they know the Worth of Water.* But this they might have known before, if they had taken his Advice; *If you would know the Value of Money, go and try to borrow some*; for, *he that goes a borrowing goes a sorrowing*; and indeed so does he that lends to such People, when he goes *to get it in again.*—*Poor Dick* farther advises, and says,

> *Fond* Pride of Dress, *is sure a very Curse;*
> *E'er* Fancy *you consult, consult your Purse.*

And again, *Pride is as loud a Beggar as Want, and a great deal more saucy.* When you have bought one fine Thing you must buy ten more, that your Appearance may be all of a Piece; but *Poor Dick* says, '*Tis easier to* suppress *the first Desire, than to* satisfy *all that follow it.* And 'tis as truly Folly for the Poor to ape the Rich, as for the Frog to swell, in order to equal the Ox.

> *Great Estates may venture more,*
> *But little Boats should keep near Shore.*

'Tis however a Folly soon punished; for *Pride that dines on Vanity sups on Contempt*, as *Poor Richard* says. And in another Place, *Pride break- fasted with Plenty, dined with Poverty, and supped with Infamy.* And after all, of what Use is this *Pride of Appearance*, for which so much is risked, so much is suffered? It cannot promote Health, or ease Pain; it makes no Increase of Merit in the Person, it creates Envy, it hastens Mis- fortune.

> *What is a Butterfly? At best*
> *He's but a Caterpillar drest.*
> *The gaudy Fop's his Picture just,*

as *Poor Richard* says.

But what Madness must it be to *run in Debt* for these Superfluities! We are offered, by the Terms of this Vendue, *Six Months Credit*; and that perhaps has induced some of us to attend it, because we cannot spare the ready Money, and hope now to be fine without it. But, ah, think what you do when you run in Debt; *You give to another Power over your Liberty.* If you cannot pay at the Time, you will be ashamed to see your Creditor; you will be in Fear when you speak to him; you will make poor pitiful sneaking Excuses, and by Degrees come to lose your Veracity, and sink into base downright lying; for, as *Poor Richard* says, *The second Vice is Lying, the first is running in Debt.* And again, to the same Purpose, *Lying rides upon Debt's Back.* Whereas a freeborn *Eng- lishman* ought not to be ashamed or afraid to see or speak to any Man living. But Poverty often deprives a Man of all Spirit and Virtue: '*Tis hard for an empty Bag to stand upright*, as *Poor Richard* truly says. What would you think of that Prince, or that Government, who should issue an Edict forbidding you to dress like a Gentleman or a Gentlewoman, on Pain of Imprisonment or Servitude? Would you not say, that you are free, have a Right to dress as you please, and that such an Edict would be a Breach of your Privileges, and such a Government tyrannical? And yet you are about to put yourself under that Tyranny when you run in Debt for such Dress! Your Creditor has Authority at his Pleasure to deprive you of your Liberty, by confining you in Gaol for Life, or to sell you for a Servant, if you should not be able to pay him! When you have got your Bargain, you may, perhaps, think little of Payment; but *Creditors, Poor Richard tells us, have better Memories than Debtors*; and in another Place says, *Creditors are a superstitious Sect, great Observers of set Days and Times*. The Day comes round before you are aware, and the Demand is made before you are prepared to satisfy it. Or if you bear your Debt in Mind, the Term which at first seemed so long, will, as it lessens, appear extreamly short. *Time* will seem to have added Wings to his Heels as well as Shoulders. *Those have a short Lent*, saith *Poor Richard, who owe Money to be paid at Easter*. Then since, as he says, *The Borrower is a Slave to the Lender, and the Debtor to the Creditor*, disdain the Chain, preserve your Freedom; and maintain your Independency: Be *industrious* and *free*; be *frugal* and *free*. At present, perhaps, you may think yourself in thriving Circumstances, and that you can bear a little Extravagance without Injury; but,

> *For Age and Want, save while you may;*
> *No Morning Sun lasts a whole Day,*

as *Poor Richard* says. – – – – Gain may be temporary and uncertain, but ever while you live, Expence is constant and certain; and *'tis easier to build two Chimnies than to keep one in Fuel*, as *Poor Richard* says. So *rather go to Bed supperless than rise in Debt*.

> *Get what you can, and what you get hold;*
> *'Tis the Stone that will turn all your Lead into Gold,*

as *Poor Richard* says. And when you have got the Philosopher's Stone, sure you will no longer complain of bad Times, or the Difficulty of paying Taxes.

   This Doctrine, my Friends, is *Reason* and *Wisdom*; but after all, do not depend too much upon your own *Industry*, and *Frugality*, and *Prudence*, though excellent Things, for they may all be blasted without the Blessing of Heaven; and therefore ask that Blessing humbly, and be not uncharitable to those that at present seem to want it, but comfort and help them. Remember *Job* suffered, and was afterwards prosperous.

And now to conclude, *Experience keeps a dear School, but Fools will learn in no other, and scarce in that*; for it is true, *we may give Advice, but we cannot give Conduct*, as *Poor Richard* says: However, remember this, *They that won't be counselled, can't be helped*, as *Poor Richard* says: And farther, That *if you will not hear Reason, she'll surely rap your Knuckles*.

Thus the old Gentleman ended his Harangue. The People heard it, and approved the Doctrine, and immediately practised the contrary, just as if it had been a common Sermon; for the Vendue opened, and they began to buy extravagantly, notwithstanding all his Cautions, and their own Fear of Taxes. – – – – I found the good Man had thoroughly studied my Almanacks, and digested all I had dropt on those Topicks during the Course of Five-and-twenty Years. The frequent Mention he made of me must have tired any one else, but my Vanity was wonderfully delighted with it, though I was conscious that not a tenth Part of this Wisdom was my own which he ascribed to me, but rather the *Gleanings* I had made of the Sense of all Ages and Nations. However, I resolved to be the better for the Echo of it; and though I had at first determined to buy Stuff for a new Coat, I went away resolved to wear my old One a little longer. *Reader*, if thou wilt do the same, thy Profit will be as great as mine.

I am, as ever,

Thine to serve thee,

RICHARD SAUNDERS.

July 7, 1757.

JANUARY

On AMBITION.

I know, young Friend, *Ambition* fills your Mind,
And in Life's Voyage is th' impelling Wind;
But at the Helm let sober Reason stand,
And steer the Bark with Heav'n-directed Hand:
So shall you safe *Ambition*'s Gales receive,
And ride securely, tho' the Billows heave;
So shall you shun the giddy Hero's Fate,
And by her Influence be both good and great.

[*Cont'd Febr.*

One *Nestor* is worth two *Aiaxes*.

When you're an Anvil, hold you still;
When you're a Hammer, strike your Fill.

☙ FEBRUARY

She bids you first, in Life's soft vernal Hours,
With active Industry wake Nature's Powers;
With rising Years, still rising Arts display,
With new-born Graces mark each new-born Day.
'Tis now the Time young Passion to command,
While yet the pliant Stem obeys the Hand;
Guide now the Courser with a steady Rein,
E'er yet he bounds o'er Pleasure's flow'ry Plain;
In Passion's Strife, no Medium you can have;
You rule a Master, or submit a Slave.

[*Cont'd Mar.*

When Knaves betray each other, one can scarce be blamed,
 or the other pitied.

He that carries a small Crime easily, will carry it on
 when it comes to be an Ox.

☙ MARCH

"For whom those Toils," you may perhaps enquire;
First for *yourself.* Next Nature will inspire,
The filial Thought, fond Wish, and Kindred Tear,
Which make the Parent and the Sister dear:
To these, in closest Bands of Love, ally'd,
Their Joy and Grief you live, their Shame or Pride;
Hence timely learn to make their Bliss your own,
And scorn to think or act for Self *alone*;

[*Cont'd Apr.*

Happy *Tom Crump*, ne'er sees his own Hump.

Fools need Advice most, but wise Men only
 are the better for it.

APRIL

Hence bravely strive upon your own to raise
Their Honour, Grandeur, Dignity and Praise.
  But wider far, beyond the narrow Bound
Of Family, *Ambition* searches round:
Searches to find the Friend's delightful Face,
The Friend at least demands the second Place.
And yet beware; for most desire a Friend
From meaner Motives, not for Virtue's End.
There are, who with fond Favour's fickle Gale
Now sudden swell, and now contract their Sail;

[*Cont'd May*

Silence is not always a Sign of Wisdom,
  but Babbling is ever a Mark of Folly.

Great Modesty often hides great Merit.

You may delay, but *Time* will not.

Lost Time is never seen again.

Poor Richard: 1758

✺ MAY

This Week devour, the next with sickening Eye
Avoid, and cast the sully'd Play-thing by;
There are, who tossing in the Bed of Vice,
For Flattery's Opiate give the highest Price;
Yet from the saving Hand of Friendship turn,
Her Med'cines dread, her generous Offers spurn.
Deserted Greatness! who but pities thee?
By Crowds encompass'd, thou no Friend canst see:

[*Cont'd June*

Virtue may not always make a Face handsome,
   but *Vice* will certainly make it ugly.

Prodigality of *Time*, produces Poverty of Mind
   as well as of Estate.

✺ JUNE

Or should kind Truth invade thy tender Ear,
We pity still; for thou no Truth can'st hear.
Ne'er grudg'd thy Wealth to swell an useless State,
Yet, frugal, deems th' Expence of Friends too great;
For Friends ne'er mixing in ambitious Strife,
For Friends, the richest Furniture of Life!
   Be yours, my Son, a nobler, higher Aim,
Your Pride to burn with Friendship's sacred Flame;

[*Cont'd July*

Content is the Philosopher's Stone,
   that turns all it touches into Gold.

He that's content, hath enough;
He that complains, has too much.

✺ JULY

By Virtue kindled, by like Manners fed,
By mutual Wishes, mutual Favours spread,

Increas'd with Years, by candid Truth refin'd,
Pour all its boundless Ardours thro' your Mind.
By yours the Care a chosen Band to gain;
With them to Glory's radiant Summit strain,
Aiding and aided each, while all contend,
Who best, who bravest, shall assist his Friend.

[*Cont'd Aug.*

Pride gets into the Coach, and *Shame* mounts behind.

Half the Truth is often a great Lie.

The first Mistake in publick Business, is the going into it.

The Way to see by *Faith*, is to shut the Eye of *Reason*:
  The Morning Daylight appears plainer when you put
  out your Candle.

⚖ AUGUST

  Thus still should private Friendships spread around,
Till in their joint Embrace the Publick's found,
The common Friend!—Then all her Good explore;
Explor'd, pursue with each unbiass'd Power.
But chief the greatest should her Laws revere,
Ennobling Honours, which she bids them wear.
Ambition fills with Charity the Mind,
And pants to be the Friend of all Mankind.

[*Cont'd Sept.*

A full Belly makes a dull Brain: The Muses
  starve in a Cook's Shop.

Spare and have is better than *spend and crave*.

Good-Will, like the Wind, floweth where it listeth.

✺ SEPTEMBER

Her Country all beneath one ambient Sky:
Whoe'er beholds yon radiant Orb on high,
To whom one Sun impartial gives the Day,

To whom the Silver Moon her milder Ray,
Whom the same Water, Earth, and Air sustain,
O'er whom one Parent-King extends his Reign
Are her Compatriots all, by her belov'd,
In Nature near, tho' far by Space remov'd;
On common Earth, no Foreigner she knows;
No Foe can find, or none but Virtue's Foes:

[*Cont'd Oct.*

The Honey is sweet, but the Bee has a Sting.

In a corrupt Age, the putting the World in order would
    breed Confusion; then e'en mind your own Business.

☙ OCTOBER

Ready she stands her chearful Aid to lend;
To Want and Woe an undemanded Friend.
Nor thus advances others Bliss alone;
But in the Way to theirs, still finds her own.
Their's is her own. What, should your Taper light
Ten Thousand, burns it to yourself less bright?
"Men are ungrateful." – – – – Be they so that dare!
Is that the Giver's, or Receiver's Care?

[*Cont'd Nov.*

To serve the Publick faithfully, and at the same time
    please it entirely, is impracticable.

Proud Modern Learning despises the antient:
    School-men are now laught at by *School-boys.*

☙ NOVEMBER

Oh! blind to Joys, that from true Bounty flow,
To think those e'er repent whose *Hearts* bestow!
Man to his Maker thus best Homage pays,
Thus peaceful walks thro' Virtue's pleasing Ways:
Her gentle Image on the Soul imprest,
Bids each tempestuous Passion leave the Breast:
Thence with her livid Self-devouring Snakes

Pale Envy flies; her Quiver Slander breaks:
Thus falls (dire Scourge of a distracted Age!)
The Knave-led, one ey'd Monster, Party Rage.

[*Cont'd Dec.*

Men often *mistake* themselves, seldom *forget* themselves.

The idle Man is the Devil's Hireling; whose Livery is Rags,
    whose Diet and Wages are Famine and Diseases.

December

Ambition jostles with her Friends no more;
Nor thirsts Revenge to drink a Brother's Gore;
Fiery Remorse no stinging Scorpions rears:
O'er trembling Guilt no falling Sword appears.
Hence Conscience, void of Blame, her Front erects,
Her God she fears, all other Fear rejects.
Hence just Ambition boundless Splendors crown,
And hence she calls Eternity her own. – – – –

[*Finis*

Rob not God, nor the Poor, lest thou ruin thyself;
    the Eagle snatcht a Coal from the Altar, but it
    fired her Nest.

With bounteous Cheer,
Conclude the Year.

VALE

Translations & Notes

TRANSLATIONS OF FOREIGN APHORISMS

Translations from French, Spanish, Italian, and Welsh are given exactly as they appeared in James Howell's *Lexicon Tetraglotton* (London, 1660), the book from which Franklin presumably drew the aphorisms in those languages.

A achwyno . . . . Who so complains with cause, should have cause given him to complain.

A noddo Duw . . . . If God saith, it must be so.

Beatus esse . . . . No man can be happy without virtue.

Bis dat . . . . He gives twice, who gives at once.

Borgen macht Sorgen. Borrowing makes sorrowing.

Con todo el Mundo . . . . With all the World have War, But with *England* do not jar.

Dyrro lynn . . . . Much liquor makes eloquent.

Eilen thut . . . . Hurrying seldom will do good.

Ex ore suo . . . . He is damned out of his own mouth.

Felix quem . . . . Happy is he who is warned by another's danger.

Fient de chien . . . . A Ducket [ducat], and a Dogs turd will be the same thing at the day of judgement.

Heb dduw . . . . Who hath God hath all, who hath him not hath less than nothing.

Ingratum si dixeris . . . . If you say he is ungrateful you say all that can be said.

Le sage . . . . The wiseman understandeth at halfe a word.

Na fynno . . . . What thou would not have done to thee,
Do not the same good man to me.

Nec sibi . . . . Nor did he believe that he had been born for himself, but for the whole world. (Lucan)

Ni ffyddra . . . . Thy hand never worse for doing thy own work.

Propria quae maribus . . . . (These two phrases occur in verses used in Latin grammars as mnemonic tags, and all students were familiar with them; the first deals with noun genders, the second with declensions. Poor Richard's punning lines may be paraphrased: "Doll, learning without book the particular attributes of men, looks like the image of generative increasing"—i.e., pregnant.)

Reniego de grillos . . . . I renounce fetters though they be of Gold.

Sapiens dominabitur astris. The wise man will be governed by the stars.

Tugend bestehet . . . . Virtue endures when everything else perishes.

Ut iam nunc . . . . So that he should now say the things which ought to be said now.

POOR RICHARD: NOTES

1.   The astronomical symbols used in the calculations are among those identified under the drawing on page 5. These three are, respectively, the signs for Conjunction, the Sun, and Mercury. See also Note 3.

2.   In his *American Almanack* for 1734, Titan Leeds replied:

"*Kind Reader*, Perhaps it may be expected that I should say something concerning an Almanack printed for the Year 1733. Said to be writ by *Poor Richard* or *Richard Saunders*, who for want of other matter was pleased to tell his Readers, that he had calculated my Nativity, and from thence predicts my Death to be the 17*th* of *October*, 1733. At 22 min. past 3 a-Clock in the Afternoon, and that these Provinces may not expect to see any more of his (*Titan Leeds*) Performances, and this precise Predicter, who predicts to a Minute, proposes to succeed me in Writing of Almanacks; but notwithstanding his false Prediction, I have by the Mercy of God lived to write a Diary for the Year 1734, and to publish the Folly and Ignorance of this presumptuous Author. Nay, he adds another gross Falshood in his said Almanack, viz *That by my own Calculation, I shall survive until the 26th of the said Month*, (October) which is as untrue as the former, for I do not pretend to that knowledge, altho' he has usurpt the knowledge of the Almighty herein, and manifested himself a Fool and a Lyar. And by the Mercy of God I have lived to survive this conceited Scriblers Day and Minute whereon he has predicted my Death; and as I have supplyed my Country with Almanacks for three seven Years by past, to general Satisfaction, so perhaps I may live to write when his Performances are Dead. *Thus much from your annual Friend, Titan Leeds. October 18. 1733. 3 ho. 33 min. P.M.*"

3.   In the Almanacks' monthly tables, each date was accompanied by such items as a weather forecast, astronomical data, Church days, anniversaries of historical events, high tide in Philadelphia, and the moon's zodiacal position; Franklin filled in the blanks with aphorisms. Astrologers related various parts of the body to the twelve zodiacal constellations, identified by these conventional symbols:

♈ Aries (the Ram).   ♎ Libra (the Balance).
♉ Taurus (the Bull).   ♏ Scorpio (the Scorpion).
♊ Gemini (the Twins).   ♐ Sagittarius (the Archer).
♋ Cancer (the Crab).   ♑ Capricorn (the Goat).
♌ Leo (the Lion).   ♒ Aquarius (the Water Bearer).
♍ Virgo (the Virgin).   ♓ Pisces (the Fish).

The "Dragon's Head and Tail" (listed by Franklin along with the planets) are, respectively, the ascending and descending node of the moon or of a planet. The Aspects are the positions of the stars relative to each other or to the observer, and these too supposedly exerted good or evil influences upon human affairs.

4.   In *The American Almanack* for 1735, Mr. Leeds once more replied to Poor Richard's joking in these words:

"*Corteous* and *kind Reader*. My Almanack being in its usual Method, needs no Explanation; but perhaps it may be expected by some that I shall say something concerning *Poor Richard*, or otherwise *Richard Saunders's* Almanack, which I suppose was printed in the Year 1733, for the ensuing Year 1734, wherein he useth me with such good Manners, I can hardly find what to say to him, without it is to advise him not to be too Proud because by his Prædicting my Death, and his writing an Almanack (I suppose at his Wifes Request) as he himself says, she has got a Pot of her own and not longer obliged to borrow one from a Neighbour, she has got also two new Shifts, a pair of new Shoes and a new warm Petticoat; and for his own part he had bought a second-hand Coat so good that he is not ashamed to go to Town, or to be seen there, (*Parturiant Montes!*) But if Falsehood and Inginuity be so rewarded, What may he expect if ever he be in a capacity to publish that that is either Just or according to Art? Therefore I shall say little more about it than, as a Friend, to advise he will never take upon him to prædict or ascribe any Persons Death, till he has learned to do it better than he did before."

4a.   William and Andrew Bradford, printers in New York and Philadelphia.

4b.   In the preface of *The American Almanack* for 1743, John Jerman wrote:

"And as for the false Prophesy concerning me, that Poor Richard put in his Almanack the last Year, I do hereby declare and protest, That it is altogether false and untrue; which is evidently known to all that know me, and plainly shews, that he is one of Baal's false Prophets."

4c.   Franklin did not write his usual Preface for the 1741 Almanack, but substituted a list of important historical dates.

5.   Samuel Butler: *Hudibras.*

Just as he took his aphorisms from a multitude of sources, effectively reshaping them in his own salty manner, Benjamin Franklin drew freely on his favorite poets to fill the pages of the Almanacks. His borrowings were rarely faithful, since he altered the poems to suit his purpose. He added and subtracted sections, changed words, and substituted verses. Poems and essays usually appeared above the monthly tables or on right-hand pages, and, especially in the later Almanacks, the longer pieces ran on from month to month. In order to preserve the magazine quality of the Almanacks we have printed each instalment under its original monthly heading, but the related parts may still be best read consecutively.

Not all of Franklin's sources are known. Many items have been identified by Dr. Robert Newcomb; these and others are cited, with the permission of Yale University Press, from *The Papers of Benjamin Franklin.*

6.   In the preface of *The American Almanack* for 1743 John Jerman wrote:

"*To the READERS*, Here is presented to your View and Service an *Almanack* for the Year 1743 according to my yearly Method, so I hope it needs no Explanation. I have put down the Judgment of the Weather as usual, and as I find the Aspects and Positions of the Planets to signifie; but no Man can be infallible therein, by reason of the many contrary Causes happening at or near the same Time, and the unconstancy of the Summer Showers and Gusts, being very often great Rain Hail and Thunder in one Place, and none at all in another Place within a few Miles distance. However, I think mine comes as near the Matter as any other if not nearer.

"The Reader may expect a Reply from me to *R---- S----rs* alias *B---- F----ns* facetious Way of proving me *no Protestant*. I do hereby protest, that for *that* and such kind of Usage the *Printer* of that witty Performance shall not have the Benefit of my Almanack for this Year. To avoid further Contention, and judging it unnecessary to offer any Proofs to those of my Acquaintance that I am not a Papist, I shall with these few Lines conclude, and give place to what I think more agreeable to my Readers. *JOHN JERMAN*"

7. With this issue the Almanack was expanded from 24 to 36 pages. The poem which follows was adapted from John Hughes: *The Ecstasy*.

8. James Thomson: *A Poem Sacred to the Memory of Sir Isaac Newton*.

9. Edmund Waller: *To Zelinda*.

10. James Thomson: *The Seasons*, "Winter."

11. The publishers differ with Poor Richard; the essay is omitted on the grounds that our public would find it neither useful nor amusing.

12. Thomson: *The Seasons*, "Summer."

13. Ibid.

14. Edward Young: *Love of Fame*.

15. Alexander Pope: *Essay on Man*.

16. Thomson: *The Seasons*, "Winter."

17. The errors are corrected in this edition.

18. Samuel Johnson: *The Vanity of Human Wishes*.

19. Edward Young: *Night Thoughts*.

20. Young: *Love of Fame*.

21. Edmund Waller: *Upon the Late Storm*.

22. Young: *Night Thoughts*.

23. Johnson: *The Vanity of Human Wishes*.

24. Young: *Night Thoughts*.

25. Abraham Cowley: *Pindarique Odes*.

26. For the public's greater satisfaction, the text of the act is omitted.

27. By Richard Savage.

28. By James Burgh. The poem runs through both the 1753 and 1754 Almanacks.

28a. Extracted from a lengthy astronomical treatise on "the GREAT Works, properly so called, of Nature; the Sun, and Planets, and the fixed Stars." It occupied several pages of the 1753 and 1754 Almanacks.

29. An anonymous paraphrase of Horace: Epode II.

30. These verses and those at the beginning of each of the other months are from Moses Browne: *An Essay on the Universe*.

31. The verses quoted from Edmund Waller: *The Maid's Tragedy*, together with the introductory paragraph, are from Charles Palmer: *A Collection of Select Aphorisms and Maxims*.

32. The verses quoted from Moses Browne: *The Consummate State of Man*, along with the prose passage, are from Palmer, *ibid*.

33. The lines from Pope: *An Essay on Criticism*, and the preceding paragraph, are from Palmer, *ibid*.

34, 35. Palmer, *ibid*.

36. Lucan: *Pharsalia*, translated by Nicholas Rowe.

37. Horace: Ode III.

38. Edward Young: *Night Thoughts*.

39. "Conversation Hints" at the beginning of each month of the 1757 Almanack are from Benjamin Stillingfleet: *An Essay on Conversation*, reprinted in Robert Dodsley: *A Collection of Poems*. (The third couplet in September does not appear in either the original or Dodsley.)

40, 41. Palmer, *ibid*.

42. Stillingfleet: *An Essay on Conversation*.

43. Matthew Green: *The Spleen. An Epistle Inscribed to his Particular Friend Mr. C. J.* — probably from Dodsley, *ibid*.

44. William Melmouth: *Of Active and Retired Life*. Franklin has followed the version printed in Dodsley, *ibid*., in which the last nine lines differ substantially from the original.

45. Green: *The Spleen*.

46. Under such titles as *The Way to Wealth* and *Father Abraham's Speech*, the Preface to the 1758 edition of *Poor Richard Improved* (the last Almanack prepared by Franklin himself) has been the most extensively reprinted of all B.F.'s writings. In it he arranged some hundred of his maxims relating to savings, industry, and stick-to-itiveness, nearly all drawn from the earlier Almanacks, and frequently in a revised form.